A Christian Walks in the Footsteps of the Buddha

BY JOHN R. MABRY

the apocryphile press
BERKELEY, CA
www.apocryphile.org

Be present with your want of a Deity
and you shall be present with the Deity.
—*Thomas Traherne*

apocryphile press
Berkeley, CA

Apocryphile Press
1700 Shattuck Ave #81
Berkeley, CA 94709
www.apocryphile.org

ISBN 9781940671307

Other Books by John R. Mabry

Spiritual Guidance Across Religions
Providing Spiritual Counsel to People of Differing Faith Traditions

Faithful Generations
Effective Ministry Across Generational Lines

Growing Into God
A Beginner's Guide to Christian Mysticism

The Kingdom
A Berkeley Blackfriars Novel

The Power
A Berkeley Blackfriars Novel

Salvation of the True Rock
The Sufi Poems of Najat Ozkaya

People of Faith
An Interfaith Companion to the Revised Common Lectionary

The Way of Thomas
Nine Insights for Enlightened Living from the Secret Sayings of Jesus

The Monster God
Coming to Terms with the Dark Side of Divinity

Noticing the Divine
An Introduction to Interfaith Spiritual Guidance

Faith Styles
Ways People Believe

God Has One Eye
The Mystics of the World's Religions

God is a Great Underground River
Articles, Essays, and Homilies on Interfaith Spirituality

I Believe in a God Who is Growing
Process Perspectives on the Creed, the Sacraments, and the Christian Life

Who Are the Independent Catholics? (with John P. Plummer)
An Introduction to the Independent and Old Catholic Churches

Crisis and Communion
The Re-Mythologization of the Eucharist

Heretics, Mystics & Misfits
A Sermon Cycle

God As Nature Sees God
A Christian Reading of the Tao Te Ching

The Tao Te Ching
A New Translation

Contents

Acknowledgements and Notes

Enormous thanks to my wife, Lisa Fullam. Often, in my travels, people would ask me, "How does your wife feel about you being away for three months?" I'd laugh and say, "Are you kidding? She was packing my bags!" I know she missed me terribly, but I also know that my own personal and professional flourishing is first and foremost for her. I will be forever grateful for that. Thanks, too, to my parents, Russel and Karen Mabry, who were less keen for me to go, but still very supportive. I'm grateful for Donna Stoneham, for sharing the first part of this journey with me, and providing nearly constant support via Facebook and text messages. Deep gratitude to the Rev. Carol Barriger for so lovingly caring for my flock at Grace North Church during my sabbatical. And big thanks to B.J. West for rendering the "A Christian Walks..." logo so splendidly.

This whole pilgrimage was financed through Indigogo and Paypal contributions, and I could not have made it without my supporters. Big thank you's to: Jamie Allen, Diane Amarillas, Jim and Annie Anderson, Michael Asteriou, Erik Bergesen, Diane Black, Måns Broo, John Edgar Browning, Jeannette Campbell, Joan Castagnone, Russel Corning, Cathleen Cox, Davy Davidson, Bill Denham, Martha & Patrick Dexter, Linda Eve Diamond, Charlotte Dickson, Karla Droste, Rosanna Ferraro, Wilson Flick, Faith Freed, Jeffrey Gaines, Leah Marsot Gapinski, Grace Gilliam, Gail Golden, Andrea Goodman, Lynn Grant, Chris Guthrey, Basil Guy, Deb Hansen, Joseph Hansen, Bob Hardy, Deni Harding, Clare Henjum, Karen Hummer, Harvey Hyman, Bruce Lescher, Mark Lodico, Russel & Karen Mabry, Reet Mae, Pat Magee, Bob Malone, Roz Malone, Laura Mancuso, Greg Miller, Joellynn Monahan,

Josephine McCarthy, Joan Morton, Suzanne Nichols, Elizabeth Niijima, the Mapplebeckpalmers, Lola McCrary, Dan Prechtel, Scott Railsback, Zulema Rashid, John Robinson, Robert Rock, Laura Rolen, Nathan Rosquist, Margaret Sharyon, Andy Shelton, Malcolm Smith, Graham Standish, Donna Stoneham, Richard Sturch, Beth St. John, Maggie Taylor, Serge Theriault, Stephanie Warfield, Kathy Watson, B.J. West, Claudia West, Jody Wirt, as well as several anonymous contributors (you know who you are).

Final thanks to my editor, Janeen Jones, who tightened the manuscript substantially and made excellent recommendations. I made several stops on this pilgrimage that did not make the final book manuscript. Feel free to read those entries at the original blog site at www.footstepsofthebuddha.org. In time that material will be moved to www.apocryphile.org/footstepsofthebuddha/.

Prologue: Why India?
Why the Buddha? Why these boots?

"They look like Frankenstein boots," I said, looking down at my feet. They looked huge. Okay, huger than usual. In my quest for the perfect footwear for my trip to India, I had thus far ordered—and returned—three pairs of boots from Amazon.com, two pair from Beck's, and another pair from Red Wing. And here I was in another Beck's trying on yet another stack of boots.

"Yeah, they look monstrous, all right," my wife Lisa agreed, frowning. "But how do they feel?"

I wiggled my toes. "They feel great." It was my turn to frown. I lifted my foot and imagined the frightened inhabitants of a Japanese metropolis beneath it, running for their lives. "But the fact is, no matter how good it feels, there's no way I'm going to wear something that huge, that heavy, and that hot for three months straight."

"That sounds like a 'no.' Next pair," Lisa said, handing me another box.

I sighed. The problem wasn't just being a size 12 with an EEEE width, it was trying to imagine everything that I would be encountering in the next three months, and finding the one pair of boots that I had confidence in. And of course, my criteria were entirely based on my own fantasy life. I've never been to India before. All of my information is based on guidebooks and memoirs and the anecdotes of other folks, mashed into the blender of my worst-case-scenario imagination. Thus, I was holding America's boot-makers to an impossible standard, despite the fact that, somewhere in the dim reaches of my trivia-flooded brain, I am aware that most people who actually live in India do just fine with flip-flops.

If it were just the boots, it would be tiresome enough, but it isn't. I have been on a similar quest for just the perfect socks, just the right jacket, the perfect suitcase, thermal underwear, the best mosquito netting, the safest neck wallet, and so on and so on. The past six months have been a mad haze of research and shopping.

As I write this, I am aware that I sound annoyed—but I'm not, really. Recently I gave my Santa Clara University students an assignment to go on a date with God, and one of them astutely noted that preparing for the date was part of the date. His response reminded me of an old Native American saying, "Preparing for the ritual is part of the ritual." Is preparing for a pilgrimage part of the pilgrimage? It feels like it. Yes.

I am gathering the proper herbs and the right stones for my medicine pouch. I am looking for signs, and searching out the proper state of mind. My dreams are filled with images of death—last night I dreamed that I found the drowned corpse of my dog Judy in our flooded garage. Usually, when my dog shows up in a dream, she represents my soul. So, that's ominous. But I keep telling myself that these are only portents of transitions and little endings.

When I tell people about the pilgrimage, they often ask me, "Why India?" or "Why the Buddha?" These are important questions, but lately they are nearly drowned out by so many others that seem much more immediate: "Why this t-shirt, and not that one? Why this shoulder bag? Why this flashlight?" and now, "Why these boots?"

So—Why India? Why the Buddha?

Religions often speak of the exoteric and the esoteric. The exoteric is the obvious, the visible manifestation, the physical, ritual, embodied expression of a faith. And the exoteric reason for wanting to go to visit the Buddha's stomping grounds has a lot to do with something that struck me during my doctoral studies.

I found that every time I learned about a new concept or practice in another religion, I would invariably find it in my own tradition, too (although it sometimes took some digging). Discovering these ideas and disciplines of other traditions cast profound light on my own tradition and spiritual journey. What I found again and again was that in learning about them and theirs, I was learning about myself and mine.

Of late, I have been immersed in my ongoing study of Christian theology (which has been wonderful and life-giving, too), but I miss the whiplash a-ha's that I remember from my heady doctoral days.

So I'm going to learn from the Buddhists. Specifically, I'm hoping that they will teach me how to be a better Christian. I am going to make connections—philosophical and theological, certainly, but even more importantly, personal and emotional. I can't just read about them. I have to meet them. I have to *go* there.

Another exoteric aspect is my work as a graduate school professor at a unique school, the Chaplaincy Institute in Berkeley, CA, that specializes in preparing people for interfaith ministry. Most of our students go on to become hospital and hospice chaplains. Instead of training them to work with only one variety of faith, we prepare our students to offer sensitive care no matter who they encounter, whether Christian, Jewish, Hindu, Buddhist, or any other faith—or none.

And just like the people they serve, our students are all over the map. Some identify as Buddhist, some as Christian, some as Jewish, some as Hindu. But the largest group simply identify as "interfaith," and are eclectic in their spiritualities. Learning how to teach such a diverse group has been challenging, especially since I am myself very committed to the Christian path. What I have discovered along the way is that teaching theology in an interfaith setting is a bit like learning another language—or perhaps several languages at the same time. Everyone in the room is talking about the same things, but using different words to describe it.

The Chaplaincy Institute brings people of different paths together to do theology, and to share their spiritual practices with one another. The fear and ignorance that separate people of one religion from another is dismantled, real dialogue occurs, walls come down, friendships are formed. The world is changed. And so, on this trip I am, I suppose, bringing the mountain to Muhammad. Instead of inviting a Buddhist into my classroom, my space, I am going to theirs.

The esoteric in religion is often spoken of as the inner core, the secret teachings, or the wisdom hidden behind the "clothes" (or, more pejoratively, the "trappings") of a faith. The esoteric reason wasn't clear to me for a long time.

It surfaced for me as my mother and I were seated together on a water taxi speeding from the island of Murano back to Venice. As we sweated in that damp, hot Venetian boat, I was discussing the pilgrimage with my Mom. She skewered me with that look of hers, the one that can pin butterflies to a spreading board. "Why are you doing this?" she asked.

My mother is a life-long Southern Baptist, and like many of her tradition, she is skeptical of the truth claims of other religions. I wasn't sure that my exoteric answers would be very helpful. So without really thinking about it, I blurted out, "I want to get closer to Jesus, using the Buddha as a lens."

There it was. The real reason I was going. And until that moment, I didn't even know.

My mother scowled. "I do not understand how your brain works," she said, simply. Then she changed the subject.

We made small talk as we bounced and rolled back to St. Mark's Square, but the whole time I was reeling inside. The esoteric reason had been revealed—which until that moment had been hidden even from me.

So Jesus and I are going to meet the Buddha. It's going to be a road trip, a buddy movie. We're going to be chatting and checking in the whole way. I've been telling people that for most of my journey, I'll be alone. But that isn't true. Jesus and I are going to India together.

I'll be asking him how the Buddha's experience resonates with his own. There are so many parallels between Jesus' life and the Buddha's. They are both historical figures, they are both reformers. Neither of them wrote anything down, but both inspired massive missionary movements. They both changed the world.

So I'll be comparing the Gospels with the Sutras, and reflecting deeply and prayerfully on the stories of my own faith as I encounter the stories of another. I expect to learn a lot about the Buddha, but I expect to learn just as much about Jesus and about myself—and about who I am *in* Jesus.

I know that kind of mysticism confuses some people. Oh, well. Barring the unforeseen—such as a cancer diagnosis or a capricious consulate or a plane crash—I'm going. If, that is, I can just find the right boots.

"Those look good," Lisa said, eyeing the black leather high-tops.

"They hurt," I said. "My little toe is smashed."

"Maybe we can have them stretched," she suggested unhelpfully.

"Let's try the next box," I said, pulling off the too-tight shoes. I didn't feel hopeful the next ones would fit, either, but I wasn't too frustrated yet. Preparing for the adventure, after all, is part of the adventure.

Part One: The Footsteps of the Buddha

Mudras adorned the walls of the New Delhi airport.

Chapter One: Going Forth

Travel day. My eyes shot open in recognition and alarm. I looked at the clock—5am. I breathed in deep and willed myself to relax. Then I felt Lisa's arms close around me. As she gently rocked me, I wondered at the gesture's meaning. Was she saying, "You are dear to me," or "Don't go," or something else? I didn't ask. Instead, I clutched her hands to my breast and leaned into her embrace, content to allow the questions to remain aloft, myriad possibilities circling in the air.

I didn't lie there long, however. In no time, my brain was buzzing with Things Yet To Be Done, so I got up and got to work. I showered and put on what I have started to call my "India clothes."

Every item felt weird. The pants are very lightweight—by design, as they'll need to dry fast in the hotel room after a wash in the bathroom sink. But they also have zippers across the knees. Weird. Likewise, the compression socks my parents very kindly sent me from Alaska feel weird. The long-sleeved t-shirt (a "trekking underlayer," according to the label) feels weird. Nothing is *uncomfortable*, exactly. Just…weird.

Dressed, I turned to a final packing of my bag. My entire life for the next three months is in that bag. It was not easy to pare my life down enough to fit.

As I finished packing, I was overwhelmed with a feeling of sadness. I wondered if this was the last time I'd wake up in this house. I banished the thought, but it kept reemerging in different forms. Is this the last meal I'll eat in this house, should something terrible happen on the road? Is this the last time I'll sleep beside my wife? Or nuzzle my dog? I felt almost overwhelmed by tragedy looming just out of sight, and an aching, anticipatory nostalgia.

In fact, the feeling was so powerful that it was hard to feel excited. Six months ago, this had seemed like *such* a great idea. But now that it was here....

I was strongly tempted to poke my head into the bedroom, but I resisted it. I knew what I'd see: Lisa on her side, snoring softly. Curled around her form with head on her hip would be her dog, Sally, snoring like an asthmatic Visigoth. As much as I love them, as much as I longed to gaze at them, I knew that if I did, I'd be sorry. It would just make a hard day harder.

Walking upstairs to put the kettle on, my mind flashed on a similar scene from the Buddha's life. At thirty years of age, he was much younger and much wealthier—a prince who would someday be king. He had been blindsided by the "wrongness" of life, by what seemed to him pointless suffering. He felt called to find a way to right it, but he knew that if he stayed where he was he would never do it. So he resolved to leave behind his wealth, his palace, his parents, his wife and son, to strip himself of every worldly good in order to find a spiritual solution.

But as he stood in the door of his bedroom, about to go, his resolve nearly crumbled. He watched his wife sleeping, and his son swaddled at her side. He wavered. How could he leave everything he loved behind in order to find...what? He didn't even know what he was looking for.

He could just stay. He could just forget all about this desperate restlessness that prodded at his soul. He could get back into bed, hold his wife close, and lose himself in the dusty smell of her hair. And he almost did. It was such a powerful temptation, in fact, that tradition says that he named his son Rahula, which means, "fetter." Literally, he named his kid "Ball-and-Chain."

No, he knew if he woke her it would all be over. She would plead with him, and in the end he would relent. He would stay. So he steeled his resolve and stepped away from the door. He stole down to the stables, swung onto his horse, and left his kingdom behind in search of an as-yet-unrevealed salvation.

There is a parallel story in the Christian tradition, although its setting is more cosmic. It says that Christ left his Father's kingdom, his royal state, and his power behind to seek us out, to make his home with us, and to heal the wound at the heart of the world. As Paul puts it, "Though he was in the form of God, he did not regard equality with God something to be held onto, but instead he emptied himself, taking the form of a servant, being born in human likeness."[1]

Both were princes, and both were so moved by compassion that they abandoned their thrones and entered the world for the sake of those who suffer and are in darkness. Both left behind everything they knew and loved and embraced the Unknown.

I have no pretensions to savior-hood, but I, too, was leaving those most dear to me in order to seek the Unknown. The Buddha's leave-taking suddenly seemed more poignant than it had when I read it last.

In his culture, those who left their lives behind in order to seek spiritual wisdom were called *sadhus*—they still are. The variety of Hinduism that the Buddha originally practiced is called *Samkyha*, and in that tradition, one who renounced the world underwent a ritual called *pabbajja*, which means "going forth."

At church last night we had a Christian version of such a ritual, a "sending forth." In the middle of our regular Sunday Eucharist, we paused to ceremonially release me from my pastoral responsibilities, and to install our sabbatical pastor, Carol. I had a hard time holding it together as I asked my congregation to forgive me for any mistakes I had made during my tenure there, for I could think of many. They offered their forgiveness and asked for mine. My eyes were moist and my throat caught as I spoke, but I got through it without crumbling.

After the service, the entire assembly blessed me with the laying on of hands. Their hands had no weight, and my heart was open. As Ric raised his sonorous voice in prayer, I felt my wife's dog Sally lick at my hand. And lick. And lick. It was a big, wet, grace-filled moment.

Just now, a big black nose flipped my arm up, causing me to misspell the word I was typing. I looked down at my dog Judy and scowled. Her patrician eyebrows raised and her brow furrowed. She knew something was up, and she knew she didn't like it. I tore myself away from the keyboard, knelt down, and hugged her close, burying my nose in her fur. She smelled of sour sunshine and dirt, the way a healthy dog ought to. My heart hurt, and I ground my teeth in anxiety.

When I'm leaving home for a trip, I am always painfully neurotic about it. My OCD kicks in, I check things repeatedly and ritualistically. I worry out loud *ad nauseum* to the annoyance of my longsuffering spouse. It makes me wonder—when Jesus "laid his glory by" to embrace the poverty of earth, did he rush around like a chicken with its head cut off, worrying whether the stove was off? I'm thinking not.

And what was I so afraid of, really? Bodily injury? Sure, that can happen. A spiritual crisis? That's a possibility, even a probability. A moral injury—in the sense that I fear the conviction of my soul for the scandalously privileged life that I lead? That's almost certain. And then there's the Unknown.

It is, of course, what I am going to discover, but it is also what has kept my sleep at bay as my travel date crept closer. And yet, did I fear something else perhaps, something not yet cresting into consciousness? It wouldn't surprise me, as I have a great capacity for hidden motives. If so, it remained obscure.

Of course, I don't need to settle on one of these reasons. They can all be true. I don't doubt that every one of them contributes to this bouncing knee and the intermittent ache in my chest as I sit on the plane typing this paragraph. I don't need to figure out *why* I'm anxious to know that I *am* anxious. I am content to allow the possibilities to remain aloft, myriad possibilities circling in the air, even as we are now, banking for a turn to the northeast, climbing through the clouds toward Amsterdam.

Unlike the Buddha, I did kiss my wife. As we stood in the parking lot of the BART station, I pulled her in and touched my lips to hers, hoping the moment would stretch out or slow down. But it didn't. It was a kiss, then it was gone, and then she was driving away. Then dragging my suitcase behind me, I walked up the ramp toward the BART station, headed for Amsterdam, headed for New Delhi, headed for Varanasi, headed for the Unknown.

* * *

Eleven hours to Amsterdam, then eight more to Delhi. The flights passed in an uneventful haze of cramped conditions, an increasingly sore tailbone, and unresponsive hand-held in-flight entertainment controllers. I tried to rest, but was mostly just restless. Just as I was on the verge of that not-unpleasant sleep-deprivation altered state so familiar to me when travelling, we touched down in Delhi. My seatmate, a young Indian woman, looked up from her phone. She smiled at me. "Welcome to India," she said. I smiled back, and she returned her focus to her phone.

Stepping from the plane into the covered gangway, I was instantly struck by a strong combination of smells—cigarettes and something sweeter. Rose water, perhaps? Just when I thought I had a bead on it, it was gone again.

Following my nose, as well as the strongly running stream of my fellow passengers, I made my way to baggage claim. I passed several brightly colored posters along the way proclaiming "Festive Dhamaal: Celebrate this Season"—yet they all showed Christmas trees, presents, and Santa. I filed it under "curious," and stepped from the corridor into a massive room, the size of a couple of football fields: the main Delhi terminal.

The Delhi Airport is a major, world-class airport, all shiny, bright, and modern. It was also amazingly...smoggy? The lights were dimmed by a clearly visible smoke that hung in the air, giving everything a noirish, cinematic, BBC WWII-era-Train-Station-in-the-Dead-of-Night quality. It was surreal.

Clearing customs was a breeze, and in no time I was rolling my bags across the street through a nippy, foggy Delhi night. I had read the warnings in the *Lonely Planet Guide to India*, so I was wary of scamming taxi drivers.

I particularly wanted to avoid a very common ploy: a driver will stow your bags in the trunk of his car and set off with you, but instead of taking you to your hotel, he takes you to a "government tourist agency" who informs you that your hotel has burned down. "Very sad," the tourist agent says, but then brightens up as he informs you that all is not lost, he can recommend a "very nice, very cheap" place. When you arrive, the place is a dump, and it costs you an arm and a leg—probably because a healthy kickback is going to the taxi driver, the tourist officer, and anyone else in on the scam. Meanwhile, you've lost the room fee you've already paid to your original, still-standing hotel.

I was determined that nothing like this was going to happen to me. As I rolled my bag out of the terminal, I remembered a section from the Jain scriptures in which a spiritual master is giving a long list of admonitions to his disciple. Each exhortation was punctuated by an almost liturgical response: "Gautama, be watchful all the while!" After about five of these admonitions, the Gautama bit gets a little tiresome. Nevertheless, it was precisely that annoying phrase that echoed loudly in my brain as I walked.

To avoid the taxi scam, the Lonely Planet guide says to head directly to a "pre-paid government taxi stand." A bright red kiosk declared itself to be exactly that, so I rolled my bag up and showed the man behind the counter my hotel reservation. "I need a taxi, please, to my hotel," I said, smiling in a way that must have betrayed my weariness.

The man looked at the hotel name and the address, clearly printed on the paper. He shook his head. "I don't know where that is," he said. "Where is that?"

I was surprised. The reviews all said it was a well-known hotel. "It's very close to the airport," I said, remembering its location relative to the airport on Google Maps. "I could probably walk."

The man shook his head, and waved over a young man who had been loitering around. He handed the young man my paper, and the young man smiled encouragingly. "I will call," he said, brandishing his cell phone. "I will find out where it is."

Within moments he was speaking rapidly in the local language. He thrust the phone at me. "Your hotel," he said. "Speak to you."

I put the phone to my ear. A thickly-accented voice said, "Mr. Mahhh-BREE?"

"Yes," I said.

"I have rented out your room. There is no room for you here. I have emailed Expedia about it. You will see the refund."

"Wait just a minute," I said, my pulse rate surging. "I called last night and you said you'd hold the room for a late arrival. You said 'no problem.'"

"I am sorry, sir, I have rented the room. There is no room for you here."

"That's not acceptable," my voice raised in both pitch and volume. "You can't just strand me in Delhi in the middle of the night."

"Good bye, sir." The phone went dead.

I uttered something blasphemous as I handed the phone back to the young man. He gave me a very compassionate look. "Would you like me to recommend a place to stay?" he asked, helpfully. "Very good. Very cheap. I help you sir, it is no problem."

I swore aloud and turned away from him, seething with rage. I decided I might as well just wait out my time in the terminal until my flight at 9am, seven hours hence. First, though, I checked my phone. There was no email from Expedia. I decided to call them.

I called the U.S. and, of course, was connected to someone in India—the voice on the other end betrayed the unmistakable Indian sing-song lilt. The irony was exquisite. I quickly explained the situation. She put me on hold and phoned the hotel. Then she apologized that she could not get through. "I will give you an address."

I assumed she was giving me a new hotel for the night, but she gave me the same address as the one I had originally reserved. "Excuse me, ma'am," I interrupted her, "they just told me there's no room."

"That is where your reservation is, sir," she said.

I moved the phone away from my mouth and roared at the smoky sky in frustration. "Let me talk to your supervisor," I demanded.

"Of course, sir," she said. The phone went dead.

"Welcome to India," I said out loud to myself.

It was only then that it occurred to me that it might be a scam. Could it be that the guy I talked to was *not* from my hotel? Was the Expedia woman in on the scam, too? I suddenly realized how conspiracy theories thrive. "Gautama, be watchful all the while!" I announced to no one. The phrase seemed a lot less annoying and a great deal more relevant.

Then I remembered that the number of the hotel was still in my phone from when I had called them yesterday. I pulled it up and punched at the number. In a moment, a familiar voice answered—it was *not* the voice I had been speaking to a few minutes ago.

"This is John Mabry—" I started. I quickly blurted out what had happened, but the man kindly stopped me.

"Mr. Mabry, do not worry. Your room is ready for you. Stay where you are, I shall send a driver. Do not worry."

In his voice I heard an echo of Jesus' favorite saying: "Don't be afraid." It was amazingly comforting.

"I'll wait right here," I said.

Twenty minutes later, the driver dropped me at a hotel that was far swankier than its $100 a night price tag should have allowed for. An immaculate room and a bathtub (!) awaited me. Too bad I only had two-and-a-half hours to enjoy it before heading back to the airport.

I had a hard time getting to sleep, amazingly. But when I finally did drop off, I slept a hard dreamless sleep and woke five minutes before the wakeup call sounded. I felt chastened by the events of the previous night. I don't want to be so paranoid of scams that I trust no one. How the hell was I going to find the right balance?

"Gautama, be watchful all the while!"

———

1 Philippians 2:6-7.

A sadhu on one of the ghats in Varanasi.

Chapter Two: Varanasi—the City of Death

The airport was a madhouse. All flights (including mine) were delayed due to fog, and there was hardly a spare seat in the entire domestic wing. My carry-on bag was becoming oppressively heavy, so I glanced around for a seat. I spied one.

"May I?" I asked the man next to the empty seat.

"Of course," he said, indicating the seat. I sat.

"You sound American," the man said. He was about ten years older than I, with a dignified, business-like manner about him. We started chatting, and I told him about my pilgrimage. "Are you Buddhist?" he asked.

"I'm a Christian pastor, actually," I said.

"I don't know much about Protestants," he confessed. "I'm Catholic myself."

"So is my wife," I said. This led us into a great conversation on All Things Ignatian, since he had a relative in the Society of Jesus.

"You must go to Ladakh," he told me.

It took me a few minutes of conversation to remember the place, but then I made the connection. "I thought the roads were all snowed in, and you can't get there until spring," I said.

"And yet, a plane leaves for there in a half hour," he smiled, pointing to the Departures board. He opened his laptop and for the next half hour showed me photos from his latest trip to Ladakh. It looked wild and cold and ancient. I resolved to go there, if I could.

I told him I was on my way to Varanasi. He nodded knowingly. "It is a city of death." I nodded, thinking how ironic that was, since one of Varanasi's aliases is Kashi, which means "City of Life." Before I could comment, though, he went on. "It is the holiest city in all of India, and so of course everyone wants to go there to die." He smiled. "You will like it, I'm sure." His smile faded as he thought for a minute. "It is a very poor place. It is very hard. It is like that in much of India."

"I've heard there's a lot of compassion fatigue here," I said.

"It is very real," he agreed. "Eventually, you just see through people."

"I have a hard time with that, as a Christian," I said.

"I have a hard time with it, too, as a Christian," he agreed. His face fell. "And yet, I do it."

"I do it too," I confessed. "We have homeless people in California."

"It is nothing like it is here," he said. "You'll see."

The flight was over in no time, and before I knew it I was climbing down the steps to the tarmac. As we approached the terminal building, a bold blue sign read "Lal Bahadur Shastri International Airport," except that the "International" part was a different color blue, as if it had been added later, as an afterthought.

Stepping out into the still-foggy street, I was met by several people holding signs. One of them said, "John Mabry" and I pointed to the man holding it and smiled. He snatched my suitcase out of my hand, uttered a curt, "This way, please" and made for the dusty, unpaved parking lot.

The hour-long ride into Varanasi was a carnival of terror. The first thing I noticed was that lane divisions are merely suggestions, not rules by any means. The next thing I noticed was that one two-lane stretch of road—with traffic going in opposite directions—held cars, buses, motorcycles, scooters, bicycles, and auto-rickshas (tiny, unlikely vehicles that look like covered mopeds with passengers—also known as "tuk-tuks").

Many of these vehicles travel at different speeds, which means that veering over into oncoming traffic in order to pass happened several times every minute. And of course traffic coming in the other direction is doing it, too. It seemed like a massive, continuous game of chicken.

The first time an oncoming car comes speeding straight at you in your own lane, it's heart-stoppingly terrifying. The 49th time it happens, it's merely alarming. I willed myself to relax, to see the crazy game of dodge-car as an interesting cultural artifact, a distancing technique that I did not expect to work, but to my great surprise actually helped a little.

Everywhere you looked there were whole families piled on top of a single motorcycle. Usually, a man was driving, and behind him was a woman sitting side-saddle. Often between them were one or two small children. None wore helmets, and all of them were riding along through this terrifying traffic with unconcerned, even placid expressions.

I took inspiration from this, and I started to look less at the road, focusing on the buildings we were passing. The main street looked very much like buildings I had seen in other developing countries, like Costa Rica or Mexico. It seemed to me that we were speeding down a main street that stretched on for nearly twenty miles, with precious little beyond it except for green hills and open land.

The storefronts were made of what looked like crumbling concrete, and yet they were often painted bright colors. Men sat in front of their shops in the kind of plastic lawn chairs you get at Wal-Mart, sipping chai from tiny clay cups. I noticed several shops here and there about the size of a refrigerator box, set up on short stilts. On each of the 4x4-foot platforms a man sat cross-legged, working away at something I couldn't discern.

Children smiled and ran, playing alarmingly close to the traffic. Stray dogs wandered everywhere, but even more numerous were yak or water buffalo, chained in place directly outside many of the shops, chewing placidly in the sun.

And then there were the cows. Every couple of blocks or so, there were one or two of them. They weren't tied to anything, they were just wandering, some of them feasting on a patch of garbage alongside a goat or two. (Wait a minute—who put the soccer jersey on that goat? And why?)

As we approached the main city, the cows became more numerous. Entering a busy roundabout at breakneck pace, I noted that navigation was complicated by the fact that two cows had decided to lie down near the center of it, blocking about half of the lane. Cars swerved to avoid hitting them and each other. I held on for dear life as we missed scraping a truck by less than an inch.

"Why haven't those cows been selected out of the gene pool?" I wondered aloud. My driver seemed not to hear. Once firmly in the city, the traffic continued to be scary, but it was slower. People took outrageous chances to cross the street. A gaggle of policemen, each clutching at long staves moved into the midst of traffic, executing what looked like a stylized dance involving hitting both one another and passing children with the staves. And yet, they did so slowly, so as not to hurt anyone. I turned my head to watch it as we passed, trying to figure out what the hell I was seeing. I still have no idea.

Eventually, my driver pulled over, and a teenager put his head near my window. "There is your boy," the driver said. "He will take you to your hotel." The teenager smiled. Grabbing my suitcase from the trunk, he set out down an alley, not looking to see if I was following. Within minutes, I was hopelessly lost.

These were not streets as we think of them in the US. In fact, they were barely alleys. At some points they were so narrow that I could put my hands on each of the buildings on either side. The streets were lined by tiny shops, each made of rusted iron and crumbling concrete. Posters announced a slick-looking guru coming to town. Women held veils over their mouths, more to protect their breathing from pollution, it seemed to me, than from Islamic modesty. Dogs slept curled up under wooden steps or on unevenly cut marble landings. A man sat cross-legged on the stoop of a building, selling chai in plastic cups—a booming business, it seemed.

Every half a block we'd have to dodge a motorcycle or a bicyclist, all the while being careful not to step into a pile of excrement. As I hurried to keep up with the boy with my bag, I was powerfully reminded of the Old City of Jerusalem or the tangled maze of alleyways that is the city of Fez, in Morocco.

One thing about Jerusalem that I remember vividly was the preponderance of cats. There were cats everywhere, lounging on steps, staring down at you from rooftops, or roving in pairs. Jerusalem may have been God's city, but it actually belongs to the cats. Yet so far, I have seen no cats in Varanasi. This city belongs to the cows. Along these tiny little alleyways, too narrow for three people to walk abreast, there are at least one or two cows every block or so. They shuffle languidly in random directions. A couple of times we had to flatten ourselves against a building to edge around one of them.

Eventually, we found the hotel. I tipped the boy and was shown to my room. It was a double, as I was expecting my friend Donna, on her way from Nepal, to join me for a few days. But she would not arrive until the next day due to the fog in Delhi. I dropped my bag and went out to explore the hotel.

As I stood on the rooftop terrace I gained my first glimpse of the Ganges, the holiest river in India. Night was falling, and boats lit by candlelight glided by. Several more were moored at the ghat that adjoined the hotel. The world's filthiest river was also the most beautiful, especially at sunset on a foggy night.

* * *

The next day I went out to see the city. I walked north along the ghats in a constant state of mild horror. All along the water, men were bathing in the foul, holy water. Women were washing clothes, and spreading them out in the sun to dry. Holy men, their ribs protruding in a frightening fashion, sat stoking fires near tiny temples large enough for only one person at a time. Other, more corpulent holy men were seated by the river underneath makeshift tents, performing ceremonies and collecting cash in exchange for their blessings. One ghat seemed to be the sole possession of barbers and I nearly had to beat away a succession of men eager to give me a shave or a massage.

Eventually I smelled the smoke. Looking up I saw piles upon piles of firewood, arranged in stacks two stories high. There were several levels of concrete structures descending down to the water. As I tried to make sense of what I was seeing, a young man approached. "It's the burning ghats," he said. "People come from all over India to die here. No pictures, please, or it makes the families upset."

"Of course," I agreed.

"You see up there?" he pointed up the hill toward the old city where I saw a large, three-story building. "This is the hospice, sir. Every morning I go out into the city and find old people who have no home and no money and are ready to die. We bring them here and we bathe them and give them medicine and make them comfortable until they die. Then we burn them." He smiled at me, as if this was the most natural conversation in the world.

"It is okay, you can come down here," he waved me down, but I stood where I was. It seemed disrespectful, somehow, to venture onto such holy ground simply to gawk. "No, it is okay, sir. As long as you don't take pictures, the families will not mind." A cow walked past him, and pushed at a tangle of wire by a pile of wood. "It is good that you are here," he smiled. "Where there is burning, there is learning." He waggled his head, proud of his quip. "We are glad that you are here to learn about our culture. Where are you from, sir?"

I told him, but was immediately distracted by a procession

coming down one of the alleyways from the old city toward the ghat. Several men—pallbearers, I realized as they got closer—were carrying a stretcher on which a body had been covered by a bright orange silk sheet, upon which red, orange, and yellow flowers had been meticulously arranged. About a hundred half-inflated balloons completed the adornment.

They carried the body to the water, and lowered it into the river. When they pulled it up again, the silk was soaked. It dripped as they carried it back up the hill. "The Ganga is holy," the young man told me. "It washes away all sins, so we can go to nirvana, to heaven. Now they will put it on the fire. Low castes down here," he pointed to where the cow was still pushing at the tangle of wire, "middle castes there," he pointed toward a pyre that seemed ready for a body a few yards up from the river, "and high castes on the other side of that temple."

I nodded, trying to take it all in. "Can non-Hindus go in the temple?" I asked.

"Yes, of course, sir," he said. "That temple there is the Shiva temple, where they smoke the ganja." I had never put together that the word for marijuana, *ganja*, might be etymologically linked to the river I was standing by, the Ganges. "And the larger temple next to it is the Durga temple. But they don't smoke the ganja there," he looked disappointed as he said it, as if he was certain I wouldn't be interested in a temple that had no intoxicating sacraments.

"So would you like to make a donation to the hospice?" *Ah, there it is*, I thought. I knew he wasn't paying me all this attention just to be friendly. As I gazed at the ghat, it struck me that it was simultaneously beautiful and horrific—the one did not negate the other.

I turned to walk up the steps of the ghat toward the old city. I reflected on how Varanasi proudly displayed much that the Buddha recoiled against in the Hinduism of his own day—

cruel austerities, the injustices of the caste system, and charla-
tan priests.

There was a frenetic, menacing quality to the city. I wanted
to be inspired by it, but instead it was all I could do to keep
my composure together. I pulled out my phone and looked at
the time—Donna should be arriving shortly. I turned right
down another impossibly narrow street, and began to pick a
meandering path back to the hotel through the City of Death.

* * *

I heard Donna's voice in the lobby, and rushed out to see a
very welcome, very friendly face. I gave her a quick hug and
left her to finish the check-in ritual at the front desk while I
made a quick sweep of the room to make sure it was room-
mate-ready. Donna and I had met about fifteen years ago. We
were both students in the Mercy Center spiritual direction certificate program, and we have been good friends ever since. To
be honest, however, my feelings for her are more brotherly—
we are twins of a common mother, the Southern Baptist Convention, from which we are both estranged. We have had
parallel spiritual struggles in many ways, over which we
bonded all those years ago.

When Donna finished at the front desk, she took in the
room. "This is an awesome place, John," she said. Donna's
Texan accent has been softened by her decades in California,
but it is still discernible. I could listen to her read the phone
book.

"It's not much on atmosphere," I complained.

"It's immaculate, though, and that's all I care about," she
said. She placed a hand on her hip, and looked me in the eye.
"You would not believe some of the places we have stayed in
the past two weeks." She had just spent the past couple of
weeks volunteering for a relief organization, working among
the poor in rural Nepal.

Soon, we were winding our way along the ghats, following

roughly the same route I'd taken that morning. I now had a general sense of the layout of things and was able to guide us with a minimum of backtracking.

"Did the ride here from the airport just absolutely terrify you?" I asked.

"Are you kidding?" she responded, "I just spent two weeks driving through Nepal. This was nothing."

"Really?" I said. "Scared me silly."

"For one thing there were no thousand-foot-drop cliff faces between the airport and here," she said. "I thought I was going to die so many times. I swear to God, John, I am lucky to be alive." We walked past a man openly peeing on a wall. "Although *that* does scare me," she said. "I must have seen twenty incidents of public urination in that one hour driving here from the airport."

I looked up and saw an enormous structure by one of the ghats made of huge round pillars. It was impossible to tell what the building was, or what it was for. Only one thing gave it away, and that was the handful of workmen applying bright pink paint to it. "Have you noticed that all of the temples are painted Pepto-Bismol pink?" I asked. Donna laughed. We stepped up onto anther ghat where a good number of people were assembled, but I had no idea for what. We made for the far corner, and passed by a holy man with only one foot. Seated directly in front of him was an enormous white cow. The man was stroking its back affectionately. "A boy and his cow," I threw over my shoulder at Donna. "It warms the heart."

I was amazed at how different it felt walking along the ghats with Donna. Previously I had felt assaulted. In the company of a friend however, I felt safer. I was no longer in survival mode. I was having a good time. I stopped resisting the experience and relaxed into the surreal carnival atmosphere that was everyday life in Varanasi. It almost seemed like a different city.

Soon we reached the burning ghat, and it was a lot more active than it had been earlier. Just as had happened to me before, a man walked up to us and started talking about what we were seeing. His script was almost a word-for-word match for the one I'd heard earlier, beginning with "No pictures, please." I realized that although his goal was to secure a donation for the hospice, his function was to operate as a sort of docent for the museum of human cremation. "We do between 150 and 300 cremations here every day," he said proudly. "Come closer."

Donna followed, so I did too. I picked my way through the milling crowd of spectators, grieving families, mud, ash, cow shit, and of course, cows. Our guide stopped at a place where at least half a dozen wood pyres were blazing away.

On one of them we could plainly see the upper torso and face of a corpse, a corpulent man of about sixty years. His head was tilted back, and flames licked away at his lower parts. One foot stuck out from the pyre, black and misshapen from the damage of the flames.

My lungs screamed from all of the soot in the air. The docent invited us up onto the balcony of one of the temples. "A very good view," he said. On the way there, we passed a handful of men sitting cross-legged on the stones, rolling what looked like balls of dough with black speckles in it. They worked slowly and deliberately, and I watched as one man carefully placed a finished ball—about the size of a racquet ball—off to the side with several others. "What are they doing?" I asked, feeling like Dante questioning Virgil regarding the inexplicable activities of the damned. "Many people, all over India, cannot come to Ganges to die. They are burned at home, and then their ashes are brought here. These men mix their ashes with *chappati*. Later, a priest will put them in the Ganges to…" he fished for a word.

"To dissolve," I finished. He smiled. "Come," he said. When

we finally reached the veranda, he spread his hand out as if to say, "Is this not a glorious view?"

It was at that point that our Virgil began his pitch for donations. Donna gave him two hundred-rupee notes. Then he turned to me. "She's paying for both of us," I said, hoping to play on his perception that we were a married couple. "She has contributed to her own good karma," he countered, "not to yours. You must provide for your own karma, sir."

"Let's go," Donna said. I agreed, but the man followed us, continuing to spout dim auguries about my eternal fate should I fail to fork over some cash. After a couple blocks of badgering, I finally gave him a hundred rupees just to get rid of him. It was worth two bucks to see the last of him.

Donna ducked into a clothing store and tried on a few things. I waited with an entire family who seemed to be in the shop for no reason I could discern other than to make jokes that I could not understand, tease one another, and pose for pictures with me. Then they all got up *en masse* and left with no explanation. Very odd.

Donna ended up not buying anything, and I was getting worried about navigating the narrow streets in the dark. Twilight was upon us and Varanasi was scary enough in the daytime. We resolved to make no other major diversions until we had reached our dinner destination.

The Lonely Planet guide had praised the Dolphin for its wonderful terrace dining and quality food. It was the closest thing to a decent sit-down restaurant that I had seen in the city thus far. "This looks good," Donna said, scoping the place out.

"Way better than the place I ate at yesterday," I said, referring to the Shiva Cafe and German Bakery. "It was a slab of concrete, with lamps that were so caked with dust that you couldn't discern their original color."

"Weren't you scared to eat there?" Donna asked, mock horror on her face.

"I was, but it was dark and I was hungry. Believe me, I ordered vegetarian."

Donna ordered a beer and I asked for a mango lassi. They informed me a few minutes later that they were out of mangoes. I ordered a salt lassi instead.

Donna's face screwed up. "Salt lassi? That doesn't sound good."

I laughed. "It kind of isn't. The mango lassis are so delicious that I drink them down in one gulp. It's like Nestlé's quick—you can't drink it slow. But a salt lassi doesn't taste nearly so good, so you drink it slow. It has more of a...grown up flavor. An acquired taste."

We ordered a rice biryani, chicken korma, and a mixed veggie dish. But the mosquitoes had begun to invade. "Are you taking malaria medication?" Donna asked. I was. She wasn't, so we moved inside. There were still mosquitoes, but fewer of them.

As we waited for our order, Donna told me more details about her trip to Nepal. When the food finally arrived, we dug in with gusto. The mixed veggie dish was weird, but good. The chicken korma did not, in fact, have a korma sauce, but one that was fluffy, white and far too sweet. We both gave up after a couple of bites. For the rest of the night I was worried that I would wake up at three in the morning with food poisoning. I resolved to eat vegetarian from now on, if not for the peace of my tummy, at least for my peace of mind.

We ate extravagantly, ordering drinks and dessert willy-nilly. Our final bill was about twenty-three dollars. We walked down the five flights of steps out into the night. It was only a short walk to the ghats, where there seemed to be a major party happening.

The manager at our hotel had told me there was a ritual every night on a nearby ghat. I figured that's what we were seeing now. A massive crowd of people was lined up along the buildings, while on the edge of the piers a line of performers held them entranced. The Ganges was thick with boats as about half as many people watched from the river. Here and there candles floating on the river winked and bobbed, lending the scene a nautical fairyland quality.

Donna and I navigated to an improbably empty step, which afforded us a decent view. She took pictures while I studied the performers. There was a line of about six of them, each with an altar at their feet. In Hindu worship, called *puja*, a camphor lamp is waved before images of a deity. To see it in the context of authentic worship can be deeply moving. But this was something fundamentally different. To an ear-splitting Bollywood soundtrack the line of performers swung gigantic flaming lamps in synchronized motion. It looked like a cross between a puja and Britney Spears' backup dancers. It was certainly impressive and entertaining. But was it *prayer*? I wondered how the grieving families who had burned their loved ones that day were responding to it. I'm sure the tourists were loving it, but the families? I cringed.

"How would you feel about this, Jesus?" I asked. Immediately, I thought of the verse where Jesus said, "When you pray, speak to your Father in secret." This was definitely prayer-as-entertainment. My heart sank as I thought of other examples that were equally problematic: the slick showmanship of our own televangelists and even the mega-churches came to mind, as did the whirling dervish dinner shows that charge an arm and a leg in Turkey.

On the other hand, no one charged us admission to this. *Who is paying for this huge production?* I wondered. Just then an orange-garbed priest approached me, carrying a silver tray. He touched his finger to a pile of bright red powder on the tray, and then reached up and touched me in the middle of my forehead.

"Now you give money," he bowed, with an obsequious smile.

"I don't think I do," I said. "I didn't ask you to do that."

"You have been blessed. It is very bad karma not to give. I do not want you to carry the burden of your bad karma." He smiled and held out the silver tray.

I rolled my eyes and dug into my pocket. I extracted a ten-rupee note and dropped it on the platter.

"That is not enough," the priest said, as if chastening a child. "Your karma is very bad."

My karma is going to be a lot worse if you don't keep your sacraments to yourself, buddy, I thought. I gave him a hundred-rupee note, and he smiled, bowed, and turned to the next mark. I seethed.

Approaching our guest house again, Donna and I kept going and explored the ghats in the other direction. Soon we came across what looked like a bonfire. Lots of people were milling about, and the air was thick with smoke and a festive vibe. Up the steps a group of drummers was frenetically banging away, providing a fitting soundtrack to the scene. Donna and I both snapped a few pictures, when a man came up behind her and touched her on the shoulder. "No pictures, please," he said kindly.

"What? Why?" I asked.

"Burning ghats," he said. "It is disrespectful to the families."

"I thought the burning ghats were up there," Donna said, pointing downriver.

"Those are the Hindu ghats," he said. His face was beatific in the firelight, patient and kindly. "This is where we burn the other people—Buddhists, Jains..." he trailed off.

Christians, too... I thought, but didn't say it.

"See there," he said, pointing to one pyre where a young man was prodding at the burning wood. "You can still see the torso."

"I'm *so* sorry," Donna breathed, horrified. She put her camera away.

"It is okay," the man smiled with compassion.

"No, I mean I'm *really* sorry," Donna said again. The man waggled his head.

"Look," he said, with a note of pride in his voice. "Those fires down there, that is where we burn the poor people." He pointed to the three fires closest to us. Then he indicated a slightly elevated part. "Here we burn the middle class, and there," he pointed to a concrete slab that was elevated by about three feet. "That is where we burn the rich."

I felt anger rise up in me as he talked. Dalits and other low-caste Indians often found in Buddhism and Jainism—and Islam and Christianity, too, for that matter—a means of escape from the oppressive caste system so central to traditional Hinduism. And yet here it was being imposed on them again after their deaths—only this time in socio-economic rather than racial terms.

Back at the hotel room, Donna and I discussed the likelihood of food poisoning from our dinner. "I reckon we'll know by morning," I said.

I turned in about 8 o'clock, still not adjusted to Indian time. Around two in the morning, I was awakened by a screaming dog. The dog wasn't howling, it wasn't barking, it was full-tilt screaming. And it didn't stop. I laid there in the dark and listened to it wail and cry in agony. I thought about how dogs always represent my soul in my dreams. This dog, wherever it was and whatever was happening to it, seemed to represent the soul of this cruel place. It went on for hours.

I felt sick, and I don't think it was the chicken korma.

* * *

The next morning was Donna's last in Varanasi—that afternoon she'd head for home. As we awaited breakfast, Donna and I leaned over the railing of our guest house terrace watching the foggy Ganges. "Look there," Donna pointed at a nearby rooftop. A little girl of about five years was prancing joyfully, performing Bollywood dance moves with abandon. She seemed completely oblivious to the fact that anyone was watching her. My heart sang to see her. In the midst of such desperation, poverty, and brutality, there was also innocence and beauty and joy.

There was also fluidity. Although her movements were imprecise copies of the elegance she was striving for, there was nevertheless a flexibility that adults can only achieve through dedicated practice. It was already becoming painfully obvious to me how much I would need some of that flexibility to survive my journeys.

Donna's taxi to the airport wouldn't arrive until 1pm, so we hired a tuk-tuk to visit the Hindu temple at Benares University. "This is the most intense thing I've ever experienced in my life," Donna said, looking around her in wonder as our tuk-tuk driver executed a death-defying, hairpin change of direction in the middle of traffic. "I had no clue." Her voice was slightly muffled because of the surgical mask covering her mouth and nose.

I made a mental note to buy one of those, because ever since I arrived in India everything comes out black when I blow my nose. "Intense," I repeated.

"I had a major insight last night," Donna said. "I came on this trip to volunteer to help poor people with eye conditions. In Nepal, we helped hundreds of people regain their sight. I thought I was *helping them*...." she trailed off. "I was the blind one, though. Not them. Me." After a couple of moments of staring out at the traffic, she added, "I feel really convicted about how I live. I never even imagined poverty like this. This is the most extreme thing I've ever seen." I felt a pang of guilt because, although I understood and agreed, I mostly just felt numb.

The University was sprawling and impressive. Goldenrodcolored buildings with blood-red roofs spread out for several miles, interspersed with lush jungle vegetation and scraggly lawns.

The main building of the temple complex towered above the campus, a rising cone of ornate stone pointing to heaven, sporting statues of deities and more swastikas than I could count. We left our shoes at the coat check and entered.

We walked past several rows of columns, entering a white marble vestibule in which several selections from the Hindu scriptures were inscribed in the stone—mostly in Sanskrit, but some also in English. I even recognized a couple of the quotations, I was pleased to note, although the translations were clunky and grammatically creative.

The next section of the building had a Shiva shrine on one side, with the faces of the *trimurti*—the Hindu trinity: Shiva, Vishnu, and Brahma—staring out from three sides of a large stone *lingam*. Across the hall was a Kali shrine, with a small statue of Ganesha beside her. Several women were leaving flowers as offerings to the Dark Mother, bowing and making their prayers.

Through another doorway we came to the inner sanctum. In one corner, a gaggle of musicians was seated on the floor, singing loudly and banging away on drums. In the middle of the room was an enormous Shiva lingam.

The Shiva lingam is an egg-shaped black stone, set up on its end. It represents an erect phallus—the great god Shiva's phallus, to be exact—the active, creative force in the universe. The lingam is seated in an elliptical platform called a yoni that represents his consort Shakti's vagina—the receptive aspect of the universe, matter—that which is acted *upon* by God.

In a way, the two forces are similar to *yin* and *yang* in Taoist thought. But whereas Taoism is content to attribute to yang masculine energies and to yin feminine energies, Hinduism makes this explicit.

Around the Shiva lingam about twenty people were gathered. Many were pouring milk over the lingam as they chanted their prayers. Some threw garlands of flowers on the lingam, and some placed leaves on the lingam before they poured their milk. One man sat cross-legged by the lingam, and it was his job, it seemed, to empty an enormous bowl of milk as it poured off of the yoni. He also gathered up the wet leaves and flower garlands and cast them aside to make room for more as wave after wave of worshippers entered the sanctuary to make their offerings and prayers.

The noise was extreme, and after a few minutes, we walked out into the relative quiet of a side hall. "Them's some Shiva *enthusiasts*," I noted stupidly. I have an appreciation for Shiva, but of the two major Hindu deities, I've always been a Vishnu guy. Shiva is scary—he can be merciful, but he can also be violent. He is the granter of life, but he is also the destroyer of all things. He is unpredictable. He is an extreme ascetic, and at the same time a family man. He makes the rules, and breaks them. He is a living paradox.

In one story, Shiva's wife Parvati wanted to bathe in private, and so she told Shiva's mount, the bull Nandi, to stand guard. When Shiva arrived, Nandi did not stop him, because his first loyalty is to Shiva. Furious, Parvati made a child out of the paste she was using for soap and named him Ganesha. She breathed life into him, and set him up as a guard the next time she went to bathe. When Shiva approached again, Ganesha refused to let him pass. It was Shiva's turn to be furious. He sent an entire army to teach this upstart a lesson, but they failed. So Shiva stepped up himself and killed him, severing the child's head from his body.

Parvati was so angry that she threatened to destroy the universe if the boy was not brought back to life. Shiva realized he had gone too far, and he sent Brahma out with orders to return with the head of the first creature he came across. It happened to be an elephant. Shiva fixed the elephant head onto the boy's body, and elevated him into the pantheon of deities. Some may favor Shiva, some may favor Vishnu, but Ganesha is everyone's favorite—even Buddhists and Jains love him.

So yes, Shiva can be quick tempered and severe. But he can also be merciful and kind. He is joy and sorrow intertwined. He is an apt patron for a city such as this.

The hall we were in led to a little alcove with a six-foot *Nataranj*—the Lord of the Dance—a statue of the dancing Shiva, ringed in a hoop of flame. Although Hindus worship many gods, they also believe that they are all aspects of only One God. According to Shaivite sects, that One God is best represented by Shiva, and the phenomenal universe is his dance. He dances all things into being, and when he stops dancing, everything will wink out of existence.

We walked back into the sunshine to see a group of people gathered around a statue of Nandi, the bull. They were laying wreaths of bright orange flowers around its neck and mumbling quiet devotions. Not far away was a pavilion. There, on a raised platform, was a square pit for the Hindu fire sacrifice. Beside it, a man was creating flower patterns on the concrete by carefully pouring brightly colored sand. After he had "painted" the flowers on the cement, he then painted three circles. Soon after another man filled those circles with round trays bearing different kinds of fruit—offerings to the gods.

Back in the tuk-tuk, Donna was quiet. "You okay?" I asked.

"I'm having a visceral reaction to all those swastikas," she said.

"There *were* a lot of swastikas," I agreed. It was true. I've never seen so many swastikas in one place before, and I've even been to the Nuremberg museum.

"I know they were originally a Hindu thing," she said, "and Hitler just stole them. But it's still hard to see them."

The swastika is the symbol of the Aryans—a warrior race

from the Russian steppes that had ridden down in a thundering horde and conquered first the native peoples of Persia and then continued on to subdue Northern India. They set themselves up as the rulers, placing their Brahmins (priests) at the top of the caste system, and the Kshatriyas (warriors) next. The native peoples became the lower castes. Aryans generally have lighter skin than the lower castes and seem to be every bit as obsessed with racial purity as Hitler ever was.

The tuk-tuk driver suddenly pulled over. Donna and I looked at each other. "What now?" I asked.

"Monkey temple," the man said. We shrugged and followed him. "Who can resist a monkey temple?" I asked. We went through a security checkpoint, and once inside, were assaulted by monkeys. There were hundreds of them, chittering and chasing each other in every direction.

"I think these are spider monkeys," Donna said. I felt a slap on the back of my leg, and a monkey cheeted and darted away. Then another did the same. Obviously they were enjoying this game. I laughed out loud.

We approached the main temple, an unremarkable concrete building next to a courtyard surrounded by booths where people were selling flowers and food to present as offerings. We slipped off our shoes and stepped up into the courtyard where we could see into the Monkey Temple. Inside was a large statue of Hanuman, the monkey god, loyal companion to Lord Ram. Ram was one of the incarnations of Vishnu and the hero of the epic poem, the Ramayana. People were lined up to offer their gifts, but it was hard to tell exactly what was happening. It was bewildering and a little overwhelming, so we didn't stay long.

On the way back, staring out of the window of the tuk-tuk, Donna gasped. I looked, and noticed an old man holding a puppy by one paw. Donna was aghast. "It's okay," I said. "It was dead."

"Was it?" she asked, clearly rattled.

"Yes, it had to be." I wanted to reassure her, but I was also trying to convince myself. "If you tried to hold a living puppy up like that, it would howl with pain and thrash around."

"Yes," she said. "Of course it would. It was dead. It's okay."

"It's okay," I repeated. She didn't speak again until we arrived, her face inscrutable behind her pollution mask. I thought about Shiva, the Lord of Death. When he comes for you, it isn't personal, it isn't judgment—it's just because you were in the wrong place at the wrong time. That poor puppy just fell underneath the great god's heel, that's all, and there's no use in thinking of it further. I shivered and prayed that I might escape that dread heel.

We must not have been far from our hotel, because we got back in time for a quick bite. Then I walked Donna out to the main street and gave her a hug. "I'm sure going to miss you," I said. "It's going to be scary alone."

"I'm just glad we could be together for the first part of your trip," she said.

"It helped a lot," I smiled, trying to look more confident than I felt. And then the taxi was speeding away.

I felt bereft. I was by myself in the most alien place I have ever encountered. I dug my hands into my pockets and walked back to our guest house.

* * *

I was hoping to be in Lumbini on Christmas Day—it's the Buddha's birth place and I thought it would be a cool bit of symmetry. But due to a Visa misunderstanding, I wasn't going to be able to make it. Since my current guest house was booked, I'd have to find another place, so I set out to find one. As my tuk-tuk pulled out into the insane traffic, I mused on the synchronicity: it was Christmas, and there was no room for me in the Inn. I also wanted to find a church to attend on Christmas morning. There were only a handful of churches in Varanasi, and finding them proved to be a task.

It was a long afternoon. I found the huge Cathedral of St. Mary, which had a Christmas mass in English at 9:30am. But every hotel I checked was full. I tried not to panic. I had one more place to check out, and it was along the ghats. I sent my driver home and struck out on foot. The place looked fine, but the innkeeper was a jerk. I was beginning to get desperate about finding a hotel.

I started praying as I walked along the ghats toward the setting sun. Rounding a corner, I saw what looked like a baby doll on the ground. Its head had been mostly severed from its neck, and a dog was eating away at something in it. As I came closer, I noticed the gore—blood covered the place where the neck had been severed.

With horror I realized that it wasn't a doll at all, but a dead baby. It was swollen, probably from having been in the river. The dog must have dragged it up onto the ghat. It was also as blue as Krishna himself. The dog was lapping blood from out of its neck.

I looked away with a jerk of my head. I desperately wished I could un-see what I had just seen. I felt like someone had punched me in the gut. I spoke aloud to myself the same comforting words that I had earlier spoken to Donna, "It's okay, it's okay. It was dead."

For the next fifteen minutes I walked around in shock. Outwardly, my body was acting normally, doing the things I'd intended: inquiring about a room, buying an orange soda—but my hands shook as I handed the rupees to the vendor. Inwardly, I was about to explode. All the accumulated shock, horror, chaos, and filth of the past week hit me at once. I was reeling.

Then I sat bolt upright. *I need to do something*, I thought. *I need to do something about that baby.* But I had no clue *what* to do. If this were the US, I'd call 911. But everything I have read about the Indian police has consistently painted them as corrupt and capricious, and I resolved to have as little to do with them as possible. I didn't know whom to call or what to do. "Arjun will know," I said, thinking of my hotel's owner.

As I mounted the stairs, I was relieved to see Arjun sitting at his desk. I sank into a chair and lost it. I told him what I had seen and collapsed in a spasm of sobs. When it passed I looked up at him. "We have to do something," I said.

He shrugged. "What is there to do?" he said. "This is no problem. This is…" he fished for a word. He found it: "…normal. This happens all the time."

"What do you mean?" I asked, incredulous.

He spoke with maddening calm. "In America, when someone dies, they put them in the ground. Here, we put them in the river. When babies die, they tie them to a stone, and drop them into the river. Sometimes, the rope…uh…" he searched for the word.

"Frays?" I offered.

"Yes, the rope frays, or comes untied, and the baby washes onto the shore. It is okay." He waggled his head.

"Shouldn't we do something?"

He looked at me impassively, seeming to not comprehend my question. "There is nothing to do," he said. "If I go to the police, they will do nothing." He thought for a moment. "There are tourist police up by the main ghat. If you go there and complain, maybe they will put the baby back in the water." He shrugged again. "But maybe they won't."

I couldn't believe what I was hearing. In spite of Arjun's words, I resolved to do what I could, and set off at a good clip back toward where I had seen the child. But when I got there, there was no sign of the baby or the dog. I looked around with my flashlight. Then I looked again. I searched farther afield. Nothing.

I felt like the bottom had fallen out of my stomach. I struggled to maintain my composure as I searched. What had happened to that poor child, that he had fallen under Shiva's heel? And what bad karma had caused that rope to fray? There would be no decent burial—or disposal, I suppose—for that innocent soul. For him, there would be no elephant-headed resurrection. He had been dog food. Never had I contemplated such a fate.

"Hey, mister, what you do?" a voice from out of the dark asked.

I shone the flashlight up and saw a young man of about twenty-five, his lean form curved in on itself in a bit of an "S." Quickly I explained what I had seen.

He nodded. "O yes? I think the dog ate it already."

"Is this normal?" I asked, still not believing it.

"Oh, yes. Especially in the monsoon. You see babies here all the time."

"Dead?"

He scowled at me as if I were an idiot. "Yes, of course."

I felt like I was in a dream. My hand moved in slow motion. I had a profound sense of the unreality of things. I did not know how to process this.

"Shouldn't we go get the police?" I asked.

He cocked his head slightly, confused at the suggestion.

Right, I thought. *And I could tell them, "Hey, there used to be a baby here"?* Best case scenario, they would pat me on the head and laugh. Worse case, they would cart me away for observation. I felt paralyzed. I felt sick.

"This is horrible," I said to the young man.

"This is India," the young man said, and waggled his head. "We are used to it."

He pointed across the Ganges, to the vast sand banks on the other side. "The other shore is *full* of bodies. Here," he pointed to the ghat wall, "they usually just float past, unless a dog catches them and gets them out." I saw what he meant—the smooth cement sides of the ghats were like the sides of a sunken swimming pool. There was nothing for a body to catch on.

"Over there, they catch on the beach," he said. "There are thousands of them."

I looked at the beach on the far side of the river, shining silver in the moonlight. It looked romantic. It looked lovely. In this place, nothing is as it appears.

"One time, a Canadian filmmaker asked me, do I know any Aghoras? You know Aghoras?"

I did. Aghoras typically belong to one of the truly extreme Tantric sects. They worship Shiva, and emulate him in his fiercest ascetic aspect. They live in the burning grounds, go about naked, and eat their meals from human skulls. They cover their bodies with the ashes of the dead, and hold taboo transgressions to be sacramental.

"I did know one Aghora, so I asked him if he wanted to be in the film for the Canadians. I told him they give him money. He said yes."

I was wondering where this was going.

"So we went to the other side of the river, and the filmmakers started shooting, and he just started eating one of the bodies." He frowned. "It bothered me a little."

I nodded. I understood. He was fishing for an incident in his own life that would help him empathize with how I was feeling. I was touched by this kind effort. I thanked him and started walking back to my guest house.

My stomach was tied in a knot and my hands were still shaking. I wasn't hungry, but I thought that food might be grounding. I made my way to the Shiva Café and ordered vegetable curry. I sat down at a table with a man who was drawing.

We struck up a conversation. He sounded like he was from Germany. When I asked him where he was from, he was evasive. "Here, now," he said, and smiled.

I told him what I had seen, and he pursed his lips and nodded. He flipped open his sketch book and turned it around. "Like this?" he said. It was a drawing of the severed lower half of a swollen baby's torso.

I swallowed. I nodded.

"Now you have seen your first dead baby. You stay, you will see more." He went back to sketching.

I didn't eat much, but the food did help. I picked my way through the alleys, stepping over the dogs and around the cows. When I got home I lay awake, staring at the ceiling. Tomorrow would be Christmas Eve. It wasn't sugarplums that danced in my head as I drifted into sleep, but visions of a dancing child, a dead child, and the child Jesus born to die.

* * *

I was still feeling sad about not spending Christmas in Lumbini. Because of my change of plans, it occurred to me that instead of beginning my Gospel with an infancy narrative like Matthew or Luke, my gospel must now be constructed more like Mark, "dropping into" the story by describing the adult Buddha at the start of his ministry.

On the other hand, it would still be Christmas very soon, and I would still be ruminating on incarnation, even if it was now ungrounded in a particular place. My approach would be, by necessity, more Platonic. So perhaps my Gospel will read more like John. I smiled at the thought. It was going to be okay.

I finally found a room in a splendid hotel, the Ganpati (another name for Ganesha). It was a bright, very Indian place, full of charm and color. It was also immaculately clean. And a sign announced a Christmas Eve party for the guests, including a Ganges riverboat ride, a live Indian classical concert, and a buffet.

I was wondering how I was going to get things from one hotel to another. Even though they're less than a mile away from one another as the crow flies, the idea of navigating from one to another on foot through the crazy, maze-like alleys—with my big bag in tow, dodging cow patties all the way—didn't thrill me. I could also walk along the ghats, but there are very, very many stairs. Arjun suggested a boat, straight up the Ganges. What a good idea!

I was a little suspicious of getting on the boat without being thrown in the water, but the boys operating the boat were pros. They trundled my bag on with nary a ripple. I had a bit more trouble, but finally reached my seat. As the teenager rowed, I watched the ghats drift by peacefully. For a moment, it almost seemed like a city I could love.

"See?" the teenager said, pointing to one of the ghats. "Sheets." Sure enough, several women were squatting in the Ganges, beating laundry, and uphill on the ghats, row after row of sheets, pillowcases, and towels were drying. "The big guest houses use washing machines, but the small guest houses wash their laundry in the Ganges." I shuddered to think of sleeping on those sheets, "washed" in the filthiest river on the planet. I was grateful I could afford to stay in one of the bigger hotels.

The hotel's Christmas Eve party was fabulous. The riverboat ride was at sunset, and none of us dressed warmly enough. Before we knew it, we were disembarking and climbing the steep stairs to the guest house. In the courtyard, the musicians were already tuning up.

The performance was fabulous. The musicians began, playing a twenty-minute set; then the dancers came out. The musicians were good, the dancers were great. I was enraptured for the first hour. Then, I have to confess, I was ready for it to be over. It kept going for another hour. The manager finally had to step in and stop the show, because the food was ready.

The buffet was delicious. I had two helpings of kheer (rice pudding), my favorite Indian dessert, and many other wonderful dishes, too. All in all, it was a splendid Christmas feast! It was way past my bedtime, though, so as soon as I'd eaten, I headed for the sack.

* * *

When Christmas morning dawned, it did not feel at all like Christmas. I had to keep reminding myself what day it was. I left the hotel at about 8am. I tried to follow the map handed out by the desk clerk, but I have come to the conclusion that tourist maps issued by guest houses ought to come with a warning label: "Caution: Bears no resemblance to the layout of actual streets."

Eventually I found my way through the maze of alleyways to the main road, where I hailed a tuk-tuk. The journey to the Catholic cathedral was shorter than I remembered it, and I arrived an hour early. The place was buzzing with activity. They were having a Christmas fair, and booths were going up all around.

Back behind the church were carnival rides. American carnival rides look sketchy enough—these were way worse. They weren't operating yet, but I wouldn't have ridden anyway. I didn't read all the fine print on my traveler's insurance documents, but I'm pretty sure "rusted-through amusement ride deathtraps" was among the exemptions.

It was cold, so I went inside even though the Hindi service was still in progress. The stairs up to the sanctuary looked like a mountain of shoes—every stair contained a row of them. Like all Hindu and Buddhist temples, the Cathedral required worshippers to remove their footwear. I left my treasured boots there, too. As I entered, I was struck by the music—it was wonderful, tribal, haunting. Most of the congregation was seated on the carpeted floor—pews flanked the far sides of the place. The choir also sat on the ground, in front of the pews, and were accompanied by harmonium and tabla. The actions of the priest were all very familiar, but the music was as Indian as it gets.

Between the services, one of the priests told me that the building was designed as an amalgam of Christian, Hindu, and Buddhist temple designs. The conical shape of the building was patterned after a Shiva lingam, while the arrangement of furniture was similar to a Buddhist temple. Instead of candlesticks, tall puja lamps flanked each side of the altar. Above the door was an enormous painting of Jesus seated in the lotus position, meditating. Very cool.

As I sat waiting for the English service to begin, I thought about the pre-incarnate Christ—whom the early Christian tradition associated with Sophia, Wisdom. In the book of Proverbs (as well as the apocryphal book of Wisdom and other books) she was the first-born of God's creation. It was through her that all things were made. She was the living Torah, God's Word, and she delivered the Law to Moses, and she was that Law. She dwelt among the people of Israel and taught them and was their light. When early Christians were trying to figure out where Christ was present in the Old Testament, they pointed to her. It was she that took a body and was born as the humble babe in Bethlehem. Paul says that Jesus is "the Wisdom of God,"[1] and the early church took that literally. I once began a sermon by saying, "Before Jesus was born as a man, he was a woman." That sermon did not go over well.

In the Mahayana Buddhist tradition, the Buddha is the incarnation of a cosmic principle, of *dharma*—a hard-to-define word that can mean teaching, or truth, or law. The Buddha once said, "He who sees the Dharma sees me, and whoever sees me sees the Dharma."[2] One myth says that before his incarnation, the future Buddha was a Bodhisattva enjoying the pleasures of the Tusita heaven. The god Brahma approached him and begged him to be born as a human being in order to teach the Dharma, to which the future Buddha agreed.

The service began, but instead of tablas, we got Western Christmas Carols accompanied by the choir and harmonium. Everyone seemed to have a copy of the carol book, but I could not figure out where to get one. I ended up sharing with a very young nun, who seemed embarrassed by my proximity. But she held her book out so we could both sing from it.

The Gospel reading was from Luke, the "shepherds tending their fields by night," who were visited by a choir of angels announcing the birth of the Christ child and declaring peace, goodwill toward men.[3] As I listened, I remembered a story I'd read recently about the Deer Park at Sarnath. It had been a favorite place for Hindu holy men for some time, because it was so peaceful. Shortly before the Buddha was born, as five hundred holy men were meditating, the devas descended from the heavens to announce his birth. As soon as they heard this, all five hundred holy men ascended into the air, and attained nirvana. Their bodies disappeared, but their possessions fell to earth, becoming Sarnath's first holy relics.

The preacher took the pulpit, and outlined briefly the Christmas story. He spoke of the Annunciation—when the angel Gabriel told Mary that "the Holy Spirit would come upon her." As he spoke, I was reminded of the Buddha's mother, who dreamed that a white elephant entered her body, without any pain.

While Jesus was born in the usual way, the Buddha emerged from his mother's side. The *Buddhacarita* says, "He came out of his mother's side, without causing her pain or injury. His birth was as miraculous as that of...the heroes of old who were born...from the thigh, from the hand, the head, or the armpit. So he issued from the womb as befits a Buddha."[4] He might have emerged "without pain," but his mother died soon after from the trauma of it. Mary lived, thankfully, yet eight days later was warned that a "sword would pierce her heart."[5] leaving her bereft and grieving.

The sermon took a sudden hard turn toward liberation theology as the priest talked about God's choice of Mary, a poor peasant woman, to bear his Son. He talked about how God's favor is always with the poor—a fitting theme for his congregation: reassurance for the poor, and an admonition for us, the rich. His sermon pointed up a major difference between the nativity stories of the two faiths. Jesus is of the royal lineage of David, but is actually born to very poor parents. The Buddha however, was the son of a king, and spent his childhood and adolescence surrounded by luxury.

There is no indication that Jesus acted in any unusual manner at his birth—although the Christmas carol does report that "no crying he makes." The Buddha, however, was clearly a prodigy: as soon as he was born, he walked seven steps and spoke aloud in a clear voice, "For enlightenment I was born, for the good of all that lives. This is the last time that I have been born into this world of becoming."[6]

There was no reading from Matthew that day, but after the service, I read Matthew's nativity account and pondered the journey of the Magi, those Zoroastrian priests who followed a new star to the place where the savior lay. Likewise, the Buddhist scriptures record that an auspicious constellation, Pushya, "shone brightly when a son was born to the queen."[7]

Luke reports that eight days after Jesus' birth, his parents took him to the temple in Jerusalem to be circumcised. There they were met by the priest, Simeon, who had been told by the Holy Spirit that he would not die until he had seen the promised Messiah. He recognized Jesus as that Messiah, and he blessed the child, and took him into his arms, saying, "Now, Lord, let your servant die in peace according to your word, for my eyes have seen the salvation you have prepared for all people."[8]

Likewise, soon after the Buddha's birth, he was called upon by the Sage Asita, who in his meditation had perceived the signs of the One who would put an end to rebirth. The Sage shed tears and looked to heaven, saying, "I am disappointed in myself. For the time has come when I must pass away, just when he is born who shall discover the extinction of birth, which is so hard to win.... To those who are tormented with pains and hemmed in by their worldly concerns, who are lost in the desert tracks of Samsara, he shall proclaim the path which leads to salvation, as to travelers who have lost their way."[9]

Being allergic to both bread and wine, I asked a blessing from the priest as I stood in the communion line. He smiled and granted it, probably relieved that the Protestant did not ask him to break the rules, asking for communion. After communion, the priest returned to his place behind the altar. I expected him to proceed with the Prayer after Communion, but I was amazed to see another line forming in front of the altar. A nun with a basket moved to meet the line, and one by one began distributing what looked like Mentos—little white candies.

"What is she giving out?" I asked the nun next to me.

"Prasad," she said. My eyebrows raised in curiosity. "Candies," she clarified. "For the Hindus." I nodded, amazed. I have received prasad at Hindu ceremonies before—it took the form of the guru placing a dollop of yogurt into everyone's hands. I remember licking it up, delighted. *So prasad can take other forms*, I thought. I was proud of this church, offering a gift, a blessing, to those of other faiths who could not receive communion. It was real hospitality. I was reminded of an Eastern Orthodox church I attended where, after communion, the deacon handed out pieces torn from large challah-like loaves of bread that had been blessed by the priest for those who could not commune.

I ate at a restaurant and went back to my hotel room to take my traditional after-Christmas-dinner nap. After which I got horrendously ill. I was on the toilet every twenty minutes for the next two days.

While so totally indisposed, I had time to contemplate the royal births of Jesus and the Buddha. Sad as it was that I could not be in Lumbini, maybe Varanasi is not a bad choice for such meditations. I have never been in a place where the squalor and tragedy of human life was more prominently on display. Jesus pitched his tent with us in the grime. Buddha may have been born to the palace, but he left it and entered the mess of the world. And it doesn't get any messier than this.

———

1 1 Cor 1:24

2 Samyutta Nikaya 22.87; this also reminds me of when Jesus said, "He who has seen me has seen the Father" (John 14:9).

3 Luke 2:8-12

4 Edward Conze, *Buddhist Scriptures* (NY: Penguin, 1983), 35.

5 Luke 2:35

6 Conze, 36.

7 Conze, 35.

8 Luke 2:29-31

9 Conze, 36.

The baby Siddhartha, as soon as he was born,
walked seven steps and pronounced this his last birth.

Chapter Three: Lumbini—Where Siddhartha Was Born

Ten days in Varanasi is eight days too long. I was beginning to feel I'd been consigned to the seventh circle of some Hindu hell by the city's patron god, Shiva. As I got into the taxi to leave for the train station, I dared not to hope. Surely, I thought, something would happen to impede my escape.

The traffic noise is very loud, and I was glad I'd packed my musician's earplugs. They're specially fitted to your ears (the folks who make them actually shoot a hardening paste into the ear canal, so they don't fit anyone else) and they allow high frequencies through—they just lower everything by 15 decibels. I always seem to forget to put them in until it's too late—*after* my ears had been blasted by a hundred competing horns.

Indians use their horns like aural headlamps. They use every means at their disposal to make sure every other driver on the road knows just where they are. All the time. And everyone is doing it. At home, I use my horn maybe once a week. Lisa uses her horn annually, if that. The longest gap between beeps I counted from my driver was five seconds.

The traffic was stop and go. As we waited for a caravan of cows to cross the street through the business district, it struck me how very disconnected I feel. I have never visited a place in which I felt so emotionally distant. I felt like I was looking at Varanasi through a telescope. I was seeing a lot of stuff, but it wasn't touching me. It wasn't moving me. My heart felt frozen.

The terminal was a huge, concrete building with no front wall. Milling around, both inside and outside, were about twenty cows and literally hundreds of people, many of them sitting on the floor. Some had started fires, burning some of the amply available cow dung, and cooking their dinners over it. Just inside the building was the big electronic Arrivals and Departures Board. My train did not appear to be listed.

I went to the door marked "Tourist Office" and inquired. The man took my ticket printout and said, "This train number is listed as this train number." He wrote a different number on my paper. *Good to know*, I thought.

Once equipped with the right number, I discovered that my train had been delayed by two hours. But eventually it pulled in, and I was frantic trying to find my car. There appeared to be no rhyme or reason to the car order, and fearing that the train would pull out before I found my place and was safely aboard, I just jumped on a random car. Some Norwegian tourists must have seen my deer-in-the-headlights look, because they lured me down, promising the train wouldn't leave before we found our places. I trusted them, and they were right. The train didn't leave for over half an hour.

It was late, and so I settled into my berth to sleep for the night. I discovered that the side berths, unlike the main compartment berths, are composed of two seats folding in toward each other, which may or may not align in the middle. Mine did not. It was frightfully uncomfortable.

My compartment-mate was a large Indian kid, about nineteen-years-old, who acknowledged me only with disdain. My intention to sleep was frustrated by his talking on his cell phone. He actually had two of them, both of them ringing and beeping, as the night progressed. I grew more and more angry and frustrated at his rudeness. Finally, well after midnight, I banged my hand on the table between us. "Turn the cell phone off!" I said. "Off!" He seemed to understand, and nodded. Ten minutes later, it beeped again. I was ready to strangle him. I roared in frustration, grabbed my glasses, pillow, and shoulder bag and moved down the hallway. Two cabins down there was an empty upper side berth. I climbed into it and drew the sticky, stiff faded red velvet curtain closed with a flourish. Free from annoying interruptions, the gentle swaying of the train lulled me into a fitful sleep.

* * *

Walking away from the train station, I dragged my Aldabra tortoise of a suitcase through the mud and grime toward the bus that would carry me to the Nepalese border. The driver was a gaunt, turbaned fellow with a *The Thin Man* mustache. Before I could reach the door, he wielded a large white metal T-shaped thing at me. He motioned me to follow, and we stopped near the rear of the bus. He inserted the T-thingy in a half-inch hole and turned it. The trunk opened up, and he heaved my suitcase into it.

"Safe?" I asked.

"Safe," he assured me. I had had visions of sitting next to it, of not letting my eyes off of it, so I was a little freaked out to just leave it unattended, even if it *was* locked up. I told myself to relax and get on the bus already.

The bus reminded me a lot of the more dilapidated school buses of my elementary school years. There was no paint that wasn't chipped or peeling, and every one of the vinyl seats was torn. I sat down about three rows from the front, and instantly discovered a major problem—these seats were spaced for people *much* smaller than I.

At home I'm not a big guy—5'9" on a good day—and more than half of the men I know are taller than I. But the seats on this bus were placed with shorter shins than mine in mind. I could not sit facing forward—my knees banged on the seat in front of me when I tried. I had to sit with knees together, turned to the right (forcing my butt halfway into the seat next to me) or to the left (forcing my knees halfway into the space of the person next to me). It was an uncomfortable quandary.

I asked when we would be going and was told forty-five minutes. *Yikes!* I thought. *That's time enough to need a bath-*

room. Which was a problem, as there was no actual bus station here—just a street where all the buses were parked. And the ride to the border would be between two and three hours—no opportunity for a bathroom break there, either.

But the fact was, in that moment, I didn't need to go. I realized that in agonizing about some future need that may or may not materialize, I was falling directly into the trap that the Buddha so often warned about. I was suffering. So I tried to stay focused on the present moment in which I was warm, safe, amply supplied with reading material, and did not have to pee. I was happy. *Huh, it's amazing how easily that actually works,* I thought.

Every now and then I'd run back to look out the back window to see if anyone was pilfering my bag—no one was. But soon, there were too many people in the bus to make this obsessive behavior possible. The bus filled up. And even after all the seats were full, they just kept coming. People were sitting on laps, standing in the aisles, sitting around the driver's feet, and climbing up on the roof.

It had to be about forty degrees Fahrenheit. I couldn't imagine how cold it must get on the roof once the bus started moving. I wasn't happy about arriving nearly an hour early, but I was glad I did—at least I had a seat.

Eventually, the driver blew his horn and, in fits and starts, pulled out into the street. There were no shock absorbers to speak of, so the bus jerked and lurched and bounced at every opportunity. As the heat grew in that little space, jam-packed with humanity, so did the smell. I tried to smile at that, and as there were no English speakers within hearing range, I put in my earphones to listen to a book as we drove.

I tried to listen to *The Tibetan Book of Living and Dying,* but it was an older recording that was not of good quality, and I had trouble hearing it over the rattle and din of the bus. So I switched to an unauthorized history of Marvel Comics, which swept my brain away to Manhattan in the early 1960s even as my eyes roamed over the foggy, grey-green fields of northeast India.

The audiobook was a good idea, because every couple of miles we'd pull over and, impossibly, cram more people in. By the end of the first hour, I couldn't raise my arms to turn the page of a paperback if my life depended on it. They were firmly pinned to my sides, and at times I had difficulty breathing because of the pressure. I fought back the claustrophobia that threatened to make things even more difficult, and focused on Stan Lee's erratic management style. After a while, I tried counting cows.

Fortunately, after the second hour, people started getting *off* the bus. I breathed a sigh of relief when I could move my arms again, and broke off a piece of chocolate. I still had no need of a bathroom, my ribs were intact, and we were almost there. Life was good.

Soon, we slowed down, entering a ramshackle town that reminded me a bit of the TV series *Deadwood*—all mud and ditches and storefronts and shady-looking characters. The bus made a sharp right turn into a field where several other buses were parked. I flagged down the driver and secured my bag.

A rickshaw driver was instantly at my side, trying to snatch the bag out of my hand. I stopped him and got him to quote me a price. It was probably too high, but okay by me, since the border was actually half a kilometer from there, and there was no way I could drag my bag through the mud that far.

There's a strange mixture of exhilaration and shame that comes from riding in a rickshaw. On the one hand, there is something of the royal palanquin about it—it is privilege in motion. On the other hand, it is cheap and efficient. At times I think, "this is unjust" and other times I hear Lord Grantham admonishing Matthew on *Downton Abbey* when the young man refused to allow a servant to dress him: "Would you deprive him of his livelihood, his honor, his dignity?" I rode and this man's family ate. And there was no shame in his honest labor. It was, in Buddhist terms, right livelihood.

He deposited me and my bag at the Indian customs office. I don't know what I expected—a building like the DMV perhaps. But no, it was a tiny, crumbling concrete storefront with three rooms in it, all of them crammed with people. I filled out a couple of forms, and the very friendly agents stamped my passport and wished me well.

I dragged my bag out into the muddy street and walked about a hundred yards, through a large yellow-colored gateway with a seated Buddha at the apex. Large blue letters declared "Welcome to Nepal." I asked the soldiers where the Immigration Office was, and they kindly pointed to a place I would have easily missed. Again, I filled out a couple of forms, paid a few rupees, and got a big red stamp in my passport. And then I was in Nepal.

It looked absolutely no different than the frontier-town roughness I'd just crossed from. Instantly, cold, half-naked children pressed in on me, begging. I was swarmed by them, and a little panicked, I set out across the street. "Hey, Mister, need taxi?" a solid-looking man said, with his arm raised.

"I need to go to Lumbini," I said.

He gave me a curt, confident nod. "Lumbini, yes."

"How much?"

"750 rupees," he said.

"I only have Indian rupees," I said.

He shrugged. "500." About ten dollars.

"Sold," I said.

"Wait here," he said, and in a moment, he pulled up beside me in a newish Tata compact. He threw my bag into the trunk, and in moments we were speeding out of town. As we left the border town behind, I felt myself relax. I'd made it. The mystery of the border crossing had not overwhelmed me.

The countryside was beautiful. It didn't look much different from the farmland in India, but it *felt* different. The people looked hale and hearty. Once we got away from the border, I saw no shantytowns. There were adobe houses, but they looked like very traditional dwellings. It may be that the people there were poor, but it didn't look like the grinding poverty that I'd gotten used to in India. I could be wrong, but that was my impression as we rode.

I chatted with the driver about life in Nepal. He told me about his family, and that most people in Nepal were Hindu, even though everyone was proud of the Buddhist heritage of the place. He asked if I were married—yes—and if I have children—no. I got asked this a lot, and most people seemed shocked when I said I had no children. First, they would give me a pitiful look, "Medical trouble..." they'd nod understandingly.

"No, no medical trouble," I'd answer.

"Wife medical trouble..." they'd nod, sadly.

"No, no medical trouble," I'd repeat. I would explain that about half of Americans I know choose *not* to have children. They'd wonder at this and think it very strange.

After about twenty minutes, I began to see signs for Lumbini. We passed a Christian church on my left, which surprised me greatly. I checked my phone, and was delighted to discover it was Saturday. Tomorrow morning, I would be going to church. "Do you know what time the church has services?" I asked the driver. He did—10am. I looked forward to spending some time with Nepalese Christians, even if I couldn't understand a word of what they were saying.

Lumbini isn't much of a town, I discovered. It has one main street and a lot of trinket carts. Scary-looking restaurants, dusty convenience stores, and shabby guest houses seemed to make up the majority of businesses. To our right, a very large park stretched for what seemed like miles. The trees waved their white spindly branches through the fog in a way that was both eerie and beautiful. A line of taxis, bicycles, and rickshaws extended from a soldier-guarded park entrance.

My guest house was only about a hundred paces from the gate. Given the general state of the buildings, I was hesitant. However, the lobby, though simple, was very nicely appointed. I asked the desk clerk if there was a room with a tub available, and against all odds, there was.

Indians (and Nepalese it seems) love bright, fluorescent colors that would never fly in the US. This room was a shocking lime green, and the plaster was beginning to crumble in places. But it was clean and there were no bugs.

Looking out the window, I saw that about a third of the people out on the street were Westerners. As I picked my way around the huge mud ruts in the road and stepped over the scabby dogs, the thought that struck me most profoundly was that there were no hawkers. Not a single person was rushing up to me begging me to buy their trinkets or to just outright give them money. *What a relief*, I thought.

It was almost bitterly cold, however. I shoved my hands deep into my jacket pockets and hunkered down into my fleece. I eyed the shops around me skeptically, looking for a place that looked inviting. I went into a convenience store and was pleasantly surprised to see a Toblerone chocolate bar—I bought one, along with an orange Fanta. It was comfort food, in a place without very much of that. Diet be damned.

When I went to pay, however, I discovered that I was almost out of money. I scoped about for an ATM, and quickly spotted three signs. One was closed up, another wouldn't take my card, and a third timed out repeatedly just short of dispensing the cash. Three ATMs in town and not one of them worked. Great…. This was going to be interesting.

Evening was not far off, and I needed to do something about dinner. I called up the Lonely Plant pages on Lumbini on my phone and looked for their top pick. They recommended Hotel Peace, but when I entered, the waiter waved me away. "Large group coming," he said. "No room."

I pulled out my phone and looked at recommendation number two—the restaurant at an upscale hotel for Japanese travelers. The hotel also sported hot Japanese baths—and as I couldn't think of anything better in such a cold, foggy place, I resolved to go there with haste.

Unfortunately, it was outside of town, on the far side of the park. I thought about walking but when a rickshaw driver pulled up next to me and gestured, I thought, *Why not? At least he'll know where it is.*

He did. And boy, was I glad I got the rickshaw. Turns out I'd seriously miscalculated the size of the park. I had been gauging it according to the average size of the other Buddha parks I'd been to. According to the map in Lonely Planet, it wouldn't be a long walk to the Japanese place. But I'd be wrong about that—my destination was well beyond walking distance, especially once it started to rain.

The rickshaw driver pulled open a canopy to keep me dry, which was very kind. Unfortunately, it was a canopy put in place for *much* shorter patrons, and every time we hit a pot hole, my head crashed into the bamboo slats above me. They really hurt, too—I kept feeling at my scalp and looking at my hand, expecting blood.

Nobody believes in electric lights in India, and apparently this is true of Nepal, too. I have never eaten in such a selection of dark, shadowy places in my life. The Japanese restaurant, for all of its claim to luxury, was no different. There wasn't a light in the place—only the dim ambient light from the foggy windows illuminated the table.

Disappointment number one came when I was told that the baths were not open, as there was no large group of Japanese tourists scheduled that day. Disappointment number two was the food itself—it was barely edible. Fortunately, however, they let me pay by credit card, sparing some of my precious cash.

The light was just fading when I reached my hotel room. It was time for a hot bath and an episode of *Smallville*. I'd come prepared with a bunch of Indian movies, but what I found once I got here was that I had enough of India by the end of each day, and what I really craved was a little bit of home. *Smallville*'s Kansas and its updating of the Superman myth was about as American as it gets—and the perfect escape at the end of a long day abroad.

The next day I rented a bicycle. After breakfast my first destination was the Christian church I'd seen about a kilometer away. In no time I was setting the kickstand and looking for a gate.

"Helloooo!" I heard a voice from above. I looked up, and saw a dark-haired man about my own age waving. He disappeared and in a moment reappeared inside a small gate. I had to duck to enter the gate, but when I got inside, he pumped my hand excitedly. "Welcome, welcome," he said. I looked around, expecting a bustle of pre-worship activity. But there seemed to be no one around.

"I was hoping to join you for your Sunday morning worship," I said.

The man's face fell. "Oh, I am so sorry," he said. "In Nepal, everyone worships on Saturday. Too bad you did not come yesterday!"

"Everyone...as in Christians, Hindus, Buddhists and Muslims?" I asked.

"Yes!" he said, bobbing in a full-body nod. "Everyone here worship on the same day!"

Well, I thought, *that solved quite a few problems.*

"I am Pastor Jisay," he said. A woman about our same age was halfway down the stairs. "And this is my wife, Carunia."

I shook her hand and introduced myself, "I am Pastor John Mabry, from America."

The couple looked at each other with evident surprise. "Pastor John," he shook my hand again, "for fifteen years I have done the Lord's work in this place, and we have had Christians visit now and then. But we have never had another pastor visit us. Not even once. Not until you." He seemed very excited indeed.

"Please, please, come in," he started upstairs after his wife. "We have no worship planned, but we will make some worship. Come!" Once on the second floor, we followed an open-air hallway and stepped through a door. Inside seemed to be the one room where the pastor and his wife lived. Nearest the door was a twin-sized bed. A large kitchen table ran along one wall, covered with brightly colored vinyl. Along the far wall were books and a computer. The fourth wall hosted a couch and a doorway into another room.

Pastor Jisay sat in a plastic lawn chair, and asked me about my ministry, so I told him about Grace North Church and Our Redeemer Lutheran in California. Then I asked him about his. His wife, seated on the bed, listened intently, and freely offered clarifications and additional tidbits of information as he spoke.

They were both from India and had been involved in a Baptist church there. Then they received a call from God to come to Lumbini, where there was no Christian presence at all. Proselytizing was illegal, and so they rented a single room and offered to teach the local children for free. No one came.

But they kept trying. After a while one family, then another, began to send their sons to school. Soon, they had over fifty students. Then Carunia asked her husband, "What about the girls? We need to educate them, too." They prayed about it, and soon began to admit girls. They now had over three hundred students enrolled—most of them Hindu and Muslim.

On major holidays they have big parties in the sanctuary,

and serve food to all who come. And lots of people come, apparently—including the Buddhist monks. They share the mission of the school with them, and they share what Jesus has meant to them in their lives.

After all this time, only a handful of people have been baptized, but Pastor Jisay and Carunia weren't discouraged by this. "We witness with our lives," he said, "by being the kind of people that other people can look up to and would want to be." He smiled confidently, like a man who is sure of his own truth. "When people see that we are honest and good, they will want to know this Lord who makes us honest and good."

A young woman entered from the adjoining room. She was wearing flannel pajama bottoms, a heavy fleece jacket, and a stocking cap. "This is our youngest daughter, Jessica," Jisay said proudly. "She plays the guitar for worship. Go and get your guitar, Jessica," he directed kindly. A few minutes later, their elder daughter Dolly had joined us, too—identically dressed. The older daughter took up the guitar and within moments, all of us were singing, "*Create in me a clean heart, O God, and renew a right spirit within me... Cast me not away from your presence, O Lord, take not your Holy Spirit from me....*"

I closed my eyes and sang loudly, to their evident delight. Then the daughters sang a song I had never heard before. It was lovely, with the tight, haunting harmonies of siblings singing together.

They passed the guitar to me and I played, "When Jesus Comes Knockin'," a song I'd written about a year ago, based on one of Luther's writings. They seemed to enjoy it very much, and afterwards, Jisay passed a worn Bible to me. "Bring us a message, Pastor John," he said.

I opened the Bible at random, and it fell to the Epistle of James. "Be not hearers of the Word only, but doers." "You know, Luther hated this epistle," I said, "because in it faith alone is not enough. God requires a response to grace, a response that reaches out to others....like you are doing here." Then I set the Bible aside and spoke to them from my heart. I told them how absent God had seemed ever since I'd arrived in India, and how much my soul ached for his touch.

Jisay nodded knowingly. "This is often the way it is," he said. "Many times in our work we have said, 'Where are you, Lord?' But he always comes back. He will come back for you."

I felt God's touch through theirs. Pastor Jisay asked us to bow in prayer, and he prayed for me, a long and loving prayer. Afterwards, I prayed for him, his family, and their ministry in Lumbini.

After this, they showed me around the school, clearly hoping that I would go back and tell my people what they were doing there. They were not shy in inviting us to partner in their work there. I promised him I would tell people what I had seen. With hearty handshakes all around, I said my goodbyes, and buoyed by the love and kindness of these strangers, pedaled back to my guest house.

After a brief pit stop, I walked into the park, and after about a half a mile, came to the grounds of a beautiful Vajrayana monastery. Several monks were practicing trumpets, providing a lovely soundtrack for my explorations. The grounds were lovingly kept, with a stunning garden. Two monks were lounging and chattering; they acknowledged me as I passed. I stepped out of my shoes and climbed the steps into the temple—it was ornate in the way that Vajrayana sanctuaries often are, all color and bright fabrics and dramatic paintings. One young monk sat in the choir stall, reading. The giant Buddha statue beamed down at me beatifically. It was hard to leave.

Passing a small lamp-house, I looked inside and saw a couple hundred butter lamps ablaze within. I remembered the sutra that I'd read just that morning, which said that when the Promised One was born, "a great measureless light surpassing the splendor of the gods appeared in the world" lighting up "even those abysmal world interspaces of vacancy, gloom, and utter darkness...there too a great measureless light surpassing the splendor of the gods appeared."

As I straightened up, I heard the echo of the Isaiah readings for the Feast of Epiphany, "The people who walked in darkness have seen a great light; those who lived in a land of deep darkness—on them light has shined.... For a child has been born for us, a son given to us; authority rests upon his shoulders; and he is named Wonderful Counselor, Mighty God, Everlasting Father, Prince of Peace."[1]

Still musing on this, I headed out of the grounds, to another temple—this one seemed to be run by nuns, but strangely, they were Hindu nuns, with images of Hindu saints side-by-side with the Buddha. I reminded myself that the Buddha was born on the site of a Hindu temple—it could be that this community saw itself in continuity with that ancient one.

Just outside the grounds there was a large, enclosed area. I followed the fence around to a place where several soldiers were operating a metal detector. This, I realized, was Lumbini's holy-of-holies. I tried to go in, but a soldier stopped me and pointed up the road. "Get ticket," he said.

I shrugged and walked to where he had been pointing. I passed two women sitting in the street. It looked like they were beggars. I stepped past them and went to the window of the ticket booth. One of the women got up—very slowly—and walked past me, through a door, into the ticket booth. "Two hundred rupees," she said.

"Here's 500," I said.

"No change," she said. And then she just sat there.

"Huh," I said, pocketing my money. "Guess I'm not seeing the holy-of-holies today."

As I was walking away, the other woman on the ground said, "No change?"

"No," I said, slowing down.

She gestured with her chin for me to come over to her. Reaching into her shirt, she pulled out a wad of bills big enough to choke a water buffalo and counted off five 100-rupee notes. I gave her the 500-rupee bill, and she stuffed the wad back into her shirt.

Feeling vaguely like I was in a dream, I walked back over to the window. "She had change," I said to the woman, "in her shirt."

Without a trace of humor, the woman took my 200 rupees and handed me a ticket. Then she went back outside and sat next to the other woman in the street. I walked back over to the metal detectors.

Once again the guard prevented me from entering. "What now?" I asked. I had to deposit my shoes in one of the little boxes off to the side. "Fine," I said, and took off my socks, too.

This time I got through the guards. Directly in front of me was the Mahadevi temple. Beside it was what was left of an Asokan pillar. I climbed the long ramp to go into the temple, and once inside, marveled at the carefully protected ruins. This was the original Hindu temple, ancient at the time of the Buddha's birth.

I circumambulated the ruins, following the white wooden walkway along the perimeter. When I got to the far wall, I got in line, although I didn't know what the line was for. As I got closer to the front, however, there was a sign in many languages. The English translation read: "This is the exact spot of the Buddha's birth."

I remembered the story vividly, having read it many times in the past few weeks. According to custom, the Buddha's mother wanted to travel to her ancestral home in order to give birth. So when she felt her time approaching, she and her entourage journeyed out to Lumbini. She reached a celebrated mango grove, and she instructed her ladies-in-waiting to erect a pavil-ion for the birth.

This reminded me of Mary and Joseph, who had to travel to Joseph's ancestral homeland—Bethlehem—for the census, just at the time when Jesus was about to be delivered.

When the time came, the Queen did not give birth as normal mothers do. Instead of lying down, she gave birth standing up—grasping the limb of a mango tree. Several times in Lumbini I would see this iconography repeated: a noble woman, standing still behind the walking child Siddhartha, grasping at a tree branch directly above her.

The woman in front of me with her three kids was standing still, too—in fact she did not move for several minutes. I could-n't move forward to see the Most Sacred Place, and I couldn't go backwards. So I just stood there. Eventually, they moved on, touching the stone wall and then bringing their hands to their mouths to kiss.

Finally reaching the railing, I looked down where hundreds of people have thrown coins and bills. In the spaces between them I could see a large white stone, shaped vaguely like a foot—the very spot, legend says, that the Buddha first touched the earth in his final incarnation.

I went out the door, and immediately in front of me was a large pool, the place where the Buddha's mother bathed after giving birth.

Beyond the pool was a large tree with a shrine in it. A cluster of people stood around the shrine, burning incense before it and making offerings. Radiating in every direction from the tree were literally thousands of strings of prayer flags—it was a spectacular, breathtaking sight.

I snapped a few pictures, but I realized that the camera could never capture the blaze of color shuddering and swaying in the breeze. The fog, the smoke of incense, the splendid stench of holiness overwhelmed me. I didn't feel God, but I felt...significance.

I exited the park and walked back to the village to get my bicycle. I sped back to explore the temples built by various Buddhist denominations. Nearest the village, on one side of a three-kilometer-long fountain was the Theravada area.

The Theravada sect preserves the earliest strata of Buddhist tradition, so I began with these. First I explored the Malaysian temple, but found it a little dumpy. Next, a nun's convent sported a tangled garden with a stupa[2] and a number of ill-groomed pillars. The temple was small, but had a lovely standing Queen. And everywhere you looked were statues of the just-born Siddhartha, striding forward on two feet, one finger in the air, already teaching, the forefinger of his other hand pointing at the earth.

I pedaled to several other temples, all of which had seen better days. Descending the steps from one particular dumpy specimen, I said to the tall Westerner next to me, "I have to admit I'm underwhelmed by the temples thus far."

He agreed, but like me he was determined to see all of them. His name was Per, and he was from Sweden. A hospice caretaker and Zen practitioner, he was on vacation, doing a bit of a pilgrimage of his own. We seemed to be going in the same direction, so without actually discussing it, we just went together. I think he was as grateful for the company as I was.

He was a little reticent, but very friendly. A few years older than I, and much taller, with a full shock of gray hair, there was a dignified melancholy about him that I found immensely appealing. He laughed easily, and we had no trouble keeping up a good banter as we cycled from one temple to the next.

The Thai temple wowed us—it was the only impressive temple on the Theravada side. The Mahayana temples promised better. Per and I found a series of bridges over the fountain, and I was inspired by Per's selective comprehension of English.

It was clear to me that the groundskeeper was telling us not to take our bikes over the bridges, but to go around—three kilometers around. But Per said, "Oh, yes, good, thank you," picked up his bike and sprinted to the top of the archway. Before the groundskeeper could object, he was halfway down the other side. I took advantage of the confusion that followed his minor act of disobedience and followed him quickly.

Feeling the excitement of naughty—but not *too* naughty—children, we pedaled off, toward the nearest of the Mahayana temples. When we got there, it was still under construction, but there was a magnificent stupa. We looked for some sign of what sect had built it, and found a sign identifying it as having been built by "France."

"Huh, France," I said, hands on my hips, "That famous European Buddhist country."

Per looked equally confused.

"Do the French strike you as Mahayana?" I asked Per, but he had already walked away toward the stupa. It was elegant, made of a dark stone of a single hue. There was nothing cheesy or ornamented about it—it was understated and elegant. "That's the way it should be done," I thought.

The next temple was a study in contrasts. It was enormous, and seemed to be an amalgam of Chinese and Tibetan styles. "Architecturally, this is one mutt of a building," I said. We asked the guard which sect had built this one, and he said, "Germany."

Per and I looked at each other, mouths agape. "*Really?*" I said, completely flummoxed. There was nothing remotely German about this building—except perhaps a slight resemblance to the baroque excess of several of the cathedrals in Germany's Catholic south. "This is crazy," I breathed.

Unfortunately, no cameras were allowed inside. Too bad, too, because it was a stunner. The main temple was built in a dome, and the whole of the inside was painted blue, the color of a bright sky. Highly stylized clouds of vaguely Tibetan provenance seemed to blow across the dome, separated here and there by wildly colorful dharma wheels depicting wrathful deities and beneficent Bodhisattvas. Stunning murals covered every inch of the outer walls, and I had to physically close my jaw as I walked around in disbelief at the outrageous beauty and startling imagination of it all.

In front, children spun story-high prayer wheels in front of a statue of the Buddha teaching a gaggle of disciples. Per and I both staggered out, shaking our heads.

As I encountered statue after statue of the Buddha, I realized how hungry I was for Christian iconography. The statues of the Buddha were designed to elicit Buddhist devotion, and I realized that part of my own feeling of disconnection from God might be the complete lack of devotional images, on which I am usually quite dependent. I typically travel with a diptych of an Orthodox icon of the Resurrection—it goes with me everywhere. But in the interest of travelling light, I left it at home. I felt struck by the loss and lack of it.

The next temple was a vertical, compact affair, which we were again flummoxed to discover had been built by the French. "Where are all these French Buddhists hiding?" I asked. We climbed the stairs to discover a very simple, very plain sanctuary made of red marble. Straight columns lined both sides of the room, ending at an altar with a large stone statue of the Buddha.

"It reminds me of a cathedral," Per said, pointing to the pillars. I saw what he meant—this definitely had a Western touch to it. It had a strangely Calvinist feel to it, too—on the altar were a complete set of sutras which must have run more than fifty thick volumes, all bound in red leather. Prayer books dotted the altar, none of them in French and most in Korean. Very strange.

There was one more temple in this particular cluster, and in some ways it was the most magnificent. We climbed slate gray steps to the top. Entering the sanctuary, we stepped into a dimly lit circular space. It was entirely made of concrete, ornamented only by dark wooden pillars at twelve points around the room. Simplicity reigned, and there was a strongly Japanese aesthetic to it. There was a gigantic statue of the Buddha front and center made entirely of beaten copper. It was very moving.

On the way out we saw that it had been built by the Nepalese government, with plenty of funding from China. There was nothing Chinese about the design or ornamentation, nor Vajrayana, either. Once again, this was how a temple ought to be built. I staggered out, stunned and impressed as hell.

"Okay, anything is downhill from there," I said. Per agreed.

And yet...not far away was a Vajrayana temple that looked Greek from a distance, although I found out later it was built by Austria. On one side of the grounds was a gleaming gold stupa, rising two stories high. Directly across from it was a shining silver stupa, a mirror image of the first. Inside was a very nice though very conventional Vajrayana temple. What made it significant were the paintings, arranged around the building like the stations of the cross, telling the life story of the Buddha in glorious detail. While we studied them, a single monk chanted and rang bells. It was haunting and beautiful and unforgettable.

We found one more Vajrayana temple on that side of the fountain. This one was much more magnificent, as colorful as any sanctuary I'd ever seen. But what really struck me was a small group of boys being given a music class in a small room adjoining the sanctuary. They played the strange Tibetan instruments in a cacophony that may or may not have been expert—I am too unfamiliar with the style of music to tell. Plus, even when it is expertly done, it is a harsh style of music, so it sounded pretty impressive to us.

Tired, and with the light waning, we pedaled back to town. Along the way, I discovered we were both fans of Emmanuel Swedenborg, and we discussed the implications of Swedenborgian theology the rest of the journey home. It's amazing the folks you find at random when you're travelling!

I was a little sad to have found Per just to lose him—the next day he'd be heading to Bodh Gaya. But it was a good reminder of Buddhist impermanence. Everything that arises—even friendships in unlikely places—passes away quickly. If you don't want to suffer, you mustn't cling. I shook his hand, wished him Godspeed, and headed back to my room.

I came to realize that I loved Lumbini. Nothing that had irritated me about India was there. There were no beggars in the street. No one was hustling me. I was surrounded by beauty—and fiercely beautiful people. It was hard to believe that the Buddha could spring from the ground of a place as garish as India. But here? Oh yes. This is a place worthy of gods—or at least of aspiring saviors. I dug my hands into my pockets against the chill and passed a rack of baby Buddhas, their forefingers all raised to heaven, proclaiming a holy birth, a magnificent light, and a pathway out of gloom and despair.

------

1   Isaiah 9:2, 6.

2   A stupa is often a building with no inside to it. I used to think that was kind of pointless, but I have come to understand it more in the sense of the Hebrew *ebenezer*, a pile of rocks that indicates a significant place. And some stupas *are* just piles of rocks, although many others are well maintained and quite beautiful.

Palace ruins at the Indian Kapilavatsu.

Chapter Four: Kapilavatsu—Where Siddhartha Grew Up

The Buddha may have been born in Lumbini, but he didn't grow up here. His father, the King of the Sakya clan, had his palace in Kapilavatsu. So that was where I was off to next— to see the boyhood home of Prince Siddhartha.

It was a bitterly cold morning as the car I'd hired for the trip wound its way through several tiny villages to the open road. As I stared out the foggy windows, I reflected on Siddhartha's boyhood. This part of his story is every bit as much about the King as about the Prince—it is the tragedy of a man losing his son and a king losing his heir.

When their son was born, the King and Queen named him Siddhartha, which means, "the one through whom all good will come"—an auspicious beginning. One scriptural source says that when the sage Asita saw the child, he prophesied that he would either be a great king or a great saint.

The King very much wanted his son to be a great king—they were of the warrior caste, after all, not Brahmins. It wouldn't be appropriate for him to be a holy man of any sort. But just in case Asita was on to something, Siddhartha's father was determined to mold him into a great ruler. To keep him focused, he surrounded him with nothing but luxury—there were dancing girls to keep his attention, beautiful gardens to wander in, and plenteous sporting events.

All throughout his childhood, the Prince had everything he could want. He never had any reason to look beyond the palace gates—which was exactly the way his father wanted it.

I wanted to see those palace gates, but I had a problem: there were two competing sites for Kapilavatsu. Both were about equal distance from Lumbini—about 20 kilometers. But one site was in India, and the other was in Nepal.

I read up on the India site first—archeologists had found inscriptions there going back to a couple of hundred years after the Buddha's death indicating that the remains of the Buddha's family, the Sakya clan, were there. That was a pretty good indication, so I went there first.

We pulled into a large park, bounded by a stone fence. Just inside, about twenty boys were playing cricket. They paused in their game to see what the funny foreigner was up to. The funny foreigner wanted to climb on the rocks, apparently, so they shrugged and went back to their game, glancing over at me every few minutes.

I was awestruck by the enormity of the ruin in front of me. I'm not sure if what I was seeing was a palace, but it was large enough to be one. There were scores of rooms. In one building, about thirty rooms were arranged around a central courtyard with a fire pit in the middle. It looked like there might have been kitchens off to one side, and storage to the other. I imagined what it must have been like for ancient visitors to step into the grand foyer. I felt like such a visitor now.

Three large buildings had been excavated. I searched all the signs in English, hoping to hear that there were more, but they didn't say so. So as I climbed about the ruins, I imagined what it must have been like in Siddhartha's day.

So it was in this palace, or in one very like it, that the young prince had heard the maids talking about the loveliness of the countryside, and he implored his father to allow him to make some excursions there as well. His father agreed, and arranged a series of day trips. But unbeknownst to the young prince, he had his men do a lot of prep work.

Like an ancient Potemkin Village, the King's men rode along the routes that the prince's entourage planned to take, razing the shantytowns, driving out the beggars and anyone who was sick or old. They fixed up the buildings and made sure that everyone the prince would encounter presented a fresh, healthy, and happy face.

On his first outing, the best efforts of the King were thwarted. The Prince's chariot slowed down in order to avoid hitting an old man tottering across the road. "What is *that?*" asked Siddhartha, since he'd never seen an old man.

The charioteer obviously had not gotten the King's memo, because he looked surprised. "What, you mean the old man?"

"What do you mean by *old?*" asked the Prince.

"Uh...well my prince," the driver ran his fingers through his hair awkwardly. "When people live a long time, they start to go downhill...like this guy here. You know, they get all jittery, they bend over, they walk funny."

"We have to help him!" the Prince cried out.

"You can't really do anything for him," the charioteer countered. "It happens to everyone."

The Prince was aghast. "Are you telling me that this happens to all people? Will it happen to my father? To my auntie? To me?"

"Uh...yeah," the driver smiled uncertainly. "Everyone knows...uh, most people know that, sire."

Siddhartha's hands were shaking, and he could barely control his emotions. "Let's go back to the palace," he said.

Siddhartha spend several days brooding. But a few days later, he decided to try again. He went out, and found that he quite enjoyed the wind in his hair and the freshness of the sun on his skin. Then he saw a woman with a crippling disease. He signaled his driver to stop. "Is she old, too?" he asked.

"No, my prince. She's young. She's just sick."

"What is *sick?*" asked the Prince.

"What is *what*, your majesty?" the driver asked incredulously. "Haven't you ever had a cold?"

"What do you mean by *cold?*" asked the confused prince.

"Oh, for heaven's sake..." huffed the driver.

"Humor me," commanded Siddhartha.

"Fine. Sometimes, bodies just break down and stop working right."

"Why does this happen?" asked the Buddha.

"Sometimes people don't get enough to eat, sometimes they get too cold at night, or sometimes evil spirits invade their bodies."

"That's terrible...." the Prince looked utterly deflated.

"But it is the truth, your majesty."

"I have lost my appetite for exploring today. Let's...let's just go home."

"Yes, my lord," and the driver turned around.

After a couple more days of brooding, Siddhartha called for his driver, determined to make at least one successful outing. This time, not long after they had set out, they came across a corpse lying in the middle of the road.

"What's this?" asked the Prince.

"Oh, for crying out loud..." said the driver. "It's a dead guy, what do you think it is?"

"What is this *dead*?" asked Siddhartha.

The driver rolled his eyes. "Dead, as in D.E.A.D."

"Do you mean to suggest that he will not rise?"

"Uh, yeah. He will not rise, and in an hour or so someone will haul him off and burn him."

"Why does this happen?" asked the Prince.

"Either because of old age or because he got sick. Or both."

"This is the end of all men?" asked the Prince.

"And women," affirmed the driver.

"This is horrible," said the Prince.

"This is life," agreed the driver.

"How can I just go and enjoy myself, now that I know this? Can we..." started Siddhartha.

"Already on it. Have a seat, your majesty, we'll be back at the palace in no time."

Siddhartha took these sights hard, but on the way back to the palace, he saw someone else his father's men had missed. "Who is that?" he asked.

"What? You mean the monk?" asked the driver.

"What is a *monk*?" asked the Prince.

"He is someone who has devoted his life to the pursuit of Truth," said the driver.

"I must devote myself to pursuing this Truth," the Prince said to himself. "I must find a solution to old age, illness, and death." And not long after, he fled the palace under cover of night, never to return to the life of luxury or wealth.

We drove a little way to another set of ruins—this one was of a stupa and an ancient monastery. As I picked my way through the stones, getting closer to the stupa, I saw a group of three monks sitting side-by-side chanting. A begging bowl was set out in front of them.

I passed by without giving, and stopped to listen to a group of Korean pilgrims listening to what sounded very much like a Bible study to me. "Sutra study," I said out loud, balancing on a crumbling wall. A large pond bordered one side of the stupa, its surface dotted with hundreds of purple lotuses.

I remembered what the Buddha had said of lotuses—that they were like the human soul, rooted in grime, but stretching toward the heavens, emerging as a thing of sublime beauty. It made me smile.

The drive back was odd. When I first got in the car, I thought I'd let in a couple of flies by mistake. I shooed them out, and thought I was done with them. No such luck. Within moments the cab was swarming with them. I opened the window again, and shooed as many as I could out. But they just kept coming. Apparently, they had their source of origin somewhere within the car itself, perhaps newly hatched and just taking to the wing. I was grossed out, and rode with the window open most of the way, huddling into my fleece against the cold.

A couple days later, I headed out to the Nepalese Kapilavatsu. The problem there wasn't flies, I discovered, but mosquitoes—I was eaten alive by them. I woke one morning to find a huge red gash across my pillow. Apparently, one of the hungry buggers didn't quite escape with my blood. It occurred to me that it isn't very Buddhist to desire the destruction of another—but then, I'm not a Buddhist.

My hotel manager called up to my room to inform me that the car had arrived. I rushed down, and just as I was about to head out, he asked me if he could tag along. I very much doubted that the driver spoke English, so having an interpreter along would be a definite plus. Also, I really liked Raji. He had been a really friendly, helpful guy ever since I arrived, and so I immediately agreed.

We ducked down through a hole in a fence, and then climbed up onto what looked like an ancient road. I realized a moment later that what I was walking on was actually the remains of several buildings, a long string of them. The buildings circled a pond, resplendent with lotuses. Now and then you could hear the *snap!* of wet clothes hitting a stone. I peered around and not far away saw a woman standing ankle deep in the murky water, doing her laundry.

Walking toward the largest group of ruins, I made for a sign that identified it as the gate through which Siddhartha had snuck out of the palace under cover of night, leaving his kingdom and his family behind. Studying the formations that were left, I could totally see how it formed a thoroughfare, with buildings close by on either side. It was, I realized, the eye of the needle. All we needed now was a camel.

In the middle of the clearing was a small shrine, although it was too dim for me to see which deity was enthroned within it. On either side of it, however, were two impressive rows of elephant statues, painted in creative colors. It looked like they were made of papier mâché. The artwork was crude, but charming.

"You can make a prayer for something you deeply desire," Raji said. "But then when you get it you have to come back here to make an offering. Go ahead."

"I don't think so, Raji," I laughed. "If I get what I ask for, it won't be easy to get back here."

"It won't?" A troubled look crossed his face.

"This is a very long way from home," I said. "And it's very expensive to fly here."

He gave me a "does not compute" look. I shook my head. "Raji, I'm not rich."

Now he really looked confused. "But look at your clothes!" he protested. I explained about the three strata of society in America. He started nodding.

"We have the same. I am middle class, here."

"Yes. So am I. It must seem like I am very rich here, but back home, I'm not. I could only come here because 200 people are supporting this trip financially."

He looked perplexed, so I explained the Indigogo campaign. He seemed to hold me in a new, higher esteem after that, although I can't say exactly why. Perhaps he saw me more as a peer, and less as a spoiled rich guy. I mean, I *am* a spoiled rich guy, compared to the vast majority of Nepalis. But he understood my place in my own society differently, and that it was more like his. He seemed to relax a bit after that. His laughter sounded more genuine.

There were several fires in the grass, and so I walked over to see what was going on. I didn't walk far, because string had been strung across the walkway. Just inside the string, several Nepali men were on their hands and knees, very carefully uncovering some very old-looking bricks. I took a step back and realized I was observing an archeological dig, and that the men were revealing a long wall.

Looking toward the fires, I saw that several large squares of land had been cordoned off by string, and that there were several men and women measuring, writing, and discussing all around me.

"John, please meet Dr. Basanta Bidari," Raji said. "He has written many books on Nepal, and on this area, too."

A large Nepali man with a very friendly demeanor shook my hand and invited me to step over the string. I did so, and he began to explain their process. The fires were to clear the brush. Then they would start digging, based on magnetic imaging of the area. A young man was laying out a measuring tape along one of the strings, and Dr. Bidari called to him. He introduced the man as a professor of archeology at the University of Durham in the UK, but I didn't catch the name. I shook the man's hand.

I told Dr. Bidari about my project, and asked him which of the two Kapilavatsu sites was the authentic one. He laughed. "They're both authentic sites," he said. "*And* they are both Kapilavatsu." He must have seen my confusion, because he quickly explained. "There was no border between Nepal and India back in the Lord Buddha's day. It was one country, his father's kingdom, the land of the Sakyas. That site is not far from this one. That is one side of the city, this is the other."

That sounded so...reasonable. I just felt silly. But as I considered it, I realized that reconciling the two sites was a fine metaphor for reconciling the two faiths, Buddhism and Christianity. Both of them are coming at several of the same truths from different directions, using different symbols and vocabularies to describe convergent ideas. For instance, the Buddhist doctrine of "no self" is remarkably similar to what Jesus was getting at when he said, "those who want to save their life will lose it, and those who lose their life for my sake will find it"[1] and "Unless a grain of wheat falls into the earth and dies, it remains just a single grain; but if it dies, it bears much fruit."[2]

We have to let go of our ideas about who and what we are, so that our true self, our real identity can be revealed—and in both faiths that true identity is divine.

It was clear that Bidari had a lot to do, so I thanked him for his time and attention, and let him get back to work. Soon Raji and I were back in the car, and heading off toward the next site. It was an impressive ruin and stood very tall over the field of yellow grass surrounding it. A sign said that it was the site of a monastery built by the Buddha's father, King Suddhodana. I remembered back on the story. Long after the Buddha had established himself as a respected teacher, he returned to Kapilavatsu to reconcile with his father.

Things were pretty testy at first, but as the Buddha shared the Dharma with his father, the King's heart melted. He said, "I understand now why you had to go away, and I no longer blame you for it. You chose the better path, and I am grateful to have had such a brave and noble son."

I remembered back to the weekend when I'd graduated with my PhD, and for the first time in my adult life my Dad told me he was proud of me. All throughout my childhood, I never remember seeing my Dad cry, not even once. But I saw a single tear escape his eye as he confessed his admiration for what I'd accomplished.

I will always be enormously grateful for that conversation. In a way, that was the moment I grew up. I had finally gotten my father's blessing. Remembering how important a moment that was for me helped me to connect to how important it must have been for Siddhartha, too. It was closure, and reconciliation, and to some degree, peace.

King Suddhodana was convinced by the Buddha's teaching, but never abandoned his throne. Instead, he became a patron of the Sangha, and supported the monastery in this place until his death. I was marveling over this reconciliation, when about six girls in their early teens, sporting matching blue school uniforms, approached us.

"Take a picture!" they demanded. So I took their picture. Then I took their picture on the steps of the ruin. Then I took their picture with Raji. Then Raji took their picture with me. Then they insisted on giving me a handful of spiced top ramen crumbs and watched until I ate them. Then they gave me an individually-wrapped mango lozenge. Then they giggled and ran away.

Raji and I just stared at each other. Later, as we were on our way to another site, we saw all six of them hitching rides on other people's bicycles, clinging to luggage racks, handlebars, or riding the bar side-saddle. We waved.

Our last stop was an Asokan pillar, built next to a stupa. "What happened here?" I asked Raji.

He pointed to a sign. "Previous Buddha."

"You don't say," I said, leaning in to read the sign. Indeed, it was placed at the legendary birth site of Krakuchhanda Buddha, the Buddha who lived about three hundred years before Siddhartha. I was skeptical, but reminded myself that this is myth, not history. I don't have to disbelieve it, because I don't have to believe it. I only have to understand the role that the story plays in the lives of the faithful.

The Buddha was not a standalone sage who single-handedly invented his teaching, but part of a long history of salvation, as one in a line of many teachers of an eternal Dharma. The story serves the same function as the history of salvation that Christians recount in their Eucharistic prayers, placing Jesus in the context of God's faithfulness to Israel as the crowning figure in a long line of Hebrew prophets. So I got why it was important and was impressed that it had meant enough to Emperor Asoka to warrant a pillar.

As we rode back to the hotel, I heard Raji start to snore in the back seat. I smiled, beginning to feel the mid-day drag myself. I remembered my own boyhood home in La Habra, and how strange everything looks to me now when I go back there. I thought of Benicia, too, where I finished high school, and which I think of as my hometown. Benicia has a very special place in my heart. I didn't grow up there, but I *finished* growing up there. And this place was the Buddha's hometown—a place that would always call to him. It was the place where he grew up, and it was the place that he had to leave to become his own person. It was the place his father grew old and died, and it was the place that he set out for when he knew he was dying himself. That's a strong pull.

Another strong pull exerted its force on me, and I sank into a drooling nap as the car bounced along the uneven dirt road.

------

1   Matthew 16:25.

2   John 12:24.

Near Vulture Peak, where the Buddha gave
some of his most famous sermons.

Chapter Five: Rajgir
—Where Siddhartha Gave Hindu Monkery a Try

I stepped out of the car and onto the dusty street of Rajgir. Horse-carts were everywhere, topped with square, brightly-colored fringes. So of course "Surrey with the Fringe on Top" played through my head as I tried to get my bearings. There was a roundabout, and a large hill. Snaking up the hill was a chairlift, it's seats polka-dotting the landscape with bright, primary colors that trailed their way up and out of sight over a ridge.

Someone tapped me on the shoulder. "You go to Buddha place?"

I turned and saw a young Indian man looking at me with curiosity. "I'm trying to figure out how to get there."

"Ski lift," the man pointed.

"Over my dead body," I muttered. He waggled his head, confused. I'm afraid of heights at the best of times. I'll get on a funicular in Israel—with some prodding. But a chair lift in India? Not on your life. "I'll walk," I said. Which way?"

He pointed up the hill. I thanked him and started off. A sign said that the road had been built 2500 years ago by King Bimbasara, the Buddha's first royal patron. I can't imagine that it hasn't been rebuilt a time or three since then, since it is in excellent shape. Every two or three paces along the way a woman in a filthy sari sat on the ground making motions toward her mouth or holding out a begging bowl. There were hundreds of them.

I steeled myself and walked past, as I did every day, in every place. I felt like a cruel, selfish jerk. And yet I hadn't seen enough 10 rupee notes since I got here to distribute to them all. Besides, fistfights are likely to break out if you give to one and not another. I chose none. The thought occurred to me that this was a rationalization. I chose to ignore that thought. Halfway up the hill, I stopped. Two women were kneeling in a ditch, and one of them was tearing open a packet of antibiotics with her teeth. It was the saddest thing I saw all day.

I refocused my attention on the countryside. It was both beautiful and forbidding, in the same way that Israel or the American Southwest can be. There were more trees, here, but they weren't green—everything was covered with a persistent brown dust. Jagged rocks the size of skyscrapers pierced the landscape, jutting up at dramatic angles through the treetops.

I was there, of course, because Siddhartha was here. After fleeing his palace, he decided to get serious about the Hindu-holy-man thing. Siddhartha first sought out a teacher. He'd heard good things about Alara Kalama, a Samkhya teacher, and put himself under his instruction. He mastered the teachings intellectually, but realized that wasn't enough. He wanted to *experience* them. He applied himself and was successful. His teacher was delighted. He offered him a place beside him as his co-teacher, saying, "As I am, so are you. As you are, so am I."

I'm struck by this verse, because there is a nearly identical verse in the Gospel of Thomas. Jesus said, "Whoever drinks out of my mouth will become like me; I also will be as he is, and that which is hidden will be revealed to him."[1] There are a lot of resonances between the Thomas gospel and the Buddhist scriptures. It's true that the theology in Thomas is nearly identical to Buddhism—in fact I call it a "native Jewish school of Buddhism" elsewhere—I'm astounded by how often verses are leaping out at me. We know from Buddhist records that there were Buddhist missionaries in Antioch and Greece in Jesus' day. Although it's unlikely that Jesus himself was influenced by them, I think it highly likely that the Thomas school of Christianity was.

But I digress. Siddhartha realized that this teaching was going to take him nowhere, so he placed himself under another teacher, Uddaka Ramaputta, a Jain. He learned everything that this teacher had to offer, too, but was still unsatisfied. "This is not the path that leads to the cessation of suffering."

So then he came here, to Rajgir, and joined himself to a small community of ascetics living in the forest. They spurred each other on to greater and greater feats of renunciation. Siddhartha impressed everyone by his dedication, and was greatly admired by his friends.

A man about my own age had stepped into pace with me. "That is Sariputta's cave," he pointed. Sure enough, just off the path, a huge jut of rock formed a low roof of a cave mouth. I walked up to it and peered in. At the back of the cave, just a few paces in, was a small shrine. A glass image of the Buddha was draped in white scarves, and several candles had been lit.

Who knows if this was really the cave that one of Siddhartha's friends actually lived in? But it had to be something very much like this. I was grateful to the man for pointing this out. But I also knew he probably wanted something. "I don't want a guide," I said, which was stupid, because a guide would have been very helpful. I was just annoyed by the constant pestering for money.

"No no, I am a businessman," he assured me. As we rounded the corner, I saw just what sort of business he was in—selling postcards to tourists. I hated to disappoint him, but I *really* didn't want any postcards.

Now that I knew they were there, I poked my head into a couple more caves. One of these could very well have been where Siddhartha lived, too. It was in a cave like this that he fell over in a faint from not breathing. It was around here that he starved himself nearly to death. He described the point he had got to this way:

"My limbs became like the jointed segments of bamboo. My

backside became like a camel's hoof. The projections of my spine stood forth like corded beads. My ribs jutted out as gaunt as the crazy rafters of an old roofless barn. The gleam in my eyes sunk far down in their sockets looked like the gleam of water sunk far down in a deep well. My scalp shriveled and withered as a green gourd shrivels and withers in the wind and sun. If I touched my belly skin, I encountered my backbone too; and if I touched my backbone, I encountered my belly skin too—for my belly skin cleaved to my backbone."

Yikes. Reading this, I flashed on the image of an emaciated Buddha statue that Donna and I had encountered. It depicted the Buddha after he had starved himself for six years. It was made of black stone and it showed Siddhartha's ribs jutting out with fierce angularity. He was seated in meditation, but unlike most Buddha statues, this one looked pained rather than serene.

It was at this point that Siddhartha had a bit of an epiphany. He said to himself, "I am too weak to meditate, so I'm not getting anywhere. And if I keep this up, I'll die without accomplishing anything." He realized that his body was the only vehicle he had to take him to enlightenment, and if he abused it, it would fail him.

So he had a bowl of rice.

His friends, disgusted, turned their backs on him. "He's a lush," they told each other, and they stopped speaking to him. But Siddhartha took it in stride. He knew he was onto something. He was discovering a "middle way"—eschewing both excess and luxury on one hand and extreme mortifications on the other.

As I climbed, I meditated on the importance of the "middle way" in religion. "Moderation in all things," is a fine aphorism to govern any aspect of life, even if you add, "including moderation" to that. But the "middle way" is a concept—and even a phrase—that keeps popping up again and again, in a number of religious contexts. Solomon said, "Be not religious over-much,"[2] which is a great statement of the middle way. The Anglicans found a middle way between Catholicism and Protestantism.

In my own spiritual life, I have swung from a very conservative Christianity that professes to have all the answers to everything, to an extremely liberal orientation that confesses so little that it can hardly be called "Christian" in any meaningful sense. At this point in my life, thanks largely to extensive readings in Martin Luther, I have found a "middle way" in which I can cling to Jesus with my whole soul without insisting that everyone else in the world do the same. I don't think I would have been able to make this journey had I not come to that place of peace. At least, it would have been a very different journey.

As soon as he was strong enough to walk, Siddhartha set out toward Bodh Gaya. One day, as he dragged himself down to a river to bathe, he encountered a young woman named Nandabala who was so moved by compassion for his emaciated state that she gave him a bowl of kheer—rice pudding. I love kheer and can only imagine how good that must have tasted to someone as hungry as Siddhartha was.

Nandabala nursed him back to health, and a stupa was built on the site where she discovered him. Later I visited that stupa. What can I say about it? It was an impressive pile of bricks, but not much else.

After a little more climbing, I came to the top. After Siddhartha gained enlightenment, he loved this place so much that he returned here often. The spot where I was standing, a Buena Vista point if there ever was one, was called Vulture Peak, and was the place where many of the Buddha's most famous sermons were delivered.

I was instructed to remove my shoes, since this was holy ground, and I rejoiced that I had found the great boots that I had. They were light, rugged, looked good, and they were really easy to pull off and on. An Asian family was seated in a small shrine having a worship service. I sat quietly nearby and pulled out my guidebook to read about the Peak. My eyebrows shot up as I read, "Pilgrims should use caution as the hills are full of bandits looking to prey on travelers." Hoo-kay, I thought, so that was close.

The Peak has other ominous associations. The Buddha had his own Judas—a disciple named Devedatta, who was also his cousin. Devedatta thought that the Buddha should retire and cede the leadership of the sangha to him. When the Buddha refused, Devedatta plotted to kill him, arranging for a large boulder to roll down on him from the top of Vulture Peak. The boulder split in two before it hit the Buddha, and each half rolled by on either side of him, leaving him unharmed.

On another occasion, Devedatta tormented an elephant until it was mad with rage, then released it into the Buddha's path. The elephant charged at the Buddha, but the holy one was so serene that when the elephant reached him, it laid its head down at the Buddha's feet, and the Buddha softly stroked its ears. The scriptures say that after doing many other despicable things—including starting a schism in the sangha—Devedatta descended into the hell regions.

The little worship service at the shrine was breaking up, and so I followed the family down the hill. *Safety in numbers!* I thought gleefully. I struck up a conversation with a young man in his late teens, a high school senior in his native Burma. He told me he wanted to study in the United States, but couldn't remember the name of the school where he wanted to go. He was pleasant company for the trip down, and I wished him well.

On the way home, my driver stopped at a Japanese temple that had been built on the site of the Bamboo Grove that King Bimbasara had given to the Buddha. It became the site of the early Buddhist community's annual retreat during the monsoons, and the location of the first Buddhist council a century after the Buddha's death, where the oldest of the scriptures were compiled and authorized. As I gazed at a plaque marking the site, it was clear that the Japanese monks were proud that their monastery stood in the same place as the very first Buddhist monastery.

Driving out of the city, I stared at the mud huts that lined the road, where family after family, hundreds and hundreds of them, were going about the daily business of living. My heart went out to them. I felt grateful just to be feeling something, anything. The Buddha had chosen his austerities, and he chose to end them. I caught the brown eye of a little girl, squatting in the dust, playing with a stick. She followed our car with a severe gaze. *She has no choice in her austerities,* I thought. *None.*

———

1   Thomas, 108.

2   Ecclesiastes 7:16.

A giant Buddha, located near the Mahabodhi Temple.

Chapter Six: Bodh Gaya
—Where Siddhartha Became the Buddha

I wasn't expecting a muezzin. There aren't actually very many Muslims in this part of India, certainly not in Bodh Gaya. I hadn't even seen a mosque. I looked at my watch—5am. Sheesh.... I lay awake listening to it, annoyed. But as I listened, I realized that the language wasn't right. It wasn't Arabic. It was Hindi. This was a *Hindu* muezzin—which is crazy, because Hindus don't have muezzins. And yet here it was, just as loud and annoying as any Muslim muezzin, and just as early in the morning.

But as it was close to the time that I wanted to get up anyway, I could hardly complain. I've taken to wearing my clothes two days in a row to cut down on laundry (don't tell my mother), so I just needed to tend to my basic toiletries and throw on a pair of pants. I eschewed my cherished boots in favor of my flip-flops this morning, since shoes weren't allowed in the temple grounds. Soon, I was ready, and heading out into the dusty Bodh Gaya dawn.

I flagged down a rickshaw, and sat back as we bounced over the crumbling blacktop. We passed numerous one-room shops and restaurants, all of which looked dangerous to eat at. We passed the Buddhaland Amusement park, with its rusty bumper cars and Samsara Tilt-a-Whirl. (All right, I'm kidding about the Samsara ride, but not about the amusement park. It's there.)

When I got to the Mahabodhi temple the sun was fully up, but there was still a ghostly mist hanging in the air. There was no line at the temple gate, so I stowed my flip-flops and went in. I paused so the security guard could wave his beeping wand over my crotch, and a moment later, joined the other pilgrims in the main park.

The temple grounds were large, stretching out over several acres, and they were meticulously gardened. In the center of everything stood the temple itself, rising over 150 feet in the familiar Shiva lingam shape that seems to be common to most temples in India, regardless of creed. The spire was made up of white stone carved in architectural patterns—arches and columns. It was breathtaking.

The park was dotted with hundreds of stupas, most of them small, and each of them commemorating either something the Buddha had done on that spot, or in memory of a Buddhist saint or benefactor. Every inch of horizontal space was taken up with thousands of small metal or glass bowls, kind of like votive candle holders, except these were filled with water, and each held a bright yellow or orange carnations. The entire park was ablaze with flowered color.

The marble steps were cold on my bare feet, and mist was still hanging in the air. I decided to head for the main temple while the crowds were thin. The temple was built directly on the spot that, according to legend, the Buddha achieved his enlightenment. Having accumulated much wisdom in his many years of Samkhya and Jain study, and having become an accomplished meditator, Siddhartha sat down beneath the Bodhi tree and vowed not to rise until he had achieved enlightenment.

Legend says that Mara, the Evil One, confronted him, tempting him to despair by calling him a failure as a prince, a husband and a father, and even as a sanyassi. When that seemed not to work, Mara tempted him with lust, sending his three daughters to entice him with their dancing. Finally, Mara challenged his right to do what he was doing. "By whose authority do you do this?" Siddhartha merely touched the earth, and creation responded, "I bear witness." Enraged, Mara attacked Siddhartha, but all of his spears and arrows turned into flowers, and drifted down around Siddhartha harmlessly. Mara fled, shouting, "He knows me! The Blessed One knows me!" And the monk was able to enter into a deep meditation in peace.

I reflected on that story as I walked down the steps toward the main temple. Of course, I could not help but think of Jesus, just before the start of his ministry, heading out into the wilderness for his own ascetic observance. He fasted and prayed for forty days, and sometime during that period the scriptures say that he was tempted by Satan. Like Mara, Satan also presents three temptations. Satan appealed to Jesus' belly, saying, "If you're really the Son of God, turn these stones into bread." Like Mara's dancing daughters, this was an appeal to appetite.

Satan then took Jesus up to the top of the temple and tempted him to jump off. "Then everyone will know who you are, and they'll listen to you!" Like Mara's final temptation, this had to do with authority. Creation herself spoke on the Buddha's behalf—Jesus just refused to be baited.

Finally, Satan showed Jesus all the kingdoms of the world and offered to let him rule them, if only he would bow down and worship him. Jesus' final temptation is about worldly power—which is fitting given the extremely political nature of Jesus' gospel. But Siddhartha had already walked away from worldly power, and so his temptation was regarding his own personal power to succeed in his quest, or indeed, anything else in his life.

The line before the main temple wasn't very long, but that didn't stop several people cutting in front of me every couple of seconds. I rolled my eyes and said nothing. Mara, it seems, was still at work—these pilgrims were *not* on their best behavior. When we reached the main door, everyone started to shove and pack in together. My arms were literally plastered to my sides, and I felt pressure on every part of my body. People were shouting and cursing and pushing at each other, which was weird, because there seemed to be absolutely no reason for it. It wasn't quite The Who at Cincinnati, but it did make me think of it.

Once we cleared the doors, however, the line moved fast. We shuffled down the left aisle, passing people seated on the floor, chanting sutras. We reached the main altar, and moved left to right. On the main altar was a larger-than-life golden statue of the Buddha, seated in meditation. On a shelf in front of him, people were leaving offerings of fruit and flowers. They paused briefly to bow and say a prayer, then they were shooed along by the security personnel. As they left, a monk scooped their offerings into a large bowl to make room for more. Then we shuffled out along the right aisle, and reemerged back into the sunshine.

I went around the building to the back, to see the Bodhi Tree. This wasn't the original Bodhi Tree, of course, but is supposed to be a third-generation cutting from it. According to legend, the Emperor Asoka's daughter took a cutting from the original tree to Sri Lanka, where it flourished. This tree was taken from a cutting of that one.

As I rounded the corner into the Tree's courtyard, I nearly tripped over someone chanting. There were about twenty of them. To one side, there was a low table set, covered with maroon cloth. A very young monk of about fourteen years was seated at one side of it, an elder monk on the other. They had just cut the boy's hair and he was taking his vows, surrounded by his proud family. It was a heartwarming moment.

I found an empty place on a low step and sat down. As pilgrims walked by, many of them chanting or praying, I decided that if ever there were a place to meditate, this was it. I softened my gaze, and focused on my breathing, but instantly I was assaulted by more of Mara's attacks—fears, anxieties, regrets, all of them rushed in to fill the tiny, brief space I had created. I tried again, but was defeated again. I arm-wrestled with the monkey mind for about fifteen more minutes before I just gave up. If it were up to me, Mara would have won. Instead of becoming the Buddha, I would have ended up as the ancient spiritual equivalent of a fry cook.

So instead of meditating (which I have never been good at), I contemplated (at which I excel—go with your strengths, I say). I thought about Siddhartha, still not fully recovered from his years of ascetic self-abuse, driven by pure determination, sitting here alone with no realistic hope of success. After defeating Mara's attack, he sank into meditation. The scriptures say that he entered into the first stage of meditation, which involves thinking and exploring (I know this stage well). Then, he sank further, into the second stage which involves "confidence and single-pointed purpose." (I have gotten there, briefly and rarely.) Then he entered into the third stage, in which he experienced true mindfulness and peace. Finally, he sank deeply into the fourth stage, which is beyond all pleasure, pain, or sensation.

And then he broke through. Suddenly, he was not Siddhartha anymore—he knew who he *really* was, and it was not the bag of bones that he had dragged to the Bodhi Tree. He saw that there was no such thing as a self, there was only the One Thing that was also No Thing.

As soon as he perceived that, other realizations followed. If there is no self, then what appears to be a self is simply an artificial construction, a collection or amalgamation (he used the word "aggregate") of phenomena—physical, mental, and emotional. These things build on one another until the illusion of a self is formed.

He saw that everything that exists is built like this—an aggregate of phenomena that seem to be separate, but aren't. All things build on those that have come before, and like them they dissolve back into their seemingly constitutive parts, all to be used again in a new aggregate. Everything that comes together, in other words, comes apart.

He saw that the self is an insatiable fiction. It can never be satisfied because a fiction can never be fulfilled. There is a lack at its very core—the lack of reality—and it feeds that lack with an irrepressible torrent of want.

The fictional self becomes a tyrant whose only concern is the equally fictional I, Me, and Mine. Craving, desire, envy, and regret follow in its wake, as it grasps after everything that it cannot possess. The Buddha saw with crystal clarity that this alone was the cause of the vast majority of human suffering—certainly it accounted for all of human mental anguish. This anguish feeds on itself, perpetuates itself, and becomes the vicious cycle of Samsara.

The Buddha also saw in that flash that there is no Self behind the universe who set these things in motion, but that the aggregates just arose. If there were gods then they were just as much caught in the wheel of delusion as human beings are, regardless of their longevity or their power.

Once he saw this, however, and knew that he saw it, its hold over him dissipated. The spell was broken. The knowledge of The Way Things Are released him from that Way. Its tyranny over him was ended. He would never again be subject to another birth. He still had one life to live, but it would be his last. And he knew exactly what he should do with it.

"Seeking but not finding the house-builder," he said, "I traveled through the round of countless births. Birth is so painful, over and over again. House-builder, you have now been seen; you shall not build the house again. Your rafters have been broken down; your ridgepole is demolished, too. My mind has now attained the formless, the extinguished, and every kind of craving is at an end."

There, under the Bodhi Tree, the Awakened One (which is what "Buddha" means) resolved to teach people what he had discovered, so that they could discover it for themselves and be liberated from endless, needless torment and suffering.

As I watched the stream of people pouring past, bowing to

show their reverence for the Bodhi Tree, it occurred to me that the liberation that Jesus brought was also done under a tree—the cross. I wondered in what way the liberations were similar. Were they similar at all?

They were, I decided, nodding. Both Jesus and Buddha preached liberation from illusion. For the Buddha, the illusion was permanence. For Jesus, the illusion was power.

Jesus' world was deeply informed by the story of the Exodus, of God's liberation of the Jews from slavery under Pharaoh. For the Jews of Jesus' time, the new Pharaoh was Caesar, and they chafed under Roman tyranny and oppression—kept submissive only by the threat of death.

But just as Moses had done with Pharaoh, Jesus showed Caesar's lordship to be an illusion. God rules the world, not Caesar, Jesus insisted. Caesar was not king, no matter what he called himself. God alone was king—but his people had been duped into thinking otherwise. Jesus said, "The Kingdom of God is spread out upon the earth, but people do not see it."[1] Jesus taught his followers who really held power—and it wasn't Caesar.

Caesar pulled out the big guns to stop Jesus' message, and leveled the ultimate punishment against him, putting him to death. But by resurrecting, Jesus showed that God was stronger than all of Rome's might, and proved that love triumphs over violence. But he also showed that God was stronger than death—so there was no longer any reason to fear Caesar at all, because the power of death had been broken. Death was temporary and no threat to those who followed Jesus. Death had been defeated.

So while Buddha liberated his followers from suffering, Jesus liberated his followers from fear. St. Paul puts this eloquently when he wrote, "For I am convinced that neither death nor life, neither angels nor demons, neither the present nor the future, nor any powers, neither height nor depth, nor anything else in all creation, will be able to separate us from the love of God that is in Christ Jesus our Lord."[2]

When the Buddha broke through, he uttered, "It is liberated." And as Jesus died he cried out, "It is finished." As I watched literally hundreds of people file by, twenty-five hundred years later, it was clear that the liberation was just getting started.

A puppy, dusty gold in color and just a few weeks old, sprang playfully onto the path where the people were filing past the Bodhi Tree. I rose and followed him, re-entering the stream of people and stepping out of line again as I rounded the corner of the temple.

Here, amidst a field of nearly a hundred stupas, even more people than that were sprawled on 6 x 3-foot plywood boards. Each board was slightly elevated, about six inches higher in the front. According to their own rhythm, these folks rose, placed their hands together in prayer, then knelt. Placing their hands on what looked like oven mitts, they slid down until they were prone on the boards, their faces to the wood. Then they got up and did it again. Rise, kneel, flatten face, repeat.

Most of those doing prostrations were monks, but as I looked around, there were a good deal of Westerners, too. It struck me as ironic that some of them—perhaps many of them—turned to Buddhism to escape the Christianity of their youth with its puritanical morality, irrational doctrinal demands, and oppressive spiritual practices—only to commit themselves to a religious system just as rigorous in each of those areas, at least in its traditional contexts. What Buddhism is free of for them, perhaps, is the baggage, the guilt—or perhaps more accurately, the shame—imposed on them by spiritually inept, abusive, or (to use kinder Buddhist language) *unskillful* leaders, teachers, and communities.

Jesus never got angry at—or opposed the beliefs of—anyone outside his own community. He only ever got angry and criticized those members of his own spiritual community who distorted its teachings in a way that hurt people. I share his outrage. I am glad that these folks were able to find a spiritual place to root themselves, and a practice that is bearing fruit. But it chaps my hide that they were driven halfway around the world to find it.

The Dalai Lama exhorts people not to change religions, but to find the authentic core of the religion that they were raised in. After my painful experience of the fundamentalist church I was part of in high school, I rebelled against my childhood denomination, but didn't leave the faith. Not that it wasn't tempting. I knew I had a choice: I could cut and run, or I could stand and fight for a *healthy* Christian spirituality. I studied world religions not to explore alternatives to my faith, but to shine light into the darkened corners of the place I had chosen to stay.

It was a fruitful and enlightening strategy, because every time I encountered something novel in another faith, when I came back to the Christian tradition and started digging, I found it there too—pretty much without exception. (Okay, we don't have prayer flags.) So I know, perhaps as well as anyone, that what those who have fled Christianity for Eastern faiths have found—mysticism, meditation, and transformative teachings—were all present in the tradition of their birth. It's tragic that these people did not have skillful teachers to present it to them in a way that was attractive rather than repellant. Our loss. And perhaps to some extent, theirs.

Nearby was a gate to a Meditation Garden. There was a ticket booth just inside, where I was told that if I wanted to walk around it would cost me 20 rupees, but if I wanted to meditate, it would cost me 25. I elected for the cheaper ticket, but was careful not to close my eyes for any extended period lest one of the many armed guards roaming the place accost me for meditating without a permit. The garden was dry, but well groomed.

Also dry was a large fountain, now rusted and its paint crackling in a spider web of decay. The bottom of it was filled with algae. Pretty much every park in India has a similarly decrepit fountain that is no longer in use.

A huge bell stood at the center of the park, and radiating from it were a seemingly infinite number of pathways that either dead-ended in no particular place or ended at a tiny gazebo with nothing in or on it. Very puzzling. It occurred to me that it was the Winchester Mystery Meditation Garden.

As I exited, a young monk came up to me. "Where you from, Mister?" he asked politely. He looked like he was about twenty-five. We played out the usual script: "America. San Francisco." He seemed pleased. I asked him his name. "Buddharata," he said.

"What does that mean?" I asked.

"It means, 'Friend-of-Buddha.'"

I smiled. What a rocking name. I tried "Friend-of-Jesus" on for size. I liked it. Then I remembered that the Gospel of Luke and the Book of Acts were written to Theophilus, which means "Friend-of-God." Close enough.

"How long have you been a monk?" I asked.

"Ten years," he said proudly. "Rejoin every five years, now."

"Wait," I said. "Are you saying that in your order, you only commit for five-year periods, and then you can go back to being a layperson if you want to?"

"Oh, yes." He smiled.

I thought that was amazing, and wondered how different Catholic orders would be if there were a similar strategy in place. How many committed Christians would devote five years of their lives to dedicated spiritual practice and service? Lots. Instead of dwindling, the orders would be swelling with young people wanting to do something a little more spiritually meaty than just joining the Peace Corps. In fact, the Catholic orders would probably have to beat the Protestants off with a stick if something like that were in place.

"Buddharata, what does the Buddha mean to you?"

He looked at me, confused. He cocked his head.

"What do you find meaningful about the Buddha's teaching?"

His puzzled look deepened.

"Relax," I said. "This isn't a test. I'm just curious. What personal benefit do you derive from following the Lord Buddha?"

Nothing. His English was good enough to follow me, so I quizzed him about some foundational Buddhist precepts. He blinked at me. "Don't you receive teaching?" I asked him.

"Oh, yes. Every day."

"So how does that teaching speak to you in your own life? How does it transform you?"

He waggled his head noncommittally. Apparently, the notion had never occurred to him. I was amazed at this, wondering if Buddharata was unusual, or if it is actually unusual for Buddhist monks to reflect on or articulate their faith. His friends called to him, and he bobbed a goodbye and scampered off.

To my left an Asian monk, arrayed in immaculate maroon robes, very slowly and deliberately opened a candy bar wrapper. Giving it his whole attention, he just as deliberately took a bite. Pleasure radiated from his face. "Now that's good spiritual practice," I said to myself. Beside him, a dog was sleeping, knowing more about Buddha nature than any of us.

To my left a group of about a thousand Vajrayana monks had commandeered one side of the park, and loudspeakers blared as they broadcast their chanting. Tibetan-style chanting is always unsettling, sounding like two chainsaws of different sizes roaring away in the distance in eerie harmony.

I walked along the back of the park, past a large, man-made lake with a statue of the Buddha in the midst of it, protected by a giant cobra's head, spread out over him like an umbrella. Studying it, I recalled the story of the snake, Mukalinda, who protected the Buddha from the rain while he meditated.

There were a cluster of buildings on my left, and I saw a flicker of light coming from them, so I headed over. Approaching the nearest building, I saw that its walls were made of glass, and inside were about thirty large tables, each holding traditional butter lamps, about 2600 lamps in all. They were all lit. An adjacent building had a similar setup. There were six more buildings, but while they had tables and lamps in place, few were lit. I walked out of the cluster of buildings, and past the contingent of Vajrayana monks, chainsaw chanting away. At the next corner, a line of prayer wheels stretched the entire length of the park. There must have been hundreds of them, and as people walked by, they spun them.

I thought about the Vajrayana theology of prayer, which holds that if you write a prayer on something, and then put that thing in motion, the prayer is being said. So Vajrayana Buddhists put prayers on flags—if they're flappin', I'm yappin'—on wheels, or in little drums on a stick with a weighted ball attached. You can hold the stick in your hand, and swing the weighted ball. It turns the drum with the prayer scroll inside, thereby saying the prayer.

I was about to go out, when I saw a small shrine on the spot of the Buddha's second week of meditation after reaching enlightenment. Inside was another statue of the Buddha in meditative repose, similar to a thousand others I'd seen the last couple of days. I turned to go, but then noticed a monk sitting in the doorway, reading a comic book of the Buddha's life. As a big comics fan myself, this made me smile. A much older monk was seated next to him. He saw me smile and, in pretty good English, asked where I was from. I told him, and asked him where he was from.

"Bhutan," he said. "I am Lama Panchan." I shook his hand

and introduced myself. He looked out over the park, a little wistfully. "In Bhutan, I am big lama. Here, I am very small lama. People in India always, 'more money, more money!'" His face was sour. He turned and looked me in the eyes. "People are not good."

St. Paul couldn't have said it any better, I thought. "Lama," I started, "what do you want Christians to know about Buddhism?"

He thought for a moment, then he said, "Christian good. Christians go up." He pointed at the sky. He nodded. "Buddhists go up. All is same." He waved his hand, taking in the whole park. "Words not same, but here," he thumped at his heart, "is same."

I decided not to give him my, "religions solve different problems, but serve similar functions" speech, and I warmly thanked him for talking to me. He seemed genuinely glad to have made my acquaintance and wished me well.

I was about to go out when I noticed a Western woman sitting on a park bench right next to the exit. I sat down next to her and introduced myself, hoping to hear her story. I told her about my pilgrimage. She introduced herself as Niosho, and said that she was from Spain. She loved Bodh Gaya, and so she came here every winter. When I asked her how Buddhism was helpful for her, she said, "Slowly, slowly, it makes my heart more beautiful."

———

1   Thomas 113.

2   Romans 8:38.

Monastery ruins in the Deer Park at Sarnath.

Chapter Seven: Sarnath
—Where the Buddha Started Buddhism

Once again in Varanasi, as I wound my way through the narrow, ancient streets, an old woman came up to me, wagged her finger in my face and started yelling in Hindi. "What?" I asked. I looked around, but nobody offered any help. Those who noticed were smiling bemusedly. "What did I do?" I asked the woman, but she advanced on me and yelled some more. I apologized profusely, but I had absolutely no idea what I had done. Finally, she spat out what may have been a frustrated expletive and turned away.

"Whooo-kay," I said to myself, completely flummoxed about which cultural taboo I had unconsciously transgressed. Her angry diatribe echoed in my ears as I picked my way past cow patties and angry, blood-red splotches where pan chewers had spit the juicy excess from the popular tobacco-and-fruit concoctions.

I finally made it to the main road, and hailed a tuk-tuk. We agreed on a price—probably too high, but oh well—and we were off. I marveled at how relaxed I had become, riding in a tuk-tuk. My first ride left me a trembling mass, but now I barely noticed the hair-raising near-misses that happened every other second. Several people stepped in front of us. They didn't wait for a break in traffic—they didn't even look—they just waded in. We swerved around them, neatly dodged a head-on collision with a pickup, then swerved within centimeters of a cow. We ducked into oncoming traffic and we did not yield when three motorcycles bore down on us. I yawned and checked my email.

I hated Varanasi, but fortunately I was only passing through for a day trip to a much more pleasant place, the Deer Park at

Sarnath. It had been a protected game reserve for thousands of years, and the reason given for it was legendary, involving one of the Buddha's previous incarnations. According to the story in the *Jakata Tales*, the Buddha had been king of the Banyan deer who lived in the park, where they lived peacefully with another tribe of deer, the Branch deer. The Human King of Benares (Varanasi) loved venison, and so he hunted daily.

His hunger for meat made life difficult for both tribes of deer. The kings of both the Banyan and the Branch deer met and came up with a plan. On one day, the Branch deer would sacrifice one of their number for the Human King's supper, and the next day the Banyan deer would sacrifice one of their own. They would alternate, so that the damage to both tribes would be equal, and the danger of extinction would be minimized. Both tribes would select the deer to be sacrificed by lot. The Human King was fine with this plan as he was growing old and frail and it would save him the trouble of hunting. He also granted that the deer kings be exempted from the lots, as a courtesy to fellow royalty.

One day a doe was selected for the chopping block. She approached the future Buddha and said, "I am pregnant. Surely the agreement is not intended to sacrifice two lives on a single day." The Banyan King was moved by compassion for her, and said, "Indeed it was not. Go and be at peace." The Banyan King himself went to the chopping block and laid his neck bare for the butcher.

The butcher, alarmed, sent for the Human King. When the Human King arrived, he questioned the Banyan King. He was so moved by the future Buddha's sacrifice that he made the hunting of deer illegal in the park from that day onward.

The *Jakata Tales* is a collection of stories—fairy tales for children, really—concerning the Buddha's previous incarnations, and it is filled with stories like this. On another occasion, the future Buddha was a rabbit who threw himself into the fire to feed a passing Brahmin. I'm not entirely sure what children are supposed to learn from such grisly stories, but then again I'm also unclear on the moral intended in Hansel and Gretel.

When we arrived, my driver agreed to wait for me for three hours, for the privilege of taking me back—all for the grand sum of about $10. The main temple was closed for lunch, so I headed to the Deer Park itself—a huge, fenced-in archaeological treasure containing a stupa that goes back nearly 2,000 years. It also hosts the ruins of an ancient Buddhist monastery. I was next in line to buy my ticket when a love-drunk Indian couple simply stepped in front of me. I was aghast at the rudeness, but I didn't say anything. It happens all the time here. Soon, as I walked over the ancient stone walkways, I let it go and relaxed.

The Deer Park is truly beautiful. I wouldn't call it lush, exactly, but it is green, with broad lawns and plentiful trees, punctuated by archeological ruins and reconstructions. Around the park are temples from various Buddhist denominations, some tawdry and tired looking, others truly grand. I circumambulated the stupa, and then found a shady spot. I hopped up on a low brick wall and opened an anthology of Buddhist scriptures to read the passages pertinent to this place.

The Buddha came here directly from Bodh Gaya, which is no small distance—about 150 miles. One legend says that once he had experienced his awakening, he longed to share it with someone. He immediately thought of his old Samkhya teacher, Alara Kalama. "He'll understand the Dharma," he thought. But invisible deities came to him and informed him that his teacher had died seven days ago.

The Buddha was terribly disappointed, but then thought that his old Jain teacher, Uddaka Ramaputta, might be receptive. "He has little dust on his eyes," he thought. (A great line.) But the deities interrupted him and informed him that his second teacher had died only the night before.

"What rotten luck," the Buddha must have said to himself. So he resolved to teach the guys he used to practice austerities with—the five ascetics he had come to know at Rajgir. He gazed out across the world with his newly acquired spiritual vision and saw that they were at the Deer Park, and so he set out to meet them.

The five ascetics had turned their backs on him when he abandoned the method of extreme asceticism they practiced. But then they saw him in the distance, walking toward them. "Hey, guys," said one of them, "Here comes the sellout." (This is a loose paraphrase.)

"Oh, yeah, look at the prince, going back to living in luxury," another sneered. "I'll bet he eats every day now. No discipline, that one. He's a lush."

"He's coming toward us, what should we do?" asked another.

"Let's ignore him," said the first.

But as the Buddha got closer, they realized something about him had changed. They were curious, awestruck, and a little confused. Their inhospitable plan was abandoned. They set out to make him welcome, and they referred to him as their friend.

Strangely, the Buddha objected to that. "Do not address the Perfect One by name and as 'friend': the Perfect One is accomplished and fully enlightened."

As I read this, I looked up and gazed across the lawn where the scene was supposed to have happened. The Buddha's words were every bit as elevated as Jesus' in the Gospel of John—both this scripture and John's Gospel are pretty late additions, so a lot of mythologizing has gone into them. But Jesus' words at his last supper with his disciples clashed dissonantly with the Buddha's words at his first supper with his. Jesus said, "You call me master, and you do so rightly, for so I am. But I don't call you servants, but friends."[1]

The Buddha's frie—er, former fellow forest-dwellers were not put off by this haughty tone. They basically said, "Tough talk for a lush."

The Buddha said, "I am not a lush, I am the fully-enlightened one."

"But you're a lush," they said again.

The Buddha said, "I am not a lush, I am the fully-enlightened one."

"Aaaaaand...you're a lush," they insisted.

The Buddha said, "I am not a lush, I am the fully-enlightened one." (Note the neat, three-fold pattern from those who were rejecting him. I'm waiting for a cock to crow, how about you?)

"How can you say that when you abandoned the path?" they pleaded.

"Fellows," the Buddha said patiently (the enlightened Buddha sometimes used dialogue out of the *Hardy Boys*), "you know me. Have you ever heard me talking like this before?"

The ascetics looked at one another. "No," they admitted.

"So there you go. I will now instruct you."

If I were there, I would have said, "Wait a minute, that's not proof! You could say 'Bob's your uncle' and start talking in a cockney accent, but it wouldn't make you the Queen of England!" but apparently it was good enough for the Sutra writer I was reading. So the Buddha launched into his first sermon.

And it was a doozy. He told them that *to live is to suffer.* As Hindus, they would have instantly recognized the truth of this. There is nothing worse than the endless cycle of reincarnation, after all. They really *did* want to stop the world and get off.

Then he told them that *the source of suffering was craving*, or desire. If you want something you don't have, then you are suffering. It's important to note that the Buddha wasn't talking about pain—he doesn't have a remedy for that. He's really addressing mental anguish—like when you're worried about the future, or envious of what someone else has, or awash in regret. All of these things come from unsatisfied desire—something you wish you had, or something you wish had not happened, or something you are afraid might happen. They are all tricks of the mind that can hold you in bondage.

They were tracking with him, so he went further: *Suffering can stop*. You just have to stop your obsessive grasping after what you don't possess. Simple, right? No. So how do you do that?

So then he told them, "I have discovered a method, a path, and if you follow it, your desire will stop. And when your desire stops, your suffering will stop."

The Buddha had just expounded the most basic of all Buddhist doctrines, the Four Noble Truths. Everything hangs on these. To summarize them briefly: 1) life is suffering; 2) suffering is caused by craving; 3) suffering can stop; 4) here's a method to make it stop.

"Okay, what's the method?" the ascetics were liking what they were hearing, and they wanted to hear more. So he outlined the path for them: First, he said, you have to develop yourselves intellectually. You must have wisdom. You must pay attention to my teaching so that you can see things clearly, and understand what's going on—what causes suffering, why we react the way we do, and so on. You have to hold *right views*.

Then he told them they had to develop themselves morally, which involves several steps along the path. The second step was to be sincere. He called this *right intention*. Third, they had to guard their tongues—to tell the truth and speak no evil of anyone. He called this *right speech*. Fourth, they had to behave themselves—no stealing or killing or sleeping around. He called this *right action*. Fifth, their employment had to be consistent with their values—so no bouncing or bartending for those on the path. He called this *right livelihood*. Sixth, they had to really work at becoming truly good people, which takes commitment. He called this *right effort.*

Then he told them that they would have to develop their spiritual practice, which involved meditation. The seventh stage involved really being in the moment and paying close attention to what was going on in their bodies, in their thoughts, in their emotions, as well as what was going on around them. That's a lot of *right mindfulness,* right there. Finally when a seeker gets the hang of mindfulness, he or she can really go deep, and can see through the illusion of separateness that keeps the cycle of reincarnation going—and can defuse it. He called this *right concentration.*

The ascetics were stunned. Many of the teachings they had just heard were familiar to them from their previous teachers, but it had never been explained so simply, so cleanly, so powerfully. They realized that a lot of what they were doing was just distracting them from the real path. They wanted to know more.

One of them, a guy named Kondanna, had a breakthrough. "Hey, if everything you are saying is true, then it isn't just suffering that can stop—everything stops. Everything that comes into being will stop being, too."[2]

One of the scriptures says that at the moment Kondanna had his breakthrough, all the deities in heaven and earth rejoiced, and that an earthquake rolled through one of the highest heavens. The passage reminds me of when Jesus said, "There will be more rejoicing in heaven over one sinner who repents than over ninety-nine righteous persons who do not need to repent."[3]

Kondanna offered himself for ordination to the Buddha's path, becoming the first disciple. The others were not far behind. This is a hugely significant event in the history of Buddhism. It was the Buddhist equivalent of the Feast of Pentecost, the birthday of the Christian church. At Pentecost the same

Spirit that was in Jesus infused the disciples, visibly manifested in tongues of fire, empowering them to go forth and continue his ministry. Everything necessary to the church was present for the first time: the Holy Spirit, the memory and teachings of Jesus, and the gathered community.

Kondanna's ordination was the birthday of Buddhism, because the same enlightenment that had transformed the Buddha had also transformed another, and it was at that moment when all three elements of Three Jewels were visibly seen for the first time.

The Three Jewels of Refuge are a very basic Buddhist creed—actually they are more like the Baptismal formula for Christians. They are the words that are said at the ceremony of initiation. The initiate says, "I take refuge in the Buddha. I take refuge in the Dharma. I take refuge in the Sangha."

There, in the Deer Park, the Buddha was visible as the Awakened One for the first time—for the first time others *knew* he was awakened. The Dharma (teaching) had been expounded for the first time. And the Sangha (the believing community) came into being with the first disciple.

I put the book down. *What a marvelous formula that is*, I thought. A few days ago in Bodh Gaya, I had seen a young bikkhu taking his vows, reciting those very words beneath the Bodhi tree where the Buddha had been enlightened. I tried to imagine what that young man must have felt as he knelt before the monk and repeated his words.

It was hard to make the connection, and so I translated the formula into something closer to home. I recited, "I take refuge in Jesus. I take refuge in the Gospel. I take refuge in the church." I felt a calm spirit descend over my being. I resonated deeply with the words. They felt right, they felt true, they felt trustworthy. I breathed the *rightness* of them deep into my bones.

What does it mean to me to take refuge in Jesus? I wondered. A refuge is a place of safety. My relationship with Jesus is one of trust, first and foremost. No matter how crazy everything in my life gets, he is the calm at the center of the storm. I can lean on him—hard. I can lean *into* him. And when I face the scariest thing life has to offer—death—it is my trust in him that will carry me over into life. Jesus is my one place of safety.

I flashed on the words of a hymn we had sung at the Lutheran church the very Sunday before I left, "*What more can he say than to you he has said, who unto the Savior for refuge have fled?*" I breathed deep and felt at peace in that quiet moment.

How is the Gospel my refuge? I didn't take this to mean the gospels, the scriptures, but Jesus' basic teachings: Caesar doesn't rule this world, God does. People create insiders and outsiders, but God accepts everyone. You have hidden from me in your shame, Adam, but I am out in the Garden looking for you and I will embrace you as soon as you show yourself. And I will do this always, no matter what you've done or how far you've run. Yeah, I trust that.

How do I take refuge in the church? That's trickier. My generation has *issues* with religious institutions. We tend to see them as dinosaurs—hypocritical at worst and irrelevant at best. And church folks are human, they're fallible, susceptible to all the *unsafe* behavior that you find in any community.

And yet, in general I have found people in the local congregations where I have worshipped and ministered to be sincere, giving, extremely loving folks. In church I have found friendship, encouragement for my own spiritual practice, as well as ample opportunity to put the Gospel (patience, forgiving each other, giving and receiving grace) into practice. And I deeply love the people in my congregations. Yes, it can get rocky at times, but overall, the church is a place of refuge for me.

I felt like I had found a place of connection with that young monk taking his vows. It took some effort, and an act of imagination to do it, but I got to a place of empathy. As I had stood watching him under the Bodhi tree I did so as a bemused spectator. But now, as I meditated on his vows in a way that I could really understand, my heart went out to him. I felt a kinship with him that transcended our religious traditions. We were people of faith together, people of trust, people of *refuge*.

I strolled around the ruined ancient monastery and pondered the first community that formed there. In light of the Buddha's new knowledge, they had to unlearn everything they thought they knew about the spiritual quest. According to the scriptures, he taught them kindly and patiently.

And their numbers grew. I leaned against a brick wall older than St. Paul and read the story of Yasa, a wealthy merchant's son who was in great spiritual distress. Fleeing to the Deer Park, he met the Buddha, who comforted him by revealing to him the Dharma. Yasa converted on the spot.

I reflected on how different that outcome was from the rich young ruler who came to Jesus in similar distress. Whatever else Jesus may have said to him, scripture says that he told him to "sell all you have, give it to the poor, and follow me." Embracing the Dharma would have meant the same thing, but while the rich young ruler went away dejected because the cost was too high, Yasa embraced the teaching and walked away from all of his earthly goods.

Yasa's father and immediate family did, too. His mother and wife became the first women to embrace the Dharma (at least in this account), and their network of friends were also eager to join. The movement began to gather steam.

Apparently sensing it was time to catch a wave, the Buddha gathered sixty followers and told them, "Go now and wander for the welfare and happiness of many, out of compassion for the world, for the benefit, welfare, and happiness of gods and men. Teach the Dharma that is good in the beginning, good in the middle, and good in the end, with the meaning and the letter."[4] He gave them the power to ordain and sent them out into the villages, two-by-two to preach.

This immediately reminded me of the time when Jesus sent seventy-two of his own disciples out, telling them, "Go! I am sending you out like lambs among wolves. Do not take a purse or bag or sandals.... When you enter a town and are welcomed, eat what is offered to you. Heal the sick who are there and tell them, 'The kingdom of God has come near to you'."[5]

So the Buddha sent them out, and his movement spread. He is still sending them out. There are now about 350 million Buddhists in the world, a number that is growing steadily, especially in the West where the Dharma is finding new, fertile ground.

I looked over toward the stupa and saw what looked like a Tibetan family enjoying a picnic. Three generations were present, a couple of teenagers, their very proper parents, and their grandparents. I smiled as I listened to their animated chatter. A white dog walked by, picking her way along the stone wall just above them. Her coat was spotty with mange, and her long, swinging teats betrayed many litters of pups.

The grandfather in the Tibetan family noticed the dog, too. Shakily, he got to his feet, leaned over to steady himself on the stone wall, and swung his cane over his head, descending with a *thwack* on the dog's hindquarters. The dog yelped and leaped away. I was outraged. The dog was only walking by the family—she wasn't begging, she wasn't being a nuisance, she was minding her own business.

I felt the heat rise on the back of my neck. I snapped. I strode toward the family, and yelled, "Hey! Why did you do that?" The old man had sunk back to the ground, smiling and satisfied with his random act of cruelty. I pointed at the old man and got up in his face. "Why did you do that?" I knew he couldn't understand me. I wasn't expecting an answer. I was *wroth*.

He smiled uncertainly and said something to his wife. I took his words to mean something like, "Who is this crazy white demon, and can I hit him with my cane, too?"

I shook my finger at him and pronounced, "Shame!" I said it over and over, "Shame! Shame!" It felt good for a few moments. Then I just felt ridiculous. I turned on my heel and stormed off.

The Buddha had sent his disciples out to preach "compassion for the world," and loving-kindness for all beings. "Where was the compassion for *that* being?" I said out loud. The Deer Park replied with silence and a gentle breeze. As I cooled down, I remembered the old woman who had yelled at me that morning, and realized that my cultural blindness and this old man's were not dissimilar. Perhaps I needed to discover empathy not only for the auspicious aspects of our respective faiths, but for the less auspicious aspects of our common human frailty and blindness, too.

I remembered something that Gandhi had said once, "Christianity is a wonderful religion. Too bad it's never been tried." In my absurd display of anger, I was perhaps exhibit A. But this day, among the Buddha's followers in this Tibetan family at least, I saw that Buddhism hasn't really been tried, either. We were people of *unfaith*, together.

------

1   John 15:15

2   Okay, now at this point I have an issue with the scripture writers. This is a huge logical leap to make, straight to another of the Buddha's major teachings, usually called "dependent co-arising." More on that later. I'm going to roll with it, but I'm just saying, dude, that's a huge leap.

3   Luke 15:7.

4   Bikkhu Nanamoli, *The Life of the Buddha* (Onalaska, WA: BPE Pariyatti Editions, 1992), 52.

5   Luke 10:1-9.

The Asokan pillar and stupa at Vaishali.

Chapter Eight: Vaishali
—Where the Buddha Admitted Women to the Sangha

For us in the spiritual guidance biz, "discernment" is a very big deal. We're constantly trying to discern an authentic way of being in the world, God's presence in various parts of our lives, and what God is calling us to. Discernment seemed to be the theme of my time in Patna.

When I got off the train, I instantly hit a discernment problem—I couldn't discern how to get to the train station. There was a stairway from the platform up to an elevated walkway that crossed all the tracks, and (usually) ends at the station. I followed the line of people getting off the train up the stairs, down the walkway, and then....the walkway dead-ended, blocked off above track number two. It looked like it had been closed for repairs, but there was no one working on it. There were no signs. You could descend down to tracks 2 and 3, but there was no way to cross to track one, to get to the station, to exit.

I scratched my head and scooted my bag back against the wall to watch how other people dealt with this problem. Some of them turned back—to God knows where—but some of them went down to track two, lowered themselves down onto the tracks, picked their way around the rocks and piles of feces, through a hole in the fence, then across track number one, where they climbed up onto the station platform. I saw an old woman struggling to get her foot over the concrete lip of the platform.

"What kind of place *is* this?" I wondered out loud. It was too noisy for anyone to hear me, even if they could speak English. I considered following the majority, here, but worried

131

about being able to get my heavy bag up and down the chest-high platform walls. Plus, it was just plain dangerous.

I decided to see what those who had turned back were up to. I got to the original stairs we'd come up, and kept going. Another staircase led down to an abandoned field where several tuk-tuks were congregated.

"That should work," I said, and carried my bag down the stairs with a groan. I wheeled it out to where the tuk-tuks were, and was instantly met by eager drivers. I told them the name of my hotel, which they didn't seem to understand. One of them quoted me an outrageous price, which I rejected. Another quoted a better one, and I allowed him to put my bag in the back. Then another driver started shouting bloody murder and started jerking my bag out of the tuk-tuk. That's when the fighting really broke out.

I grabbed my bag myself, and without another look headed back up the stairs, over the walkway, and down to track two. I forced myself not to think about what I was doing as I lowered myself to the tracks, carried my bag through the hole in the fence, crossed the second set of tracks, threw my bag up onto the platform, and scrambled up.

Outside the station I tried to find a tuk-tuk, but there seemed to be a rare scarcity of the usually ubiquitous contraptions. A bone-thin driver with a beard down to his knees pointed at his rickshaw. I had no idea how far the hotel was. If it was a kilometer or less, that would be fine. But if it were more, a tuk-tuk was a better—and much faster—bet.

But there seemed to be no other choice. Fortunately, it was only a few blocks away, and I overtipped him in my relief. My relief grew as I was shown to my room. This was the nicest hotel I had yet seen in India. Strangely, it wasn't expensive. It was modern, bright, and—most unusual of all—clean.

As an added bonus, its restaurant was picked by Lonely Planet as the best place to eat in town, and even though I was still leery of food due to lingering Delhi Belly, I knew that I either had to eat something or add hypoglycemic shock to my list of maladies. The restaurant opened at 7pm, and I and a woman about ten years younger than I were both waiting by the door. When they finally opened—about fifteen minutes late—they tried to seat us at the same table.

I laughed, "No, we're not together."

She echoed this, but paused. "On the other hand, it seems silly to eat alone in a big empty restaurant. Care to join me?"

"Why not?" I said, and sat myself down. We started chatting, and such was the relief—on both of our parts—to be with someone who speaks English that it actually took us a while to get to the menu.

Kim was from South Africa, but had been studying nursing in England. She had a job starting in Australia in about a month, and was taking a bit of a vacation as she wound her circuitous way there. She was keen to try the chicken, since Lonely Planet had raved about it, but I was wary. I told her about my history of digestive distress since I'd arrived, and was amazed that she'd just spent a month volunteering in the villages in Nepal and hadn't gotten sick once.

"My rotten luck," I muttered under my breath. We ordered, and I told her about my project. She didn't seem particularly interested—I got the impression she didn't have much use for religion—but she was polite and cheerful.

I ate about a quarter of what they brought me, and then ordered the butterscotch ice cream. About halfway through, I fished something leathery out of it. I have no idea what it was, but I lost what was left of my appetite. I shook Kim's hand and wished her safe travel.

When I got to my room I fairly collapsed, and was asleep instantly. And I dreamed. It was one of those Big Dreams, too, which are always wonderful and fun. I dreamed I was cuddling in bed with an old flame. She started talking about our lives together in the future, and I interrupted her. "Hey, I love my wife," I told her. "I'm not leaving her. She's my home."

Then I woke up. I lay in bed as the dawn light was just beginning to peek in through the curtains. I snatched greedily at the wisps of the dream and got most of it back. As I went into discernment mode, its meaning became clear very quickly.

In my spiritual direction experience, erotic dreams are almost always about intimacy with God—including the creepy or violent ones. This dream was a snapshot of my trip. I am snuggling with the Buddha here in India, but I'm not going to leave Jesus. I'm married to him. He's my heart's true home. The thought of this was bittersweet. My commitment to Jesus is absolute...but I wondered about his commitment to me. I was still having a very hard time discerning God's presence. I felt very alone.

My stomach was behaving, so I went down early for breakfast. A man about my same age was at the table next to me, very intently poring over some handwritten notes. A bible was on the table next to him, but at first I mistook it for a Day Planner, and assumed he was a businessman.

I am annoyingly chatty in such situations, so I introduced myself. He did the same, and I asked him what he was doing in India. He told me he was a Presbyterian pastor, and he was leading several of his church's young adults to observe a ministry that they support here in Patna.

I was overjoyed, told him he'd found a colleague, and filled him in on my pilgrimage. He didn't look too sure about what I was doing, but he was polite about it. He asked me what I was "planning to do about worship on this Lord's Day." My jaw dropped. I had no idea it was Sunday. For the past couple of weeks, I couldn't have told you the day of the week if my life depended on it.

He was preaching (I realized then that he was going over his sermon notes), and the service was at one of the house churches in the area. My heart sank, because I would have dearly loved to join them. Not only was I hungry for English speakers, but I was aching to be in the company of other people who love Jesus. It's hard to explain why that is to folks who aren't religious, but it's true. We don't just go to church because it's an obligation. We go because we hunger for it.

Unfortunately, I had already hired a car to take me out to Vaishali that day, and it was too late to cancel or postpone. By this time, several of his folks had come down to breakfast, and a lively conversation ensued. I hated to leave them, but my car would be arriving soon, so I made my apologies and my exit. I wondered how long it would be before I would be able to share in that fellowship again, or how long before I tasted another Eucharist.

I re-read all of my materials on Vaishali as the car dodged water buffalo, rickshaws, and potholes. We were never able to reach more than 40 mph because of the conditions of the road. Plus, there were speed bumps in non-intuitive places that my driver somehow was able to divine. They were a mystery to me.

After about an hour and a half of driving, we reached Vaishali. We drove past the Buddha Fun and Food Village, with its 40-foot-high angular purple Tyrannosaurus Rex flashing its fangs at us, and a moment later, parked next to a trinket cart.

Scratch that. There were about fifteen trinket carts, each with gleaming gold Buddhas reflecting the midday sun. There were also row after row of pictures of Shiva and spinning plates bearing the image of Krishna and Radha. There was also a poster of the sacred heart of Jesus. Most trinket carts, I have discovered, are deeply ecumenical.

My driver, a solid man who reminded me of an Indian Martin Sheen, led me through a gate and pointed. He didn't speak any English, but he could gesture with aplomb. He waved away, and I looked in the direction he indicted. An enormous, gleaming white stupa filled the landscape. He sat down and started to clean his nails. I walked to the stupa.

It was easily seven stories tall. It had an onion-shaped dome on it with a gold crown. A nearby sign said that the crown contained some of the Buddha's ashes. I removed my shoes and sprang up the stairs to the main platform. I walked around it, and discovered that there was a large gold statue of the Buddha facing each of the four directions. To the south was the infant Buddha, stepping forth boldly and declaring his final birth. To the West there was the familiar Buddha in meditation. Facing North was a Buddha with his hand raised in a mudra of teaching. I walked around to the East side, and saw the Buddha reclining—the moment of his death. His face didn't look old, but as young as the day he'd been enlightened. His trademarked serene smile played on his lips as he entered nirvana.

Next my driver took me to the archeological museum, a dusty, dim building in which there were nevertheless many impressive pieces of ancient statuary—some of it Hindu, some Jain, some Buddhist.

Our next stop was a large park containing the ruins of several monastic buildings and a sizeable stupa. As I walked around the peaceful park, I meditated on the significant events that had taken place there. In the Buddha's day, Vaishali had been one of the largest, most thriving cities in India. It was the capital of a confederacy of nearby city-states that became the world's first democratic republic—long before Greece. The peace and prosperity that followed in the wake of all that cooperation made it the envy of people far and wide.

The republic had invited the Buddha to come and preach the Dharma to them, and legend says that King Bimbasara had a road built all the way from Rajgir to the stream that bordered the confederacy's land, just so the Buddha could travel easier. The Buddha enjoyed such a warm welcome there that it became a favorite place, and he returned many times, delivering some of his most celebrated sermons there. He was so impressed with their system of government that he based the polity of the sangha on it.

(As I write, a lone cockroach is exploring my desk, its antennae aquiver as it discerns the provenance and composition of these strange computer cables....)

During one of his stays there, a prominent prostitute invited the Buddha to dine with her. He accepted her invitation. But several leaders of the city had hoped the Buddha would join them for dinner the same evening. When they extended their invitation, he shocked them by saying that he already had plans to dine with the prostitute. He went to dinner, shared the Dharma with his host, and she became a disciple. Seems the Buddha had a Magdalene, too.

That event isn't the only reason that Vaishali is important for Buddhist women, however. The Buddha's wife had become a disciple of his, as had his stepmother, and they had repeatedly begged him to allow them to become monks. Time and again he refused them. Then, while on retreat at Vaishali, the Buddha was informed that his wife and stepmother were approaching. Concerned, he went to greet them, only to discover that they had walked, in the company of 500 other women disciples, all the way from Kipalavatsu. His stepmother had shaved her hair and donned the ochre robes of a monk. They demanded ordination.

The Buddha said, "I have to think about this." It was a major discernment, and so he retired to consider the matter. When his beloved disciple Ananda attended him, he confessed that he worried what might happen to the women. If he ordained them, they might be subject to all kinds of cruelties. In their culture, a woman who remains unmarried is often looked upon disparagingly. "They might be raped or accused of being prostitutes," he said.

"But, Lord," Ananda reasoned with him. "Can women achieve enlightenment?"

"Yes, of course," the Buddha affirmed.

"Then why should we deprive them of the support of the sangha in their practice?" Ananda's reasoning carried the day, for the Buddha realized he could not deprive half of the human race of one of the three Jewels: refuge in the sangha. The next day he ordained his stepmother, wife, and 500 other women who had come on the protest march. (Just for the record, the Buddha's concerns were not trivial—Buddhist nuns were often openly reviled by Hindu culture as being "loose women.") Just last year, Vaishali was the site of the 13th International Summit of Buddhist Women.

Pulling my safari hat down to shield my eyes from the sun, I explored the large stupa at the center of the park, crumbling but still two stories high. Nearby, one of the pillars of King Asoka towered over the park, an ornate lion at its top, still looking fierce after all these years. Like all the Asokan pillars, this one was covered with writing, reportedly from the emperor's own hand.

I wandered over to what looked like a man-made pond the size of a large swimming pool. Legend has it that the pool was dug specifically for the Buddha by a tribe of monkeys, whose King offered the Lord honey. Strangely, although so many significant things happened in Vaishali, it was the monkey's gift that made it a popular pilgrimage site. Never underestimate the power of monkeys, I always say.

As I surveyed the pool, I noticed a group of about seventy kids, all around high-school age. They were standing in front of the stupa, but none of them were looking at it. They were all looking at *me*. I looked behind me to see what they were looking at, but there was nothing. It was unsettling. I waved at them, pathetically.

An advance party of about six boys broke away from the

main group and approached me. "Where is your country?" they predictably asked.

"America," I said, for the millionth time since I got here.

"We would like a photo of you, please sir. Okay?"

I shrugged. "Okay," I said.

One of the boys turned and yelled back at the other kids. Instantly all seventy of them broke into a run and mobbed around me. One of them ran a short distance away and clicked the photo. Then, amidst shouts of thanks, they all ran away.

Very strange. I scratched my head.

After we returned to Patna, I gratefully hopped in a rickshaw and asked the driver to take me to the Patna Museum. The Museum didn't disappoint, but it did amuse. The Natural History wing looked like it hadn't had an upgrade since Sir Edward Gait had founded it in the early 20th century, pith helmet and all. I marveled at the stuffed tiger, wondered over the string of stuffed rats....there must have been about eleven of them. (Wouldn't one stuffed rat have done the job?) What really stumped me, though, was the crocodile, which looked like it had been fashioned of papier mâché, based not on an actual crocodile but on someone's verbal description of one. I could have sworn its beak was carved out of wood.

But the statuary was stunning. It instantly took visitors back to the time of Patna's imperial glory, when it was the capital of known India in the third century, BCE. It had been united under the merciless King Asoka, who murdered all of his brothers as rivals to his throne—all except one brother, who was a Buddhist monk. A nominal Buddhist, Asoka waged war after bloody war, adding kingdom after kingdom to his empire.

Then, after one fateful battle, he was brought to his knees by the horror of what he had instigated. At his command, 150,000 men had died, and as he wandered the ruined landscape, picking his way over the corpses of horses and men, he cried out, "What have I done? If this is victory, then what is defeat? Is this justice or injustice? Is it glory or shame? Is it valorous to kill innocent children and women? Did I do it to increase my empire or to destroy another's kingdom? This woman has lost her husband, someone else has lost his father, someone else has lost a child, someone else an unborn baby. And what about all these corpses? Do they indicate victory or defeat? Are these vultures, crows, and eagles the messengers of death or evil?"

His own bloodlust shook him to the core, and precipitated a true conversion of spirit. He embraced the Dharma with a whole heart, proclaimed it the creed of the empire, and began a period of remarkable peace and prosperity.

Asoka undertook his own pilgrimage to all of the holy sites of the Buddha's life, and erected pillars testifying to the events that happened there. Asoka lived only two centuries after the Buddha, so his locations are considered authoritative, and indeed, we only know some of them because of the testimony of his monuments.

Asoka saw the great potential of Buddhism to unite his empire, and so when a schism threatened the Sangha, the emperor called the Third Buddhist Council to settle the matter. The doctrine of "eternalism" (the idea that people possess an unchanging self) was condemned, and unity was restored to the sangha.

As I toured the rest of the museum, I pondered just how similar Asoka's story is to Constantine's. The emperor Constantine converted to Christianity in the third century after Christ, also because of events on a battlefield. He, too, hoped his new faith would unite his empire, and when schism threatened to split the church, he called the Nicene Council to decide the matter.

The museum was closing so I grabbed my bag from the coat-check and headed out to find a rickshaw. I hailed the first one I saw, and the driver seemed weirdly animated. I told him where I wanted to go, and he nodded vigorously—he knew where that was. I asked him how much, and he looked offended. "Nothing, nothing! I do for Jesus!"

"Uh, okay," I said, "But I'm still going to pay you *something*. How about twenty rupees?" That was what the rickshaw driver had charged me on the way there, after all. He waggled his head and agreed.

I climbed in and we were off. "Are you a Christian?" I asked.

"Yes, yes!" he answered, and as if to confirm this, every time we started to enter an intersection, he made the sign of the cross. If ever it were an effective ward against danger, we needed it now. All drivers in India seem reckless by American standards, but this guy took the cake. He charged out in front of racing tuk-tuks with no hesitation, making no effort to merge. Fortunately the other drivers were on top of their game, and we escaped unscathed.

Throughout the ride, he kept reaching back and touching me, which was weird because his right hand seemed floppy and boneless. I noticed a long scar on the back of it. He also looked back a lot, causing me to shout, "Please watch the road!" at regular intervals.

Several times he asked me which way. "I thought you knew were we were going!" I shouted above the car horn din. Good thing I'd been paying attention on the way there. Finally, though, he stopped in front of my hotel and held out his hand. I placed a twenty rupee note in it, along with a ten rupee tip.

He swore and threw the money down at my feet. He started yelling. I thought maybe he was offended that I'd tried to pay him, since he'd said he wanted to do it "for Jesus." But as a crowd gathered around, some people started to translate. "He says you owe him seventy rupees," said one young man, laughing. He was probably laughing because that's about three times the going rate for a rickshaw.

The crowd was growing but the rickshaw driver was just

getting started. "He drunk," said an older man next to me. He shrugged apologetically. I picked up the money from the ground, added another twenty rupee note to it, and placed it in the man's good hand. He stopped yelling instantly, got up on his rickshaw and started pedaling away.

"That was frustrating," I said as the crowd started to dissipate. I wasn't sure what I'd done wrong, or what I could have done differently, but it was a matter for discernment that I pondered for a couple of hours afterwards.

That night, I found prayer harder than usual. I realized that I had a large backlog of spiritual frustration built up, and I just let God have it. "Where the hell *are* you?" I demanded. "This was supposed to be a buddy movie, a conversation, but you're completely absent!"

I'd tried everything, every discernment method I knew of. I tried chatting like Brother Lawrence, I tried checking in several times a day, I tried to "be still and know that" God is God. I hadn't flagged in my regular prayer practice, either. And yet, it seemed like the moment I'd hit India, God just winked out of existence.

It was almost as if I'd entered a henotheistic universe, where there are many gods, each with their own jurisdictions. When I got off the plane in India, I stepped out onto Shiva's soil, and the God of Israel was too far away to hear or help me. I don't think I've ever felt so alone. The only ray of hope I'd received, the only nudge from the Spirit I could discern was the dream that morning. I clung to it.

Then I raged and railed and cursed and shook my fist, and vented my feelings and my frustration at the One who is *supposed* to love me. Afterwards, my rage spent, I wondered what God was up to with this absence stuff. It wasn't like him at all. I usually feel his presence quite easily and often throughout the day. In fact, I couldn't do my work without it. Was he trying to teach me something? Is there some kind of soul work going on that I need to endure, that will be clear to me soon? India is a scary enough place *with* company. To be forced to face all of this alone just seemed cruel. I couldn't figure it out.

So I said Compline, and prayed, "Lord, you are in the midst of us, and we are called by your name—do not forsake us, O Lord our God."[1] But it didn't ring true. It sure didn't *feel* like God was in my midst. It felt like God was on another continent, far beyond the sound of my voice. I felt abandoned. Do not forsake us, indeed.

———

1 Jeremiah 14:9, 22.

The reclining Buddha at the site of the Buddha's death.

Chapter Nine: Kushinigar—Where the Buddha Died

My night was dreamless, a lowering into unconscious extinction, and then a sudden jerk into consciousness as the maintenance men began to pound on the pipes just outside my door. "Well, good morning to you, too," I mumbled. I did a quick surveillance—how sick was I this morning? I sat up. Slightly nauseous, with a mild thickening of the head. My cold was still in full effect, but it wasn't getting any worse. So...not too bad, considering. I threw on my pants and went downstairs to breakfast.

Lingering over cornflakes (the only thing on the menu that I could eat and/or looked edible), I read in *The Times of India* about an overnight train out of Mumbai—three sleeper coaches had caught fire at about 3am. No one in charge of the train noticed until everyone was already dead.

I had just taken one of those a couple of days ago, and shuddered. Thinking back on it, I didn't remember seeing the familiar "pull in case of emergency" cord. That was what, 19th century technology? Was that too much to ask?

I headed out to catch the bus and casually asked the guys at the desk how long the journey was. "Why take bus?" they asked. "Take car."

I thought, *My bowels are unpredictable. Two hours on a bus without any control over where we stop?* I chewed on my lip. In a car, I could ask the driver to find a bathroom. He might not understand English, but everyone knew the word "toilet," I have discovered. That decided it. "How much for the car?"

"1600 rupees," the man said, smiling. He knew they had me. That was about 27 dollars, for a minimum of five hours. Okay, that wasn't so bad. "Okay," I said, feeling like a wuss. A chubby, rich, privileged, contemptible wuss. "I'll take the car."

The driver arrived promptly, and soon we were off, zooming recklessly into traffic in near-zero visibility fog. We hadn't yet reached the outskirts of the city when the driver pulled into a gas station. He filled up, and when the attendant came to the window to collect, the driver gestured to me to pay.

"What?" I said. "I don't think so!" The bill was 500 rupees. That would instantly bring my total cost for the outing up to 2100 rupees. The driver insisted, raising his voice. I felt trapped. I gritted my teeth and paid the attendant, but as soon as the window was shut, I turned back to the driver. "No go," I said to him. "Hotel."

"Whaa?" the driver cocked his head. "Hotel??"

"Hotel," I said firmly. It wasn't too late to take the bus, I decided. I wasn't going to just sit back and be fleeced.

The driver looked concerned, but he pulled back onto the road and wound his way back to the hotel. By the time we got there, I had worked myself into a livid lather. I confronted the guys at the desk, explaining what had happened.

The manager exchanged quick words in Hindi with the driver, who shrugged, confused. The manager turned back to me with an obsequious smile. "Sir, I think there has been a misunderstanding. You pay the gas, but take that off of your final bill." He handed a 500-rupee note to me, "But it is okay. Here is the money you paid. Now you pay usual, yes?"

I wasn't at all sure that taking the 500 rupees off of the final bill had been my driver's plan all along. He looked slightly cowed, and I felt a pang of shame at my hot-headedness. I offered my hand for him to shake. He did. "Let's get going," I said.

This time he headed directly for the freeway. As we were stopped for the light, I saw a one-legged man crossing in front of us, supporting himself on a single crutch made from a rough branch. His pants had fallen down around his ankle, and he dragged them along as he jerked across the intersection, completely naked from the waist down.

In the next couple of minutes I saw a dog hobbling by the side of the road, one broken back leg swinging uselessly. Five minutes later, we stopped briefly beside a boy who must have been about twelve. He had stumps for hands, and was so impoverished it was clear he had never seen—and would never see—a doctor.

I marveled at the staggering number of wrecked and ruined lives in this country. The fetal position called, but I resisted it—there was simply too much of it. One or two instances of it are enough to make you enraged. The degree of brokenness in India that I witnessed went so far beyond what I could comprehend that the little mechanism in my brain that says, "get mad" or "do something" had completely short-circuited. All I could do was stare in fascinated horror.

As a Christian, I believe that God's ultimate project is to fix everything broken—every wounded soul, every scarred body, every ruined landscape, every damaged relationship—to bring everything that is or ever has been into healing, harmony, and wholeness. God has his work cut out for him in America. In India, it seemed simply hopeless. The sheer magnitude of brokenness seemed beyond even God's ability to heal, or even touch. In that place I find I needed to clutch at my faith with both hands.

Everywhere you look in India—not just in this city, but in every city I have been in so far—trash is not collected, but burned in little piles. Anywhere you walk, you're walking from one smoking heap to another. The noxious smell of burning plastic is ubiquitous. I turned my head to see a cow lower her nose into the flames of one such fire, braving a nasty burn in the desperate hope of finding a morsel of food.

Stopped at another light, motion in my peripheral vision caught my attention. I turned my head to see a little girl of about ten scampering to and fro, playing badminton with herself. The crumpled stained shuttlecock hung on the foggy air, as she stood poised with her racquet below, a look of sheer joy lighting up her face. She wore a red shawl tied around her neck like Superman's cape. She was resplendent.

I choked down the swelling in my throat and wiped roughly at my eyes. I'd steeled myself against the tragedy, in fact I was becoming numb to it. It was the beauty that did me in.

There are no actual on-ramps in India—only intersections where streets meet freeways. I rolled my eyes as I realized that we needed to be on the other side of this freeway. There is, of course, no way to get there except to wait for a break in oncoming traffic, then to simply drive across the road, entering our direction's traffic in the middle of the high-speed lane.

India may have city planners, I mused, *but they keep them all drugged and chained in a basement in Mumbai. There is simply no other explanation.*

Successfully crossing traffic without a tragic collision, the little Tata economy sedan struggled to get up to speed. Once we did, we passed two motorcycles, each of them transporting about twenty-five stackable lawn chairs, tied to the seat behind the driver. The stacks of chairs rose about fifteen feet into the air, swaying like mobile twin towers, or the antennae of a gigantic cockroach emerging from the pavement. There had to be a Kaiju name for such a beasty, but I couldn't think of one.

About ten minutes later, we were behind a four-seater jeep in which thirteen people had been packed. Two teenage boys were positioned precariously, balancing on the rear fold-down gate. They had mujahedeen scarves wrapped around their faces. Their dark eyes looked directly into mine with a hatred and ferocity that unsettled me. In spite of this, I was worried that at any one of these pothole bumps that regularly threw us from one side of the road to the other, one of those boys could lose his perch and fall under the wheels of the next car. I was struck not only by the precariousness of life in that place, but the nonchalance with which it was treated.

As if to reinforce this, my driver was texting instead of watching the road. This is bad enough in America, where people generally drive defensively, but here? It was suicide. I didn't say anything, but visibly relaxed when he put the damn thing away.

Finally reaching our destination, we pulled through a large double-decker golden archway. We were in Kushinigar—the place where the Buddha breathed his last.

It was an unlikely place to die, and probably not according to plan. The Buddha had been in Vaishali when he realized his end was near. He was probably intending to go to Kapilavatsu, in order to die "at home," in the company of his family in his boyhood home. But he didn't make it that far—he only made it *this* far. When the Buddha informed his beloved disciple Ananda that he would die in Kushinigar, he was incredulous.

It reminded me of Peter's reaction when Jesus said he was going to Jerusalem. Both teachers said, "I'm going to die." Peter responded, "Surely not," but Ananda said, "Surely not *there.*" Kushinigar was not deemed an auspicious place to end one's life, apparently. It was known for nothing—nothing important had ever happened there, and it had no resonance for the Buddha or his community.

It was certainly famous now. Concessions carts lined the street on both sides, all selling street food that looked delicious, but which my cautious intellect recoiled at. This was symbolic, I realized, because the reason that the Buddha didn't make it to Kapilavatsu was probably because he contracted food poisoning from the last meal served to him. He fell very sick after eating it, and was only able to walk another six kilometers before collapsing. There is only one way in which I surpass the Buddha, and that is in the vulnerability of bowels. I gave the food carts a wide berth.

We passed a stone building with a bright blue painted sign, "State Ayurvedic Hospital." I scowled—there was so much wrong with that. First, I can't imagine the State of California running a homeopathic clinic, and second, the place was hardly large enough for a convenience store, let alone a hospital.

My driver pulled up and set the brake. He pointed to a gate. I opened the door, and instantly a man appeared, offering himself as a guide. He spoke good English and I was tempted. "How much?" I asked.

"700 rupees," he answered. "I go everywhere with you."

I fished my cell phone out and opened my iTranslate app. I spoke, "Is this a good deal?" into it, and held the screen up to my driver. He looked at the resulting Hindi text, and shook his head. He pointed to himself. Of course, he didn't speak any English and the iTranslate app only works in one direction for Hindi. I thanked the guide, but told him, no. This was an expensive enough day as it was. Besides, I had my guidebooks, and they were pretty thorough. I'd have a good idea what I was seeing.

We set off through the gate and entered a large, beautiful park. In the center of it was an enormous white stupa, looking for all the world like a gigantic Shiva lingam. Attached to the stupa was a shrine with a long flight of marble stairs leading up to it.

As we approached, I marveled at the enormity of the stupa. A large crowd of Asian pilgrims was listening to their own guide in what must have been Korean or Vietnamese.

I "put off shoes" as the sign insisted, and climbed the marble stairs into the barrel-shaped shrine. Inside was a very large statue—nearly nineteen feet long—of the Buddha lying down. This was the dying Buddha, and according to legend the stupa was built at the very spot where he died. What I thought was ironic, or at least a very neat bit of symmetry, was that while

I was standing here on the spot where the Buddha died, my beloved wife was in Jerusalem, and could at that very moment be standing at Golgotha, the spot where Jesus died.

I thought about those two deaths as I stood there gazing at the golden serene face of the Buddha statue. Both deaths were chosen. Jesus chose to set his face toward Jerusalem, determined to walk into the political hornet's nest he knew was waiting for him there. He would put off the inevitable showdown with Rome, death, and hell no longer. Time to take your guns to town, Billy Joe.

The Buddha told his followers that an Awakened Being can live to the end of the age, if he chooses to. But the Buddha chose to die within the normal span of a man's life. "Everything comes to an end," he told his disciples. "I have done what I could do, both for myself and for others. To stay here would from now on be without any purpose. I have disciplined, in heaven and on earth, all those whom I could discipline, and I have set them in the stream."[1] The Buddha died a friend of chiefs and princes, while Jesus died an enemy of the state. The Buddha died of old age, while Jesus was violently executed—still a young man. Both, however, *chose* to die.

It seemed kind of unfair that the Buddha got nearly fifty years to teach, while Jesus barely got three. It makes you wonder if Christianity would have thousands of scriptures, as Buddhism does, had Jesus taught for so long. And what further teachings would he relate?

On the other hand, their opponents were different. The Buddha was battling ignorance, and teaching is the best method for such an enemy. But Jesus was battling oppression and coercion, and unfortunately opposing these often involves placing one's life on the line. Teaching was important to him, but his life was the great object lesson that would turn everything around.

As the Buddha was lying there awaiting death, a Hindu ascetic named Subhadda heard that the Buddha was nearby and would die soon. He instantly set out to see him. Ananda tried to shoo him away, but the Buddha called out, and bid him draw near. Subhadda had several questions for the Buddha, and the master patiently answered all of them, and with the last of his strength, taught the Dharma one last time.

As Jesus hung on the cross, he extended grace to the criminal being executed next to him, comforting him and assuring him that on the other side of this ordeal was paradise. Then Jesus cried, "My God, my God, why have you abandoned me?" and surrendered his spirit.

At his end, the Buddha called his closest disciples to him, and said, "All things decay. Keep working toward liberation." Then he closed his eyes, and entered into a deep meditation from which he never emerged.

The scriptures say that at the moment of his death, "the earth quivered like a ship struck by a squall, and firebrands fell from the sky. The heavens were lit up by a preternatural fire, which burned without fuel, without smoke, without being fanned by the wind. Fearsome thunderbolts crashed down on the earth, and violent winds raged in the sky. The moon's light waned, and in spite of a cloudless sky, an uncanny darkness spread everywhere. The rivers, as if overcome with grief, were filled with boiling water."[2]

This is what scripture reports at Jesus' death: "From noon on, darkness came over the whole land until three in the afternoon.... The curtain of the temple was torn in two, from top to bottom. The earth shook, and the rocks were split. The tombs also were opened, and many bodies of the saints who had fallen asleep were raised. After his resurrection they came out of the tombs and entered the holy city and appeared to many."[3]

Okay, it's not exact—the Buddhists get meteorological fireworks, but (as my friend Steve Case points out) Christians get zombie action. Seems like a draw. And it *is* remarkably similar. I never get tired of this crazy stuff. I was still musing on the comparisons as my driver pulled up to the next site, the ruin of a massive stupa built on the spot where the Buddha was cremated. Again, the park was immaculate, and the stupa, built of brick and decaying in a jagged, irregular pattern, was still impressive....well, as impressive as a four-story mound of bricks can be.

As I circumambulated, I wondered what had happened to the Buddha after he died. The answer to that depends on what variety of Buddhist you are. For the low-Buddhology Theravadins, the simple answer is "nirvana"—which only sounds simple. We in the West think of "nirvana" as the Buddhist equivalent of heaven, but it isn't.

Once a wandering ascetic asked the Buddha what happened to enlightened people after they died. The Buddha said, "Why don't you make a fire from these sticks?" The ascetic complied, after which the Buddha said, "Okay, throw some more sticks on it." The ascetic did. "What's happening?" the Buddha asked.

"It's going pretty good now," the ascetic looked pleased.

"Good. Now stop throwing sticks on it," the Buddha instructed. After a while the fire went out. "What happened?" asked the Buddha.

"The fire went out," the ascetic answered.

"Where did it go?" asked the Buddha. "Over there? To the right? To the left? Up? Down? Where is the fire?"

"It's not anywhere. It just went out," the ascetic answered, looking wary.

"Exactly. That's what happens to enlightened people when they die. They just go out." The word "nirvana" actually means "snuffed out," like a candle flame. The cycle has stopped. No more karma is being handed out. Karma and consciousness and life are all likewise extinguished.

It doesn't sound like much of a happy ending to Western ears. But if you've been trying to get off the Ferris Wheel of Horror that these countless lives are to those in the East, perhaps we can approach the feeling of relief that it offered.

A more subtle understanding of Nirvana is that what was extinguished was duality—the Buddha left behind all two-ness, and entered into a state of unity with all being. Mahayana Buddhists lean closer to this understanding, although for them the Buddha didn't go into Nirvana at all, but eschewed Nirvana until all beings could also be liberated.

Most Mahayana Buddhists teach some form of Trikaya, or doctrine of the three bodies. They teach that the Buddha's physical body (*nirmanakaya*) died, was cremated, and is gone. The Buddha's Dharma-body, however (*dharmakaya*) is at one with all things, and is found everywhere and in all things. We encounter this Dharma being consciously, however, through a mediating body (*sambhogakaya*), which is how the Buddha comes to us through meditation, prayer, and visions.

I'm describing this in deceptively simple generalizations. Your mileage may vary, however, since every Mahayana school has a slightly different spin on this. What I find interesting, of course, are the parallel ideas within Christianity.

When Jesus died, he didn't go to heaven, as most people assume. Instead, scripture says that he went to hell, and while there he "preached to the dead."[4] Tradition says that he liberated every being held in captivity there—or at least all those who *wanted* to be liberated—and led them to paradise. Then he came back to earth, and was resurrected in a glorious, perfected body.

After Jesus' resurrection, he continued teaching for another forty days or so. Then he ascended into heaven, "to fill all things"[5] as pseudo-Paul puts it. Eastern Orthodox theology makes much of the Cosmic Christ, the result of Christ's wedding of himself with all creation, who is even now in the process of divinizing all things, converting all that is into God. The medieval Catholic mystics expanded on this theme. Mechtilde of Magdeburg said, "The day of my spiritual awakening was the day I saw—and knew that I saw—God in all things and all things in God." And Martin Luther affirmed this theology for Protestants by establishing the doctrine of ubiquity—Jesus is present at all places, at all times, in all things, and in all souls.

"Okay, we go now?" my driver said.

"What?" I asked. We'd been in town for maybe an hour.

"We go now. Hotel," he looked at me hopefully.

"I...huh..." I had to think. All around were temples from various denominations of Buddhists, but when I'd tried to go into one of them, my driver had refused, and waved me elsewhere. I didn't come all this way to do the whirlwind circuit and then go sit in my hotel room. I didn't care how much this driver wanted to get home.

On the other hand, perhaps he assumed I'd wanted a quick spin about the place and had another commitment that afternoon? I tried to be fair to both of us. Which meant, of course, that we'd have to part ways. It looked like I'd be taking the bus after all, if only one way.

I signaled for him to stop and pulled open my neck wallet. (I secretly loved the fact that whenever I went to pay for something I got to flash the Indians my belly. It's my own quiet subversive action.) I pulled out 1600 rupees and placed them in his palm. Then I added another 100. "And that's for you," I said. "A tip."

He looked at me, confused. "You go back to hotel," I said, pointing at him. "I go by bus." I smiled. "Thank you." Then I got out of the car. I felt the exhilaration of freedom, although instantly the foggy cold snapped at my chin and I wondered if

I'd been wise, given my iffy health. "What's done is done," I said, and headed over to the first of the monasteries I'd seen.

In a moment, my driver was tugging on my arm. I turned and he handed me a cell phone. It was the concierge from the hotel. "Sir, what is the problem?" he asked. I explained the situation, and told him the driver could return. I handed the phone back to the driver, who spoke rapidly. Then he handed the phone back to me. "Sir, the driver will wait for you. It is no problem. At what time would you like to return?"

It was 11:30am, and I knew that most of the monasteries would be closing about now, reopening after lunch at 1:30pm or so. I did a quick calculation based on the number of temples I'd seen. "How about 3pm?" I asked. I handed the phone back to the driver, who talked back and forth several times with the concierge. Finally he put the phone away. He scowled at me. He must have thought I was the world's biggest pain in the ass.

He pointed to the car. He held up three fingers. "Three," he said. "There."

"See you then," I said. I was free. *And* I had a ride home. Sometimes you *can* have your cake and eat it, too.

Unfortunately, it looked like some of the temples were under construction and not yet open to the public. I walked up the street to the State Museum, but it too was closed—for renovations. That was a pity because the Lonely Planet had said good things about it.

I walked over to the impressive Thai temple, noting that it opened again in an hour. Then I noticed a sign—it indicated a dusty path next to the temple, and announced the village where the Buddha's ashes had been distributed. My eyebrows leaped up. That seemed like a promising destination.

Unfortunately, an old man appeared next to me, and tried to get me to follow him down the path. I groaned. Yes, I wanted to check out the village—no, I didn't want to pay this old man to "accompany" me. I didn't know what to do, and hated being in that situation. It doesn't matter where you're walking in India, if someone comes up alongside you and walks with you, when you reach your destination, they'll demand money for "guiding" you. You can set your watch by it.

I heard a commotion, and turning around, discovered a group of about thirty students crossing the street, coming straight toward the little path. *Saved!* I thought. *I'll just walk with them.* I found the teacher and introduced myself, and we chatted amiably as we walked.

After a couple hundred yards, we went into a gate to a small courtyard. At one side was a makeshift tent made of a large yellow tarpaulin. Inside I could see a straw mat where, it seemed, the old man lived. My feelings toward the poor man softened.

He was clearly overjoyed to have so many visitors. The kids kicked off their shoes and made for the other side of the compound, where they climbed up on a marble platform and examined the statue of the Buddha set upon the spot where his ashes had been divided among all the claimants. There were eight of them, according to a nearby plaque.

Of course, the class wanted their pictures taken with me, so I posed for half a dozen of them. There would have been more, but I was mindful of my time. On the way out, I gave twenty rupees to the old man. He bowed to me in a namaste gesture that seemed genuinely grateful.

The Thai temple was amazing—a spotless collection of gleaming white marble buildings, all in that inimitable Thai style that seems both weightless and ascending. Unfortunately, the great Buddha hall was blocked off, so all I could do was peer in. It was dark, but what I could see was lovely.

On the way back to the car, I saw a little curios shop—the first such shop I had seen in town. Oh, sure, there had been souvenir carts, but nothing like this. Most of the store was given over to saris, but in a glass case there were several sculptures. Near the front was a black stone carving of the reclining Buddha. In fact there were several of them. As I examined them, I realized that they differed. These weren't epoxy knock-offs, these were each carved in granite by hand.

"How much?" I asked.

"1200 rupees," the man said.

"I'll give you 500," I said.

The man shook his head. "My shop not like other shops," he explained. "I don't jack prices. My prices are low, and my profit is low. This not cheap. This take a lot of work, cost a lot of money."

His price was about 18 dollars. Hardly expensive. I loved the statue. Reclining Buddhas are rare—I hadn't yet seen one on my trip. And to have one from Kushinigar, the place where the Buddha had died? Priceless. "I'll take it," I said. After all, I'd been here almost a month, and hadn't bought a single souvenir of any value. It seemed important somehow.

As I walked away, I stowed the statue in my shoulder bag. I thought it would make a fine compliment to my assortment of crucifixes once I got home. I'm a Christian, after all. I collect dying saviors.

———

1   Conze, 62.

2   Conze, 63.

3   Matthew 27.

4   1 Peter 3.

5   Ephesians 4:10.

A Brief Interlude: Kathmandu

By this time, I was due for a break. While I was in India, my wife Lisa had been chaperoning a group of students on a trip to Israel and the Palestinian Territories. When her students got on a plane to fly back to the States, she flew in the other direction, to Kathmandu for a romantic rendezvous.

India had worn me out. I liked Nepal, and a little more time there would be a welcome relief. Lisa and I would have about ten days together, and to be honest, looking forward to those days really helped get me through the last couple of weeks. I arrived the day before she did and got a sense of the neighborhood.

After her plane landed, we got her settled into our hotel, and set out to explore. Soon Lisa said, "I'm starving."

"Well, right up there is the number one-rated restaurant in Kathmandu, according to Trip Advisor," I said, pointing to the sign for Rosemary's Kitchen and Coffee Shop. "I ate there last night and I'm still standing."

"Good enough for me," she said. It was about three o'clock, my preferred dinner time while travelling anyway, so I was ready. As we walked in, I hailed the rowdy Nepali youths that had been drinking there last night. They raised their glasses in greeting.

Lisa ordered a chicken dish. "You're awfully brave," I said.

"If I'm doubled up in the hotel room retching into the toilet at three in the morning, you have my permission to say 'I told you so,'" she answered.

"That will be no consolation," I said. I had learned my lesson early and ordered the Nepalese Thali—an assortment of traditional food, usually involving a vegetable curry, rice, lentil soup, and yoghurt.

So after our little jaunt, where will you be headed in India?" Lisa asked.

I hunkered a bit in my seat. "Actually, I have a confession to make," I said.

Her eyebrows raised.

"I can't believe I'm saying this, but...I *hate* India. At least, if the rest of India is anything like the northeast, I hate it. If I have to go back there again, alone, then I think I'm just going to go home when you do." There. I'd said it out loud. It was hard enough admitting it to myself, but now I'd admitted it to Lisa, too.

"You *have* been through the wringer," she said. "Do you have to do what you're doing in India? I mean, haven't you done all the major Buddha sites already?"

"Yeah," I agreed. "I did all four of the primary sites. And I've done three out of the four secondary sites."

"Which one did you miss?" she asked.

"Sravastri," I said. "It's the site of some miracles, but no major event happened there. I'd hoped to go, but it's really hard to get to." I stared at my glass of soda water. "But I've been thinking about this a lot. Let me try something out on you."

"Okay," she said, leaning in.

"What if I spent the rest of my pilgrimage time exploring the Buddhist diaspora?"

"Meaning what, exactly?"

"Meaning exploring Buddhism's theological development through time, by visiting places that exemplify the three major strands of Buddhism."

"I thought there were only two main strands of Buddhism."

"There are," I said, "Theravada and Mahayana. Vajrayana is a subset of Mahayana, but it's so distinctive that many people treat it as its own thing. And they see themselves as very much a progression beyond Mahayana. So I think it's fair to talk about it as a distinct strand."

"Okay. Tell me more about what you're planning."

"So the earliest stratum of Buddhist teaching is preserved by the Theravadin tradition. So why not spend some time in a country that is predominantly Theravada?"

"Like where?"

"Like Thailand," I said. "I could go to the various temples there, talk to people, and read up on Theravada theology."

"That sounds wonderful," Lisa said, sitting up straighter, an excited smile spreading across her face. "Where else?"

"Well, the next major development is the Mahayana schools. So I'd go to a country that is predominantly Mahayana."

"Where would that be?" she asked.

"Ideally, China," I said. "But the visa situation would be impossible at such short notice. But I could get into Taiwan with no trouble at all. And they have some magnificent temples. I could read up on Mahayana thought, and talk about Bodhidharma and so forth. Then I could go back to India to visit those predominantly Vajrayana places that are still accessible. I can't go to Tibet on such short notice, but I can go to Ladokh and to Dharamsala, where the Dalai Lama lives." I waited and watched her face.

She was beaming. "I think it's a *great* idea," she said. "I think you should do it."

"I'll go crazy if I have to spend the rest of my time in India alone," I said.

"I get that. I don't blame you," she said. "I think this plan is wise."

"You don't think my supporters will balk?"

"You're still following the Buddha, aren't you?"

"Well, if not his footsteps, certainly I'm following the path of his teaching."

"I think they'll love it. They'll get to see some new places, too."

I relaxed. That was what I was most worried about. I am deeply grateful to all the people who supported me on this journey, and I want to make sure that I honor my covenant with them.

"How expensive will this be?" she asked.

"Negligible," I said. "It's about $150 for each flight—just a tiny bit more than my flights *within* India would be. And the hotels there are no more expensive than they are in India—at least the Indian hotels worth staying in."

"You should definitely go," she said.

So I went.

Part Two: In the Footsteps of the Buddhists

Outside the Grand Palace in Bangkok.

Chapter Ten: Thailand—The Theravadin Revelation

The flight to Bangkok was brief, only three hours. On the plane I studied the Lonely Planet guide. There are over 40,000 Buddhist temples in Thailand. Since I'll only be there for ten days, I'll probably miss a few. Still, I resolved to do my best. I breezed through immigration and customs (US passport holders are just waved through, apparently), and collected my bag. I wheeled it out to the metered taxi stand. They soon matched me up with a driver, and we were on our way.

As the city lights started to speed past, my irritation and travel exhaustion conspired, sapping my strength, and I sank low into the back seat. I was irritated because of a horrible snafu—my hotel didn't send me a car and claimed that they never received my email. Fantasies of what I would say to the receptionist played out in my mind, and several times I reminded myself of what the good Buddhist approach to this would be ("you only suffer so long as you resist what is" so just let it go and stop suffering) as well as the good Christian approach ("love one another; forgive your brother seventy times seven times"). I decided that the longish taxi ride was a good time to pray, so I opened my ipad and called up my *iBook of Common Prayer* app, navigating quickly to the service for Compline.

The familiar and comfortable words of the service soothed my nerves, and got me out of the resentful rut I'd been spinning in. At the place in the service for free intercessions, Jesus and I had a very good exchange, and I asked him to be more available for the next leg of this journey, pretty please. I took comfort in a "burning in the breast" (as the Mormons marvelously describe it), and asked Jesus to help me leave all my resentments behind—including what I'd been feeling toward him. I felt comforted and renewed as we exited the freeway, and hit the surface streets of Bangkok.

The strange, noodly script of the Thai language flashed at me in a rainbow selection of neon lights, interspersed with snatches of English. I had been expecting another juxtaposition of third-world and first-world structures here, but it was first-world all the way. Bangkok was sleek, modern, and bright.

I braced myself as we pulled up at my hotel—I'd been disappointed so many times in India. I had already forgotten the taxi snafu, so I was completely taken aback when the woman behind the desk dropped her eyes, hunched her shoulders, and said, "I am sooo sorry about taxi."

"Ah," I said. "You found the email, did you?"

She nodded. "How much you spend on taxi?"

"600 Bod," I said. About fifteen dollars.

Within seconds, six 100-Bod bills were laid out in front of me. She renewed her apology. I waived it away. "This is very generous," I smiled at her, ducking in order to catch her downcast eyes. "Thank you so much for your apology."

She smiled and I checked in. A rambunctious, talkative porter showed me to my room, and when I saw it I relaxed. It was spotlessly clean. It was in good repair. It was cheery. *Oh yes,* I thought, *this will do very nicely.* I'd been worried, since I was only paying about thirty dollars a night for it.

I rose late the next morning (well, late for me, about 8am). I went down for breakfast, not expecting much, and was bowled over by the rice and chicken with spicy Thai pepper sauce that greeted me. Okay, room, food…Thailand was *definitely* an upgrade.

I left my laundry at the desk and set out with a Top-10 list of wats (temples) to see. I walked the block and a half to the metro station and rode the crowded, shiny car three stops. I bounded down the stairs to the street, and was instantly met with a lovely olfactory assault from street vendors roasting chicken and pork and deep frying dumplings. I'd just eaten, and I was already salivating.

I quickly made my way to the dock, where I purchased a one-day ticket for the water taxi. "Where do I board for the orange line?" I asked an employee. "All boats go same," she said, "just get on boat." So I did.

I was lucky to get a seat, and searched out the map of stops posted over the door of the boat. I had about seven stops to go. As people poured onto the boat, a man's voice blared over the loudspeaker in English, "Too many people on the boat. Get on the boat!" I frowned. It was very confusing, but apparently not to everybody—people continued to get on the boat until there was standing room only.

I looked around and noticed that about half of my fellow travelers were Westerners. The air was so thick with a babel of languages that it was almost intoxicating. I smiled and made good use of the time by putting on some sunscreen.

I also read up on my first stop. This was the Grand Palace, built in the 1700s, side-by-side with the Temple of the Emerald Buddha, the most sacred Buddha image in Thailand, although I have yet to run across the story of why it is so special.

I paid for my ticket, passing by a pharmacy (why is there a pharmacy at the entrance to the most popular tourist attraction in Thailand?) and a Nepalese handicraft store (wait, *what?*). I passed through the turnstile and walked out into a square that made my jaw drop.

Building after glittering building wowed everyone in the crowd. Each building was covered in jewels, reflecting the sun in a million sparkling patterns of color. Gold stupas stretched to the sky beside bright blue pagodas. The inside wall of the compound was covered in dazzling murals all the way around, depicting palace scenes, mountain monks, and fiery monsters feeding on innocent flesh with such regularity that Godzilla would be green with envy if he weren't already...well, green.

I watched those making offerings before the Temple of the Emerald Buddha. About fifty incense sticks sent smoke and fragrance into the air, while braziers blazed away. Platter after platter of flowers and fruits were set out, but it was not clear whether they had been offered already, or were ready to be taken in as offerings.

A question nagged at me: to whom were these being offered? To the Buddha? But that made little sense. Theravada Buddhists embrace a "low Buddhology," meaning that the Buddha was just a man. He was a very important man, of course, and they believe he was just one Buddha in a long string of enlightened beings—way-showers and prophets who have guided the spiritual evolution of humanity through long ages. There were Buddhas before him, and there would be Buddhas in the future. But his Buddhism—Siddhartha Gautama's Buddhism—was supposed to endure for five thousand years. *Two thousand five hundred down,* I thought, *two thousand five hundred to go.*

That notion reminded me of dispensational theology in the Christian tradition—the idea that God has ordained discreet ages in human history, and that the rules are different in each age. According to this theology, we are now in the "Church Age" between the first and second comings of Christ, which is ruled by the Holy Spirit. Dispensational theology was disseminated throughout the United States through the evangelical Scofield Reference Bible, and the popular "rapture" theology is also part of this dubious schema.

Needless to say, more historic Christian theologies sneer at this, and I don't give its detailed series of "dispensations" much credence myself, although I do find it fascinating as a "frontier theological artifact." And yet, the idea of dispensations in general—that there are different ways or methods of relating to the Divine in different historical and cultural settings—seems beyond dispute. It seems the Buddhists agree.

I had been reading up on Theravada theology, and discovered that there is some academic disagreement about it—no big surprise there. The joke that Jews tell about themselves (put three Jews in a room and you have four opinions) is equally true of academics. Kate Crosby, for example, says that the idea that Theravada Buddhism preserves the original, ancient teaching of the Buddha is a reductive distortion promulgated by Western scholars.[1] In fact, Theravada Buddhism, far from being stuck in the third century BCE, is a tradition that continues to evolve and adapt, even today.

But she acknowledges that the Theravadins themselves see their tradition as a direct continuation of the Buddha's teaching, preserving its integrity. I'm sure the Mahayana would say the same, but I get what she's saying: The myth that Theravada preserves and transmits the earliest and most accurate teachings of the Buddha is foundational to Theravadin identity. *And it is still a living and evolving tradition.* Where she faults Western scholars is in trumpeting the Theravada claim uncritically, when it is a much more nuanced reality.

I shed my shoes and entered the Temple of the Emerald Buddha. Taking a seat on the carpeted floor, I gasped at the beauty all around me. Bright paintings covered every inch of the temple, while the altar was a glorious, crowded jungle of gold and glittery statuary. Standing and sitting Buddhas spread out across the altar, forming a jewel-encrusted pantheon presided over from on high by a tiny, almost completely obscured deep-green enthroned Buddha, draped in bright orange monk's robes.

Beside me, a woman knelt, placed her hands together in a mudra of prayer, and bowed three deep bows before the altar, her mouth moving silently as she prayed. Again I wondered, *To whom is she praying?* Theravada Buddhists, after all, believe that when the Buddha died, he entered into nirvana. He was *outta here*. So if the Buddha is gone, who is hearing her prayer? To whom does she address it?

I'd get my answer soon. First, however, I made sure I saw every inch of the temple grounds, and then exited to explore the palace. Very few of the palace rooms were open to the public, which was very disappointing. I wanted to see where the royal family lived—what their bedrooms looked like, how the kitchens were arranged, how the toilet worked—you know, how people actually *lived*. Instead, I saw a tiny arms museum (how many spears can you really look at before you start looking *past* them?) and two throne rooms—one of which was grand and the other was undergoing repairs with draped furniture tossed here and there at odd angles. I stopped at a café and texted Lisa and my folks while enjoying two scoops of Häagen-Dazs and an icy cold sparkling water.

I was starting to sweat. Up until now, I had been absolutely freezing at every stop of my pilgrimage. But in Thailand, it was hot—not oppressively hot, not Spain-in-July hot, but enough to make my t-shirt cling to my back. After all the weeks of cold, it felt *good*.

I left the Grand Palace and headed south along the wharf. Before long I came to Wat Pho, the second most important site on my list. No sooner had I paid for my ticket than I was approached by a guide. He spoke very good English, and introduced himself as Phalang. His fee was about seven dollars for forty-five minutes, which sounded fine to me.

We set off at a brisk pace, and headed straight for the main attraction: a long temple in which was housed the longest reclining Buddha in Thailand, measuring 46 meters. The statue was enormous, and the building was not much larger—there was only room for the pillars and a narrow walkway on either side.

As we strolled the length of the giant Buddha's body, Phalang explained that Buddhism was a fairly recent import to

Thailand. It had arrived only about 750 years ago. Previous to that time, most people had been animists, although some had been Hindus. Then monks from Ceylon had preached to the King, who was convinced and took refuge in the Buddha, the Dharma, and the Sangha and strongly encouraged his people to do the same. "But we still love the gods," Phalang added.

"Wait," I said. "You believe in gods? Which gods?"

"You know, Ganesha, Vishnu, Shiva—"

"You believe in the *Hindu* gods?" I asked.

"Oh yes," Phalang assured me.

"Just you, or all Thai people?"

"Most," he nodded. I found that incredible, since 95% of the Thai people are Theravada Buddhists. "I pray to Ganesha every morning," he added.

"But you're Buddhist," I said.

"Oh, yes."

"And there's no contradiction in that?" I asked. He looked troubled, like he didn't understand the question. I shrugged it off.

Exiting the temple of the reclining Buddha, we paused by a small shine where people were making offerings to a small, seated image of the Buddha. "In your religion, you make confession, yes?" Phalang asked.

"Yes," I assured him, not bothering to explain that different Christian traditions did this in different ways.

"We do same. This for purification."

I watched as one young army officer knelt, bowed three times to the image of the Buddha, and offered incense. He stayed on his knees praying for some time.

"What do the three bows mean?" I asked.

"He bow once to Buddha, once to Dhamma, once to Sangha," he answered, visibly pleased at my question. "It show respect."

"The three jewels," I nodded, thinking how very cool that was. "And who is he praying *to?*" I asked.

Phalang looked confused. I redirected. "Is he praying to the Buddha?"

"Oh, no," he said. "Buddha gone. Nibbana." Nirvana. That squared with normal Western ideas about what Tharavadins believed. Yet Crosby spent a whole chapter on the phenomenon of Buddha worship among the Theravadins, so I didn't know whom to believe.

"So who is hearing his prayer?" I asked.

Phalang's eyebrows knit together as he thought about how to respond. Finally, he said. "Image not Buddha, but remind us of Buddha teaching. He pray to teaching."

"He's praying to the *Dharma?*" I clarified, using the Sanskrit word.

"Yes," he smiled broadly, "to Dhamma," using the Pali word.

It was my turn to knit my brows together. I'm used to praying to the Father, to Jesus, or (less often) to the Holy Spirit, but the idea of praying to the Gospel seemed strange. I couldn't quite wrap my head around it. This would definitely take further pondering.

Crosby wrote that even though Tharavadins believe the Buddha is no longer present, he continues to be present through the things that he left behind: his relics, his teaching, and through the ongoing presence of the Sangha, the gathered community. She writes about installation ceremonies for new Buddha statues, before which the sutras are read, and to which the Buddha's powers are transferred. A Buddha statue has the same power to transform a seeker that the Buddha's presence did when he walked the earth—the power to challenge, to inspire, to enlighten.

I asked Phalang about that. "Do Buddha statues have the same powers that the Buddha did?"

He scrunched his face up and shook his head. "They just statues," he said.

"But it looks like these people are worshipping the statues," I said.

"No worship," he said. "Reminding."

His response triggered a memory, when as a child I was being taught about the Lord's Supper. As Southern Baptists, we were told that the Supper reminded us of Jesus' death, but it wasn't magical in any way, as the Catholics wrongly believed. It was just a symbol that served to remind us of Jesus' death.

Having spent several of my adult years as a Catholic, I recognize how reductionistic that assessment of sacramental teaching was, but it wasn't entirely inaccurate. Phalang was saying something similar. There's nothing magical about the Buddha statue—it isn't an idol. It just serves to remind believers of the Buddha and his teaching.

In the Christian tradition, we make a big deal of the distinction between worship and reverence. The whole iconoclastic controversy in the 8th and 9th centuries hinged on that very distinction. A church council finally decided that icons could be used as aids to devotion, and they could be *revered*, but they were not to be worshipped.

That's a tricky distinction, and one that continues to plague the Christian tradition. Catholics are supposed to revere Mary, they they're not supposed to worship her. Protestants revere Martin Luther, but they don't worship him. But Lutherans are better at this than Catholics are. Catholic theologians can make this distinction until they are blue in the face, but it isn't going to stop a theologically unlettered peasant woman in Guadalajara from worshipping the Blessed Virgin. The less educated people are, the more difficult the distinction between worship and reverence becomes.

I guessed that it was the same in Buddhism. Theravada Buddhist teaching might officially say that the Buddha is gone and the statue is just a reminder, but that isn't going to stop the hoi polloi from worshipping those images. I wondered at just how theologically literate Phalang was. He seemed to know a good deal.

I was just about to ask him about it, when we entered another sanctuary. Yet another grand altar assembly towered over us. "Over there is where the monks sit," Phalang pointed at an elevated section of the floor. "I used to be monk," he smiled.

"You did?" I asked, surprised.

"Yes, all Thai boys become monks—for few months, at least. Some stay monks. Some go to work." He lowered his head conspiratorially. "I stay only a month. Like female too much." He bobbed his head and smiled wickedly.

I'd known about Thai boys joining the monastery, but it hadn't occurred to me that it was a way to educate the laity—make all of them (or all of the boys, in this case) monks—let them eat, sleep, and walk the life of a dedicated religious, including intensive instruction. It seemed to work: Phalang really knew his stuff. I was impressed, and wondered again why Christian monastics didn't allow "temporary" ordinations.

Apparently, anyone can be ordained a Buddhist monk, even non-Thais. There's a website called "monk for a month" in which anyone can be placed in a monastery for thirty days, complete with temporary Buddhist ordination. You'll even be placed with a spiritual director who speaks your language. What a great idea.

I thanked Phalang for his excellent guide work and tipped him well. Then I took a ferry across the river to the Temple of Dawn. Once again, I was awestruck by the beauty of the place. There was no actual temple to go into, but an impressive collection of stupas, all based on Indian temple structures in tall

Shiva-lingam style. And each of them was covered, top to bottom, in multi-colored Chinese mosaic tiles.

I climbed up the steep stairs to the first platform, intentionally not looking down. The view was so spectacular, that I decided to brave the even steeper stairs to the second platform. I gritted my teeth and looked only at the stairs in front of me. The whole time I thought of my best friend Lawson, and tried to absorb a little of his devil-may-care recklessness, which is always good for me.

Standing at the top, I saw a guy who—in true Lawsonian fashion—faced outward and simply bounded down. "Impossible," I said to myself, as the stairs were almost a stepladder. I turned to face the wall, looked *only* at the wall, and did, in fact, make it down.

Phalang's answers were still ringing in my ears, so I resolved to try to talk to a monk. This proved more difficult than I expected. I found the temple's main office, and opened the sliding door just as a monk walked past me and into the building. I said, "Excuse me, is there a monk who speaks English? I'd like to talk about the Dhamma." But he completely ignored me. He simply pretended that I wasn't there, and shut the door in my face.

I had the same response several other times. It started to make me angry, and I wondered where all that Buddhist loving-kindness I'd heard so much about had gone. Finally, I came across a building that said, "Education," and stepped in. Then I froze in my tracks.

The place was crawling with rabbits. Rabbits ran in packs down the hallway to my right, and straight ahead an enormous fat one sat chewing on a piece of straw, staring right at me. "Okay...this is weird," I said out loud. A teenage girl walked around the corner and jumped a bit at the sight of me. I explained that I wanted to talk to a monk who spoke English about the Dhamma.

"Yes, there is a monk who speaks English, but he's at the church with the other monks," she said. She shrugged. "Sorry."

I was struck by her use of the word "church" instead of "temple," but I let it go. I thanked her, but before I walked away, I asked her about the rabbits. "They for the students," she seemed amused by the question. "To take care of. Good for them."

I smiled and nodded. "Good for them," I repeated, meaning something different by it.

I snagged a tuk-tuk and asked the driver to take me to the Golden Mount Temple. We agreed upon a price, and I climbed in. I had a devil of a time trying to figure out how to sit in it. Thai tuk-tuks are shaped differently from Indian ones—instead of seats with room for actual legs, they have shallow platforms on which you're expected to perch. The canopy is so low, that in order to see anything (and not bump your head) you are forced to actually lay down in the thing. I found it extremely uncomfortable, and my stomach muscles got the best workout since I tried doing forty sit-ups about five years ago.

The driver went about four blocks and stopped by a wat. I got out, scowling. This didn't look anything like the Lonely Planet description of the Golden Mount Temple. "Golden Mount?" I asked.

He nodded. "Wat." He held out his hand for the cash—150 bot, as we'd agreed.

"No way," I said angrily. "Not just *any* wat—Golden Mount wat!" Did he think I was an idiot? I started to walk away without paying him anything, at which point he said, "Okay, okay," and motioned for me to get back in the tuk-tuk. So I folded myself in once more and we sped away.

I was angry for about two minutes, and then I was able to just shake it off. I was getting used to being the intended victim of rip-offs, and I was getting pretty good at noticing them and shutting them down, too.

As downtown Bangkok zoomed past, I thought about how tame Thai traffic was compared to Indian traffic. It's still crazier than American driving, but even so it was a welcome relief from the hair-raising antics I'd been used to.

Feeling the late afternoon sun on my neck, I returned to musing on the worship question. Crosby points out a fundamental discrepancy between theology and praxis. Theravada theology says, "The Buddha is not present," which Phalang corroborated. But she says that the emotional need that Theravadins have for the Buddha to still be present and active in their lives is so great that they act (and practice) as if he is. From what I'd observed at the temples I'd visited so far, that seemed accurate as well.

The conflict hit home—I could certainly relate. For many years, I'd been a big fan of liberal Christian theologies that championed what Lisa calls a "snake-belly low Christology." This kind of theology says, "Jesus was a reforming rabbi—he was just a man. After he died, human myth-making turned him into a god." Such a position appealed to my reason. "Yes," I could agree, "that is the most logical reading of history and the tradition."

But I was never satisfied with such theologies. They were fine by light of day, but in the dead of night, when you're really confronted with your soul, they left me cold. Also, regarding the core of one's spiritual life, they tended to replace intimacy with God with social justice. Social justice is a fine thing, but I want more than justice—I want to be *loved*.

The thing that most often stops me in my tracks—repeatedly and often—is the overwhelming feeling of being loved by God, wholly and completely, in spite of my numerous and obvious flaws. It brings me to tears regularly, and it isn't the distant Father that inspires such feelings, but the Jesus who has come to share my lot, who pitched his tent in the muck with me in my sad little life, and who has, in fact, ennobled my life by joining it to his. This kind of intimacy and emotionality just doesn't square with a low Christology. To be in loving relationship with a living Jesus he needs to be more than a cool, famous dead guy.

Several twentieth-century theologians have articulated the difference between the Jesus of history and the Christ of faith. But I have problems with that, too, as the distinction has always felt disingenuous to me. There has to be continuity between the historical, human Jesus and the eternal, divine Christ. If the Christ we worship is the invention of St. Paul, then our faith is in vain.

I struggled with this for some time until I read deeply in Martin Luther's work. I discovered that where translators wrote "faith," Luther meant "trust." And with that realization, a major cog clicked, and everything turned on its head. Relationship with Jesus isn't about believing a list of metaphysical propositions (like the Creed), it's about trusting that I'm loved. It's about trusting that if I stumble, I'll be caught.

Suddenly, God wasn't someone who demanded that I keep my ducks in a row, but was someone that I could lean into when all my ducks have gone to hell. It was a huge shift.

It was helpful, profound, and life-giving, but it wasn't *rational*. But I didn't really need it to be rational. Like the Theravadins I've been reading about and watching with my own eyes this week, I really *could* have it both ways. I was able to hold logic and its low Christology in one hand and affirm it as reasonable, while holding emotion and its high Christology in the other hand and embracing it as my heart's deep need and desire. I don't need to sacrifice one to the other, because I have no need to be logically consistent in my inner world. In fact, I'm such a mess I can't even imagine a logically congruent inner life.

I am, most of all, a feeling person—much more than I am a thinking person. I *do* think, but when information comes in through my senses my brain is not the first place that it goes. It goes to my heart first, *then* it goes to my brain. I *feel* my way into life (in stark contrast to my wife, who thinks her way through life—we're happily complimentary that way). So the emotional connection, the focus on a deep relationship with Jesus—and the high Christology and continuity between the historical Jesus and the Christ of faith that this necessitates—isn't optional. Friedrich Schleiermacher, after all, said that it isn't our intellect, but our *emotions* that connect us to God. That is certainly true in my experience.

And so what if it isn't rational? The universe is, rather gloriously, filled with irrational things and truths that defy reason. And I learned a long time ago that being "successful" at this religion thing necessitated the capacity to hold conflicting truths in tension.

And besides, the logical left brain and the emotional right brain need each other, don't they? If either insisted that the other work as it does, we wouldn't be able to pick up a spoon, let alone play the violin. Both sides of the brain provide a different set of tools, each of which is needed for a whole human life. Just so, faith and reason are different tools, each required to address different human needs. If we try to confuse the two we do violence to both, for we either prostitute reason to a pre-decided faith, or we sacrifice faith in order to stuff all of life into an arbitrary box we've labeled "the possible." It is true that the ambiguities of mystery sit uncomfortably beside the certainties of reason, but I'm fine with that discomfort. As Walt Whitman said, "I contain multitudes."

I was certainly beside myself by the time we reached the temple. It seemed like we'd been going in circles for a half hour, and I later discovered that we actually had. Thai cabbies and tuk-tuk drivers are notorious for setting off without a clue as to where they're going. Part of this, I'm sure, is the language difficulty—more pronounced here than in India—but another part of it seems to be pure wishful thinking. There's often a lot of slowing down and chatting with other drivers during any given tuk-tuk journey.

At the temple I paid for my ticket and joined a gaggle of other tourists tramping up a long, circular ramp winding its way around a man-made hill. We walked through mystical, Disneyfied tropical forests filled with artificial mists, past Chinese deities posing beside waterfalls (you could hear the hum of the electric pumps bringing the water up), to a platform where teenagers were gleefully ringing a row of temple bells.

That brought us to the stairs. I took them two at a time, and was profoundly out of breath by the time I got to the top, where a two-story-tall stupa pointed to the sky. I leaned against the whitewashed plaster of the railing and took in the magnificent view. Bangkok spread out before me in 360 degrees as I circumambulated the stupa. Unlike India, which seemed tired, dusty, and inept, Thailand said, "Watch out. I'm young, I'm driven, and I'm *hungry*." This was a city as slick and modern as any in America, and it was buzzing like a high-voltage wire.

A tune nagged at my brain. The first night here, my earworm had been, predictably, "One Night in Bangkok," from the Broadway musical *Chess*. But the next day it had reverted to a song that had been inexplicably haunting me for days. It was a Beatles B-side called "You Know My Name (Look Up the Number)," an interminably silly song in which the title is, pretty much, the only lyric.

I'm a big believer in earworm-mancy, the practice of "reading" one's earworms as a tool for divination. In my case, I always assume that the earworm, no matter how obnoxious, is a message from God. If that is so, the meaning of this earworm was painfully obvious: "You need to pray more." And that was probably quite true. I sighed and clutched at the handrail.

I resolved to check in with Jesus more often each day, and to spend a longer, more relaxed period of time with God in the evening.

A yellow flag bearing the red image of the Wheel of Dharma snapped in the breeze, as if claiming this land in the name of its spiritual sovereign. I turned to behold the great golden Buddha, enthroned in splendor, his hand touching the ground in the mudra for subduing all doubt and deception. Before him, a woman was on her knees, at least half a dozen lit sticks of incense clasped between her praying hands. She brought them to her forehead, she brought them to her heart. She bowed.

"Jesus," I said, "let me worship you as she worships—with my head *and* with my heart. It doesn't matter if my head and heart don't agree with each other—as long as they are both pointed toward you." It was a good prayer. The earworm ceased momentarily. The incense smelled exquisite as it wafted upward, carrying with it the young woman's prayer—and mine.

———

1   Kate Crosby, *Theravada Buddhism: Continuity, Diversity, and Identity* (Wiley-Blackwell, 2014).

Ruins at Sukhothai.

Chapter Eleven: Ayuthaya, Phitansulok & Sukhothai —My Faith in Ruins

When I got back to my hotel room, I sighed and began to unpack my bag. The door rang, and I opened it to find a bell-hop holding my finished laundry. Except that it wasn't *my* laundry. I frowned. "Not my laundry," I said.

He looked horrified. "No your laundry?"

I shook my head. "No my laundry. *Please* find my laundry." Remembering the forgotten airport pickup, I wanted to say, "You guys really kind of suck at this hotel-running business, don't you?" but I held my tongue. He looked concerned and turned to go.

"They'll find it," I said out loud to myself as I closed the door. "Don't worry about it, just enjoy your evening." I was tired. The last thing I needed to do was obsess.

The next morning the laundry inquiries would have to wait, as I had scheduled a day trip to Ayuthaya, the former capital of Siam and the site of some truly amazing Buddhist ruins. I was the first pickup, at 6am but by 9:30 we had a full compliment of Western tourists—mostly Francophones, oddly—and had hit the road. By 10am, we were there.

The first site was awesome. It was also crawling with tourists. There's a fine line between pilgrim and tourist, so I can hardly complain, but it was difficult to get photos without a whole gang of people obscuring the view. But I didn't let that get in the way of my joy at exploring the site. Entering a walled enclosure, I discovered a series of about 100 Buddhas seated on stone risers all around the perimeter. At first glance, they looked identical. Each of them was in a meditative pose, sport-ing the "subduing Mara" mudra, their right hands touching the earth. Each one of them was draped in a bright ochre shawl. The effect was stunning.

In the center of the enclosure was a large temple. It was shaped like a stupa, but at the top of a long set of stone steps was a doorway. I shed my shoes and socks and climbed the stairs. Stepping through the doorway, I saw several people applying gold leaf to various Buddha statues arranged around a large well that appeared dry but deep. I watched respectfully as people prayed.

I imagined myself in a ruined Cathedral in Europe, before a statue of Jesus. I wouldn't be worshipping the statue, but the statue evoked emotions, emotions that connected me to....

I stopped, aware that I was onto something. I walked around the perimeter of the landing, snapping photos of the statues in the courtyard below, but my attention was actually far away.

As soon as I got home I'd be teaching a class at Santa Clara University in inter-religious dialogue, and I had been reading a lot of material looking for a "way in." After all, what could I contribute to an area that so many good, brilliant people had been working in? How could I bring "added value" to my class, an "a-ha" element that the students couldn't get from reading a bunch of books?

Descending the stairs, I stepped out of the courtyard, past several street vendors selling cheesy Buddha statues and deep-fried dumplings, sometimes from the same cart. I headed for another walled enclosure and discovered there a large reclining Buddha. I was once again struck by the unfairness of it: the Buddha had gotten fifty years to walk the earth and teach his disciples. Jesus had gotten three. I wasn't resentful of the Buddha, I was glad for him. I was just sad for Jesus.

I circled the large statue, also draped in an ochre cloth that shone in the late morning sun. I stopped and watched more Thai families gathered before the image, putting several incense sticks in a huge cauldron-like burner, and then bowing three times. Then they knelt there, praying, often for quite a long time.

They were connecting with something. I would call that something God, they might call it the Dhamma. Lawson defines worship as "connection." Anything that facilitates connection, he classifies as worship. It's a damn good definition. I was still unclear as to whom or what the Theravadins were worshipping, but they were undoubtedly *connecting*.

I understand the need for that connection deeply. I also understand that we need connection with each other—we call that "community." I felt uncomfortable with the fact that I, as a deeply religious person, was watching other deeply religious folks worshipping with the same detachment that a scientist observes an insect. My heart wanted to go out to them. I wanted to connect *with them*.

It occurred to me that my entire trip was an exercise in interfaith dialogue. I was talking to people along the way, yes. But the primary work was internal. I realized that to be successful in my project, I would need to connect with the religious feelings and experiences of these people. And that would require an act of imagination.

St. Ignatius uses the imagination as such a fundamental tool in prayer, that for him, the imagination is an organ of perception. I think this is a profound insight, because I believe that all acts of connection—with God, with other people, with our deepest selves—all require acts of imagination.

I am trapped inside my own head. I don't know what anyone else is really feeling or thinking. All I have is what they tell me and what I can infer from their behavior. That's all. In order to really sympathize with someone, I have to imagine what the world is like from his or her perspective. This requires a feat of imagination, and my ability to feel empathy is directly proportionate to my talent at and willingness to daydream into the sufferings, mundanities, and joys of another person.

The old Native American dictum, "You only understand a man when you've walked a mile in his moccasins" neglects to point out that it isn't feet that fill those moccasins. It's the imagination.

When I saw those folks worshipping the image of the Buddha, and I translated it in my imagination to myself worshipping before an image of Jesus in a cathedral, my heart leaped. I understood what they were doing in a way that was not clinical but soulful, emotional, profound. I *got* them.

To some degree, I had been doing this kind of reflection during most of my trip, but I wasn't really doing it consciously, and I wasn't reflecting critically on *what* I was doing. Noticing what I was doing, so that I can be mindful of it and consciously do it again was a significant piece. In retrospect, it seems obvious, but as I gazed on those worshippers, I felt like a veil had been pierced, that I had been let in on an occult secret, and I reveled in it like the euphoria of gnosis.

Our next stop was at another enormous reclining Buddha. As we all piled out of the bus and towards the enormous feet, I cocked my head, noticing that the toes were distorted. They were too long, for one thing. They were stacked like sausages of uniform length, perfectly round. But wait—one or two of them bent at barely perceptible angles. There was a surreal aspect to them, an intentional distortion of the human form that I could not understand. It intrigued and delighted me, especially as I reflected on the fact that this statue was over a thousand years old.

A sign nearby revealed that the statue did not represent the Buddha's death (as most reclining Buddhas do) but a legend about a giant who was exceedingly proud of his height. Wanting to take him down a notch or two, the Buddha pulled a Hank Pym, growing himself until he was larger than the giant.

I walked around the giant Buddha and smiled at the face, which was almost cartoonish. I had noticed that about a lot of Thai Buddhas. How are we supposed to take him seriously when he looks so goofy? It was fascinating to see how the Buddha's image was morphing across time, and across great distances.

A film I'd seen recently discussed how the first Buddhists used symbols to represent their faith, such as the lotus or the footprint—much like early Christians used the fish. But Greek Buddhists began carving statues, just as Greek pagans carved marble likenesses of their gods. These Greek statues migrated (with a little help from humans, no doubt) to India, where their popularity really took off. These early Indian Buddhas still look very Greek, with impressive Mediterranean noses.

I was amazed to learn about the Greek connection, and it answered a lot of questions about why early Buddhist statuary looked so different from Hindu statuary from the same period. It was so much more lifelike, more sedate, more dignified. Fascinating. But that was not true of this reclining Buddha. His face was whimsical, and his nose was a flattened Asian nose like you see on many Thai faces.

As I waited for our bus, I walked through a series of shops, which opened out into a large covered area where several elephants were walking around. Some of them wore saddles covered with bright red tassels, while others just walked around. A baby elephant stuck close to his mother, who used her trunk, it seemed to me, to straighten his hair.

One elephant and a human minder were front and center snapping photos with tourists. We had about ten minutes before the bus left, and it was only thirty bod to pose with the elephant (about a dollar), so I said, "What the heck." I paid my bod and stepped up toward the elephant. I faced the camera, and was thrilled when the huge trunk fastened itself around my waist and gave me a little hug.

I didn't realize I'd needed a hug, but it felt great. I looked into the eye of that great, intelligent beast, and felt a strange kinship with him. The elephant opened his mouth and posed with his tusks over my head. I laughed out loud, and it was part nervousness and part sheer joy.

* * *

The next day I took a train to Phitansulok, which the Lonely Planet had recommended for some awesome temples, and as a launching point for another day trip to some of the most amazing ruins in the country. We arrived at about 1pm. I was relieved that there was no delay, as I would need that afternoon to explore—the next day I was determined to make a day trip.

A short taxi ride deposited me at Wat Phra Si Ratana Mahathat. I was instantly taken aback, because the place was packed with pilgrims. It was also surrounded on all sides by an open market selling everything from flower offerings to fish cakes to Hello Kitty jumpers.

Eventually I found the entrance to the wat, and depositing my shoes outside, tried to squeeze in among the worshippers. It was a stunning temple. It had been built in the 14th century, but had surely undergone restorations fairly recently, because it simply shone. It also had been decorated with a contemporary flair that still succeeded in looking traditional and powerful.

The walls were a deep blood red, while the numerous pillars were jet black, inlaid top to bottom with a gold diamond pattern. Chandeliers lit the space perfectly. The altar wall was slate black adorned with floral patterns in gold, with two gold Thai...well, angels was what they looked like...flanking both sides of an enormous gold statue of the Buddha. His schnozz was huge, his hand descended, defeating Mara. His head was crowned with a halo of fire.

All around me, people were kneeling and bowing, touching their heads to the carpet. Some eyes held tears. *Would I bow before Jesus like that if I saw him?* I wondered. *Oh, yes,* I thought to myself. *In an instant.* My heart leaped at the thought of it. I connected with what they must be feeling.

This works, I thought to myself. As I walked out into the courtyard to the rear of the main sanctuary, I reflected further on my breakthrough about empathy. Connecting with the religious experiences of others is an *emotional* endeavor, not really a *logical* one. Crosby had used the word *affectional*, which I like a lot. Once again, this logical-emotional distinction was arising. I paid attention, figuring there was more gold here than just what people were sticking on the Buddha statue.

When people try to turn inter-religious dialogue into a logical endeavor, it turns into a "we believe this, you believe that" affair, which really is of very limited use. It can get downright ugly when the matter of who is "right" or "correct" rears its head. In fact, you might as well just pack up and go home at that point.

For inter-religious dialogue to be fruitful, both parties must come to the table with humility. Both parties must eschew the notion that they have all the answers or that they have everything right. Both parties, in fact, must be teachable. They must come with a willingness, even an eagerness, to learn from one another. In fact, both parties must be willing, and even desire, to be mutually transformed by their conversation.

This transformation isn't going to happen by making a list of divergent or even similar theological ideas. It's only going to happen by imagining your way into the universe of the Religious Other. One must be willing to enter the mythic, symbolic, and emotional world of one's dialogue partner.

This requires an act of will, just as other affective connections do. We can only do inter-religious dialogue when we *choose to love* the Religious Other, and it requires effort and dedication to do it well.

Stepping into another pagoda, I discovered a modest museum. Dusty shelves showed a haphazard collection of items from the temple's past. Here were certificates of some kind, signed by the king. Here were photos of prominent laypeople. Here was a lovely set of china. All around me were the things the people of this temple loved too much to toss or to sell. It was a shrine to their history as a sangha—a community of people who loved each other and the Buddha. Respect for them welled up in me as I poured over the items on display—worthless to a pawnbroker, but priceless to this community.

How do we build intimacy with God? I asked myself. *How do we build intimacy with family? How do we build intimacy with partners? Surely we build intimacy with people of other religions using precisely those same tools, those same methods, those same skills.*

Inter-religious dialogue requires a commitment to love these people we are talking to, to be vulnerable with them, to trust them and to be worthy of trust. We must show our human sides, our frailty, and admit our uncertainties and questions. We must ask forgiveness for how we have failed, and we must humble ourselves to ask for help. To do this well, we have to look for the deep humanness of the Other, and to be willing to reveal the deep humanness in ourselves.

God, what a risky business. No wonder we have so rarely done it well. I thought of Nanak, the first Sikh guru, setting dogmas aside and just putting his love of God *out there* for any and all to see…and inviting them to join in. I thought of the Mughal King Akbar, who invited Hindu and Muslim scholars together for evenings of tea and mystical poetry. No debates allowed—only the sharing of experiences and emotions. Friendships between Brahmins and imams were made there. In other words, miracles happened.

Deeply moved, I stepped out of the museum and headed back to the main sanctuary. A little girl of about nine blocked my path. "Would you like to hear about our temple?" she asked in imperfect but eager English.

"Why yes," I said, assuming an air of mock seriousness. "Yes I would. Please tell me about your lovely temple."

A badge pinned to her dress read, "Youth Volunteer Guides." I was delighted by her boldness. In a loud and confident voice she started in on her spiel. I couldn't follow all of it—she was speaking English all right, but her accent was so thick I was missing every third word. The upshot of it was easy to follow, however. The best part involved the making of the gold Buddha statue. It seems that three statues were being forged at the same time. Two of them came out fine, but the third had to be recast again and again. Finally, an old man appeared. He was really a god in disguise, and he oversaw the casting of the third Buddha. When it was removed from the mold, it shone, and was instantly recognized as being far superior to the other two, and in fact, it was the most beautiful Buddha statue in the whole of Thailand.

By the time she finished, a crowd had gathered around her, and we all applauded. She gave a little bow and, mildly embarrassed, she ran off to do it all again. My emotions were really up by that time and I was deeply touched by her obvious pride in her community and her faith.

I said Compline with a greater spaciousness than usual that night. I consciously brought myself into God's presence, and talked with Jesus. He showed up. I almost cried with relief.

* * *

The next day I had a cold, but I didn't feel tired. I slept as long as I could, had breakfast, and wrote for a couple of hours. Then I looked at the clock. There was still time to go, if I wanted to. I did.

So I snatched the key out of its faceplate cradle by the door and headed out. I took a tuk-tuk to the bus station, and then wandered around, bewildered at more than thirty windows where one could buy tickets for a staggering variety of bus lines. As I walked in circles, a small, plump Thai woman came up to me, and said, "You go to Sukhothai?"

"Uh, yeah."

"50 bod. Sit over there." She pointed to a row of chairs. I gave her a few bills, and she gave me a ticket with 10:55 written at the top. I didn't feel like sitting down, so I walked around the convenience stores and street venders boiling things with tentacles in oil. I wasn't at all sure I'd done the right thing, but decided to just trust and go with it. I bought a soda and some cookies made from puffed rice, and returned to the seats.

A couple that looked like they were about ten years older than I were sitting there, looking uncertain. "Going to Sukhothai?" I asked, taking a seat in front of them.

"I am not sure," the man said. "We bought tickets. From her." He pointed at the small, round Thai woman. I nodded and turned back to them. "Where are you from?" I asked.

"Montreal," he said.

"Oh, I want to go there sometime!" I said. "I've heard it's beautiful."

"Oh, *oui*. It is," he said. His wife smiled warmly, but I got the impression that his English was better than hers.

"My favorite band does a whole weekend convention there every year," I said. "I keep telling myself that one year I'll go." He hadn't heard of Marillion or the annual Montreal convention, but showed polite interest. He had been to San Francisco, however, and he told me effusively how much they'd loved it.

"Come," the Thai woman commanded, and the three of us rose and joined several other people marching behind her. She led us out to the street, turned right, and continued past several shops to a major highway. I furrowed my brow and leaned over to the guy from Montreal. "Where the hell are we going?"

"I have no idea," he admitted, giving an exaggerated shrug.

In a moment a road-worn bus pulled up, and we all piled

in. There was just barely enough seats for all of us, and of course we kept stopping to pick up more people as we went along. By the time we reached our destination, it had taken over two hours.

We were dropped at a convenience store near the gate of a lovely park a sign identified as Old Sukhothai. Across the street was a store that rented bicycles, the favored way to see the park, since its many sites were some distance apart. But I was keenly aware of my flagging energy level, and I did not want to exacerbate my cold, given that I was travelling on again the next day.

I crossed the street and spoke to the woman running the bike rental. I pulled out my phone and called up the iTranslate app. "I want to hire a tuk-tuk to take me around the sites," I said. In a moment, the Thai translation popped up on the screen, and the robotic voice read it out in what I assume was passable Thai, because the woman nodded, and said, "Five minute."

The couple from Montreal walked by. I mentioned my head cold and my concern about not depleting myself with a bicycle. The man's eyes grew wide. "I have a cold, too!" he said. "Do you want to share?"

"Sure!" I said. "And it'll be cheaper for all of us if we go together and split the cost."

The man, who had been slightly reticent back at the station, put out his hand. "I am Serge. And this is Joanna." I shook both their hands and introduced myself. "Ah, Jean, that's easy to remember," he smiled.

Joanna and I headed out for the toilets before our tuk-tuk arrived, and I was happy that I had some extra tissue to give her. (As in India, there is no toilet paper in any public restroom, anytime, anywhere.) When we got back, we were met by the strangest tuk-tuk I'd yet seen. Instead of pulling the passenger platform, it was literally a motorcycle, pushing it. The rear side of our platform served double-duty as his handlebars. He revved the bike and pushed us off.

He headed into the park, and stopped at several points where he recommended we take pictures. We dutifully did. Then he let us off near the entrance to a major site, and I gasped.

I've seen a lot of ruins since I've begun my journey, but nothing like this. A chest-high platform stood lined with pillars like a smaller version of the Parthenon. At the far end of it was an enormous stone Buddha statue. Behind it was a large temple. To one side was a tall narrow building about three stories high. It had a two-meter wide opening in the middle that ran floor to ceiling, revealing a standing Buddha statue that was every bit as tall as the sheath-like building that contained it.

The area was shaded by large, leafy trees, and green, well-tended grass covered the ground, rolling down to the edge of a pond. Lily pads dotted its surface—or were they unblossomed lotuses? I couldn't tell. It was one of the most beautiful places I have ever seen. I wove my way in between a score of stupas and statues, snapping pictures and trying not to trip over my dropped jaw.

When I caught up with Serge and Joanne again, I shook my head. "That was worth the whole bus ride, the tuk-tuk rental, and the price of admission right there. We could go home right now, and I'd be happy."

Serge agreed wholeheartedly. "This is amazing," he breathed.

The rest of the park was just as well tended, and many of the sites were impressive, but nothing compared with that first stop. As we rode, Serge and Joanna warmed up to me, and they told me about their son, who was considering studying at Berkeley. I gave them my card and told them I'd be delighted to show him around Berkeley if and when he comes out west.

When we finished the last of the sites inside the park, the

driver pulled out a map and showed us that there were still several ruins outside the park. "Inside park, 200 bod," he said, "outside park, 400 bod."

We put our heads together and discussed it. Finally, Serge said, "Only 200. Take us back to the bus stop." The man nodded, but after only a few minutes, pulled over next to an amazing site.

I thought, "Oh, how nice of him to stop at a cool place on the way back to the bus stop," but what I should have been thinking was "If we set foot out of this tuk-tuk, he's going to charge us 400 bod instead of 200," because that's exactly what happened. The thing was, it really was a cool site he'd brought us to, with the largest standing Buddha we'd seen yet.

He kept stopping at placess, and after a while, Serge said, "I think he is going to charge us the 400."

"I think you're right," I said.

"We told him to take us back," Serge protested to me. "I don't want to pay it."

"But we got out of the car," I said. I shrugged. "He's clever. He knew just which one to bring us to, in order to crumble any resolve we might have."

Serge nodded and in the end, we paid the 400—but we didn't tip. Serge and I commiserated over the endless scamming everywhere you went. He agreed with me that it was exhausting. "It doesn't happen at home," he said. "I won't miss it." I laughed my agreement.

On the way back, I thought about the metaphor of ruins. I'd certainly seen enough of them in the past couple of days. It occurred to me that my entire journey of faith as an adult has been an attempt to salvage Jesus from the ruins of my childhood faith.

I don't mean the Southern Baptist faith, I mean the naive faith that all children have, and must outgrow. The God who serves us as children rarely serves us well as adults. As we grow up, we grow out of a God who acts like superman, who demands strict obedience (or else), or who draws in clear black and white lines.

The real world, and the real God, isn't clear, isn't black and white, and doesn't always come to the rescue. The real God is messy. The real God lets us down. The real God needs to be forgiven as much as he forgives. As adults we must step up and take responsibility for our own spiritual lives, we must think deeply and critically about religion, and we must come to our own conclusions, and not just parrot the ones handed to us by our teachers and parents.

The little girl yesterday had clearly memorized a script. I wondered what she would have to say as she grew into adulthood—about her faith, about the Buddha, about her sangha.

It's a leap that too many people don't make. They assume that the God they were given as children is the God their religion actually espouses, and so instead of growing into a mature, thinking, idiosyncratic expression of faith, they reject their religion and its childish God, missing out on so much rich teaching, tradition, and real relationship they might have found there.

It is a leap I am still trying to manage for myself. I had rejected much of what I was taught, only years later to come back around to it again, to embrace it all again, but holding it in a very different way. It seems like a profoundly important project, one that I have been trying to do in a very public way through my writing, my preaching, and my teaching. With so many of my peers abandoning Christianity like rats from a sinking ship, it seems a vital and important endeavor. It is my deepest hope that at least a few of my parishioners or students or readers will see the joy I take in this Christian path to God and might give it another look. There are a lot of bad "Christianities" being promulgated out there, but when the faith is properly understood and aptly presented, this tradition, this savior, this path is so deeply transformative, so wise, so profoundly *good*.

And yes, the irony that Jesus might need saving is not lost on me. I think the Buddha is popular with a lot of Westerners precisely because he *isn't* Jesus. He's a replacement savior. But is that good enough? I certainly wouldn't want to marry someone who pointed at me and said, "You'll do." I want to marry someone who is madly, deeply in love with me.

I am madly and deeply in love with Jesus. So it's heartwarming and deeply satisfying to stand back and watch these people who are obviously over the moon about Buddha. It's a bit like watching your best friend fall in love with someone whom you would never in a million years consider dating yourself. You're happy for him, but you're equally sure that she just isn't for you. That's how I'm feeling now, watching the devotion and the love playing out in front of me. I understand it, I get it, because that's exactly how I feel about Jesus. It's not *my* relationship. But I can, and do, honor it as *theirs*.

At the market in Chiang Mai, procuring items for cooking class.

Chapter Twelve: Chiang Mai—Now We're Cooking

The ride to the train station was surprisingly quick, so I wheeled my bag over to some of the streetside vendors, just to kill time. To my amazement, I stumbled upon a very large covered market with literally hundreds of vendors. I carefully navigated my large rolling bag through the crowd—though not without a pinched toe now and then. The vegetables were often confusing, and the open-air butchers were horrific. I brushed away flies as I stepped past the faces of pigs, stripped from their skulls and hung up on display, their jowls spread and flattened outward like the pink, fleshy, flightless wings of porcine angels.

Having exhausted my browsing possibilities and beginning to tire, I went back to the train station, grabbed a soda, and sat in the shade. Unfortunately, the soda I grabbed was a flavor of Fanta I'd never seen before: banana, pineapple, and coconut. I made a face as I tasted it—it was very close to cough syrup. "Ech..." I said out loud, once I'd swallowed. "Should have stuck to orange."

"Not great, huh?" a chipper voice near me said. I turned to see a man about my own age standing casually nearby. He was balding and wore shorts, a polo shirt, and sunglasses.

"Terrible," I said. "I think I'm just gonna leave that...right there." I said, placing it on a nearby plastic table.

"First time in Thailand?" he said.

"Yeah."

"What do you think?"

"I love it," I said, enthusiastically.

"That's what I'm sayin', right?" He was gregarious, that's for sure. He introduced himself as Marc, "That's Marc with a C," he said, narrowing one eye at me. He sidled over to stand by a matronly Thai woman seated on the pavement next to a younger woman who was reading tarot cards.

"This here's Maude," he said. "She's my girlfriend's auntie."

Maude squinted up at me. "You wan' fortune? My girl give you good reading. Cheap. Good love, good life, you see."

"Uh, thanks, but when tragedy strikes, I want it to be out of the blue," I answered. I'm a real "the glass is half full" kind of guy, and I don't care who knows it.

"You hungry? Maude can get you something." The man waved at all the street vendors. "Lots of great food, here, man. And you can't beat the price."

I hadn't tried street food yet, still being a bit gun-shy after my Indian culinary misadventures. But it *was* lunch time, and I wouldn't get another chance to eat again until about 9pm. I was tempted...but I just couldn't do it. I comforted myself with the fact that I had a large supply of peanuts. And chocolate. They'd have to do.

I told Marc about my project, and he seemed not the slightest bit interested. Some folks just switch right off the moment you mention religion. But he seemed interested in me as a person, so that was nice, and we kept up a good banter. "How about you?" I asked him. "Are you on vacation?"

"Nah, I'm retired," he pointed to his chest proudly. "I had to get out of America. Things are getting too wacky, you know?"

I didn't, but I laughed and nodded anyway. I thought about the riots going on in Bangkok at that very moment, trying to overturn the democratically elected government. Marc, apparently, did not deem that "wacky."

"I was in real estate, and made a little bundle. I got no wife, no kids, nothing to hold me down, so I came here. I love it!" He turned in a circle. "I feel like a new person, here." He leaned in. "Do you know how much I pay for my apartment?"

"Uh...$250 a month?" I guessed.

His eyebrows jumped. "Yeah. That's it exactly—how'd you know that? $250. In a brand new building, air-conditioned, in a great part of town. It's a fuckin' great deal."

"Sounds like it," I agreed. "That could really make your retirement savings stretch. What about health care?"

"Are you kidding me? I had a little heart incident, so I went to the hospital—not the public hospital, the private hospital, mind you—and they did an EKG and a full blood panel, the works. They give me the bill when I left. Guess what it was?"

"No clue," I said. I knew my monetary mind-reading luck wouldn't hold.

"21 dollars," he said, his hands on his hips. I was impressed.

"America is wacky," he asserted. This time, I nodded with genuine assent.

He pulled out his wallet. "Here's my girlfriend," he said, showing me a picture of a very attractive woman who couldn't have been more than thirty. "They're crazy about Americans here," he said. "They don't even care if we're old!"

My train was due to arrive, so I had to go. I thanked Marc for the conversation, shook Maude's hand, and wished them well. As I wheeled my bag toward the platform, I felt a little sad for Marc. He seemed so over-the-top effusive that it made me wonder whether he was trying to convince me or himself how great things were for him. Thailand *did* seem like a great place to retire, especially on a limited budget. I filed it in the old bean under "possibilities," and hopped my train.

The trip to Chiang Mai took about three hours, and unfortunately I had a window seat—my way to the bathroom perpetually blocked by an unfriendly elderly American. The time went by blessedly fast, however, and before long we had arrived and were piling into a beast I'd never seen before. It was a cross between a tuk-tuk and a pickup truck, with long benches in its bed for passengers. It was covered, and the whole thing was fire-engine red. And these contraptions were *everywhere*.

It took the driver a long time to find my hotel. It was thirty minutes outside of town But it *was* a wonderful hotel—brand-spanking new, sparkling clean, with a helpful staff and a wonderful breakfast. There were a few puzzling things about it, though. The yard around the place was thick with chickens. They rented bikes, but where would people ride them to? There was absolutely nothing around for about twenty miles as far as I could see, other than dusty highway and a few trees. The place did have a refreshingly whimsical side, however. The storage room on my floor boasted a beautifully etched sign that read, "Stuff only." Nice.

When I woke, my cold was worse, so I gave myself permission to take it easy that day. I'd see a few wats, then come home. So much for good intentions. I walked myself into the ground, as I usually do when traveling. As I walked, something Marc had said struck me. He said he felt like a whole new person in Thailand. I don't walk myself into the ground at home, what makes me do that when I'm away? In what way am I a different person when I'm away from home?

It struck me that this is a fundamental question about pilgrimage. At home, we are constantly being pushed and pulled by family, work, and society. In fact, without these things we don't really know who we are. We go on pilgrimages because when we're not bending over backwards to conform to the various peer pressures that—seen or unseen—are always surrounding us, we find out who we really are. I think that prospect scares some people. It often provides an opening for the Sacred to make its presence felt. This, of course, scares people even more.

I, however, was so frustrated I was ready to beat the Sacred with a tire iron if it didn't speak up now and then. Still, I am willing to concede that the magic that pilgrimage works on people was indeed happening to me. I may not be finding God in the places that I expect, but I am looking for him more, and missing him more, and I am strangely more homesick for God's embrace than I am for my wife's. (I don't think she'd mind me saying that, either, which is one of the reasons I love her so. In our relationship God comes first, and she wouldn't have it any other way.) I thought that I'd go away and say, "God is everywhere. He's just as much in Asia as in America." But that hasn't been my experience. Intellectually, I know it's true. But in my daily life on the road, it's been a long Dark Night of the Spirit.

In St. John of the Cross' mystical theology, there are two Dark Nights. In the Dark Night of the Senses, the seeker loses all interest in anything but God. The later stage is the Dark Night of the Spirit, in which God winks out of existence, leaving the seeker alone and bereft. The reason God does this is that, in order to enter into full union with God, the seeker must be shorn of all of his or her images or pre-conceived ideas about who God is or what God is like. The Seeker is faced with only the void, the nothingness, and is invited to follow God into that nothingness. Since God is no-thing, the seeker, too, is drawn in to discover his or her own no-thing-ness.

This is amazingly close to the Buddha's idea of no-self, that a seeker must abandon any notion of an enduring self. In the Christian vision of this, it isn't self altogether that is being left behind, but all *illusions* about the self—and about God. And because this isn't work that we can do ourselves, we are drawn into the Dark Night so that God can work *on us.*

What images of God do I need to be shorn of? I'm certainly surrounded by images—Ganesha winks at me around every corner, even here in Thailand. I cannot escape the power of The Trunk. And of course, images of the Buddha are not, strictly speaking, images of the Divine, at least not in Theravada Buddhism. But as I've seen, they *function* like them. But these are not *my* images. These are not the pictures that pop up in *my* mind when I hear the word "God." Meister Eckhart's words echoed in my head: "I pray that God will rid me of God for the sake of God."

I am open to this. I want to discover who God really is, away from the religious and cultural conditionings and pressures of my home environment. I'm also open to discovering who I really am. *Better get to work, Jesus,* I prayed. *We've only got another month.*

I stepped into Wat Phra Singh, the most glorious temple in Chiang Mai. In America, if you step into a cathedral, they will yell at you if you don't remove your hat. In India, no one cares about your hat, but you'd better not have your shoes on. In Thailand, both your hat and your shoes come off.

The sanctuary was splendid, with deep red walls and white marble pillars. At the altar sat a gigantic gold Buddha haloed by a Dharma wheel with bright blue spokes. At his feet were several smaller Buddha statues, and a collection of what looked like small, 18-inch-high stupas, each of which was fitted with what looked like a bright purple knitted tea cosy. Were they indeed small stupas, or perhaps reliquaries? It was hard to tell.

In the middle of the room was a life-sized Buddha statue, around which a small crowd had gathered to stick gold leaf to its body. Close up, this Buddha looked like someone with a very bad, very shiny case of psoriasis. He positively glowed… flakily.

To one side of the altar, I was arrested by a disturbing sight. An elderly monk was seated on the altar, in a meditation position, facing us. His eyes were open, but he was not blinking. I watched him for several minutes. No blinking. I started overblinking sympathetically.

Eventually I figured out that he wasn't real, but an exact fiberglass replica of one of the senior monks in that community who had passed on. Madame Tussaud has nothing on these monks. Wax museum figures always look a little fake. This guy looked like the real thing—spookily real. So real I was sure it was taxidermy. If Roy Rogers can do it for his horse Trigger, what's stopping Thai Buddhists?

The Lonely Planet had said to come around 11am to see the monks eating. I wasn't sure why monks masticating was a tourist-worthy event, but sure enough, low tables were scattered all around the sanctuary, and plates were being set out. I smiled wryly, thinking of how excited I'd get as a child, getting goat chow out of the gumball machines at a petting zoo. Perhaps there'd be a place to purchase some monk chow?

I bowed in reverence to the Buddha image, and then put my shoes on. I wandered the immaculate grounds, watching how the gold on the pagodas reflected the sun. Turning the corner to see the back of the sanctuary, I was surprised to see an elderly European monk in gray robes sitting on the back steps. At his feet was a hand-drawn sign announcing, "Buddhism, in English."

I was still very confused about the Theravada doctrine of the soul, so I'd been hoping to have a chance to talk to a Buddhist monk. I'd started making a list of my questions, and it was getting quite long. I introduced myself, and discovered the man was an American Zen master. "Thailand is a strange place for a Zen Buddhist," I said, "What are you doing here?"

"Oh, you know," he said, tossing his lean bald head one way and then the other, "I meditate. I eat. I pass solids." He smiled impishly. "And liquids, in case you were wondering." I was instantly reminded of Fr. Richard, my dear friend and mentor, who is also often rather impish.

I told him I had several questions about Theravada teaching, and asked if he could help. He said he'd try, so I asked him about the doctrine of no-self, and my understanding that what passes on from life to life isn't consciousness or personality, but only the ongoing force of past actions, karma.

He stroked his chin and leaned back. He then launched into

a long story about General MacArthur destroying most of the temples in Japan following World War II. I kept waiting for him to circle back around to the doctrine of the soul, but as the minutes ticked by it was clear that he wasn't going anywhere near it. Other questions met with similarly oblique replies.

Charming and entertaining as he was, I was beginning to get exasperated. Suddenly the prospect of watching monks chew rice seemed like a must-see event. "Well, thank you for your time," I said. He nodded and smiled, and I went to watch the monks chew their food.

I was in for another surprise, because as I stepped up and into the sanctuary, I saw that there was meat on the tables. I was under the impression that Buddhist monks are vegetarians, as part of their vows. I've done some reading since then, and discovered that Theravada monks cannot kill animals for their own food, but if someone else kills it...well, break out the fish sauce. Mahayana monks, with their emphasis on compassion for all beings, are much more likely to eschew meat except in emergencies.

This actually accounts for a discrepancy I'd noticed earlier. In my posting about the Buddha's death, I related the story of how he'd accidentally eaten a poisonous mushroom. Someone wrote me and said, "I thought it was pork!" Mahayana Buddhists tell the mushroom story—since the Buddha would not eat meat, of course. Theravada Buddhists tell the pork story—but theirs is a better story: apparently the Buddha killed a demon in a previous life. That demon got revenge by reincarnating as a pig, whose flesh poisoned the Holy One.

The monks were mostly young boys, and I remembered Phalang from Wat Pho in Bangkok telling me about his month as a monk when he was a boy. And here they were, about fifty teenagers, all with shaved heads, clothed in identical bright orange robes, laughing and teasing and having a grand time under the beatific, heavy-lidded gaze of the giant Buddha. If the Buddha himself were here, I can only imagine that he would have smiled. I sure did.

I moved on to the next wat, only half a block away. I ducked into every building I could find, and eventually came upon a sign that said, "Monk Chat." One monk was holding forth, explaining to a Western couple the proper way to meditate. It was entry-level stuff, and I waited patiently for him to take a breath.

When he finally paused, I held up my hand. "Do you mind if I ask a question?" The Western couple gestured, *Of course.* "I'm wondering about the persistence of personality across lifetimes," I said. "Do Theravada Buddhists believe that there is a soul that survives death?"

The Western couple sat up straighter, clearly interested. They looked at the monk, who licked his lips uncertainly. "That is *philosophical* question," he said.

"Yes?" I prompted, implying, *So?*

"You say 'Theravada.' I just tell you what all Buddhists believe. Life is full of suffering. When we stop and focus our mind, suffering ceases...." and he continued in the Buddhism 101 vein for a while.

I understood what he was doing. The Buddha had refused to answer philosophical questions. When one monk didn't get the answers he was looking for, he famously said, "Whether the world is eternal or not eternal, whether the world is finite or not, whether the soul is the same as the body, or whether the soul is one thing and the body another, whether a Buddha exists after death or does not exist after death—these things the Lord does not explain to me. And that he does not explain them to me does not please me, it does not suit me."[1]

I totally understand how that monk felt. Of course, the schools that followed in the Buddha's footsteps *did* make metaphysical claims, and that was precisely what I was trying to get clear about.

When he stopped, I leaped in again. "That's great, but it's not what I asked. Listen, I understand about dependent co-arising, and about the aggregate nature of all being. When the aggregates that form one being dissolve, does anything survive to be transferred to the new bundle of aggregates being formed?"

He looked at me like I was out of my mind. *Surely,* I thought, *I'm not talking over his head. He's a friggin' monk, for Christ's sake. Maybe it's a language issue?* I put it as simply as I could. "Do Theravadin Buddhists believe in a soul?"

He smiled a fake, patient smile. "Yes, we believe in a soul."

"What *is* the soul, then?" I asked. "It can't be an aggregate, because then it wouldn't endure."

"Memory. It just memory."

That made sense. The Buddha had remembered his previous lives. They weren't *him,* as we think of enduring consciousness. If I was understanding him right, one aggregate being dies, and all of the aggregates of which he is made (matter, feelings, perceptions, thoughts, and consciousness) dissolve their union, handing on the former being's karma—and, apparently, memories—to a new aggregate being forming around the karmic energy. That all made sense of what I'd been reading. I nodded. "So when the karma gets handed on from one being to the next...."

"It not like that," he interrupted me. "Kamma not a thing. Not like a rock. It..." he fished for a word. "...it a pattern of actions."

Karma actually means, "action" in Sanskrit. I'd recently read a wonderful article on karma in *BuddhaDharma,* a major Buddhist magazine, so I clued in quickly. Karma isn't an accumulation of bad or good energy, it was a tendency of character, formed out of long practice.

My wife specializes in a flavor of moral theology called Virtue Ethics, which is very close to this same idea. Instead of saying, "this behavior is right, this behavior is wrong," Virtue Ethics asks, "what kind of person do you hope to be?" and then encourages behavior that is congruent with that hope.

Likewise, karma in Buddhist teaching isn't a tally of rights and wrongs, but a recognition that a person will likely continue on the same moral path that he or she is on now, and that the choices that have gone into forming that path will have consequences that will affect that person now and for some time into the future. There's nothing magical about it: a person who makes a decision every morning to light up a cigarette will most likely light up another one tomorrow morning as well. And eventually, this behavior will lead to emphysema or some other ailment.[2]

Buddhism is simply saying that this pattern of behavior continues to have an effect after our deaths as well. There is a similar teaching in the Christian tradition. The Anglican theologian Charles Williams says that the longer we walk in any one direction, the harder it is to turn around (although we always can). He also says that the decisions we make—he frames the great moral questions as being choices toward either community or isolation—continue after death as well. If we spent our lives spurning community and isolating ourselves, then we will find ourselves isolated after death (hell). On the other hand, if we have spent our lives cultivating intimacy and trust and relationship with God and others in this life, we will find ourselves enjoying the same pattern of community in the next life (heaven).

But I still didn't feel like the monk had completely answered my question. Other people had arrived, and I wanted to make way for their questions too, so I walked over to the side where I was joined by the original Western couple. They were from

Canada, and thought my questions were deep and fascinating. I told them about my project, and we had a great conversation.

I did finally get an answer to the question of continuity of personality, and it's pretty slippery. Rupert Gethin says that what survives from one life to the next is a pattern of causal relationships. That certainly squares with my understanding of karma. He goes on to say that Buddhism rejected as heretical the "eternalist" view (people have souls that are eternal), while also rejecting the "annihilationist" view (everything that a person is is annihilated at death). Instead, Theravada Buddhism embraces a middle ground that is neither "this" nor "that."[3]

So is there continuity between one life and another? Yes, but not in the way we would prefer, and not in a way that is easily explained or understood. As I rambled to the next wat, I meditated on this question of continuity. I remember my life as a child, but in what way is that child the same as my current self? There is no physical part of me now that was alive back then, is there? If I let go of the idea (momentarily) of an enduring soul that is somehow the "real" me (that was in that boy then and is still in me now), then what I am left with is the accumulating choices that the boy made as he grew that turned me into who I am now. That, and the memory that I have of my childhood. Action and memory, exactly what these Buddhists are saying. *Fascinating.*

The next wat looked much older, the wood of its beams ancient and rugged, but what really caught my attention was the dog lying in the middle of the sanctuary floor. Two more were lazing by the open doorway, and as I went out into the courtyard, I saw an entire pack of dogs sprawled in the sand, enjoying the sun's heat. Formally known as Wat Chiang Mun, I nicknamed it, "Dog Wat."

There's something about having a cold that makes me hungry easier and faster. Usually, my tummy wouldn't start rumbling until about 3pm, but here it was noon, and I was starving. I happened upon a restaurant in which several tourists were ensconced, and saw the "recommended in Trip Advisor" signs on the tables. I was in! I ordered the green chicken curry and a cold soda water.

Unfortunately, the food was only so-so. Later, I looked the restaurant up on Trip Advisor and found that it only got two circles out of five! I was a little horrified that such a poorly reviewed place would advertise itself as "recommended," but I made a mental note to check the app before believing a place's hype.

That night I dreamed that I was at church, and a little boy came up to me to talk. His parents were close behind and so I shook their hands in greeting, and then sat down on the pew next to the boy. "I like the people here," he said, "but I'd rather go next door." In my dream, there was a mosque next door. I feigned concern. "They have a very fine mosque next door—I go there sometimes myself to pray. What do you like about it?"

"I like to go to the cave with a bucket," he said.

With exaggerated excitement, I said, "That sounds great! I think I want to go to the cave with a bucket, too!" A cave with a bucket sounded like a novel worship experience. After all, Islam had started in a cave, since that was where the angel Gabriel had first appeared to Muhammad. I'm not sure where the bucket fit in, but I didn't have time to explore it further, because I woke up.

If dreams are a snapshot of what's happening to me right now...I was puzzled. Was the child a reflection of my musings on my childhood self? Is digging in a cave a metaphor for rooting around and trying to bring something to surface consciousness? And all of this in a sacred context? And what did Islam have to do with it? Islam means "submission," and truly, I am trying to submit my own will to God's, if I can just discern what it is. I get glimmers of the dream's meaning, but it is not clear.

Passing by the desk on my way to breakfast, the clerk waved me down, and handed me a package. It was my laundry, completely dry (rare), folded (normal), and sealed in plastic (very cool but very odd). I thanked her profusely, and headed for the buffet.

It was a great spread. The problem was, it was a buffet, and Lonely Planet strongly warns against buffets, or any other place were meat is set out for a long period of time. This food had been setting out for about three hours, since breakfast had been available since 6am, and so far there were few takers. It was probably fine, but I simply couldn't take any chances. It killed me to do it, but I passed up a tasty-looking Thai buffet for corn flakes. Did I feel like an idiot? Yes. Did I get strange looks from the kitchen staff? Yes. I ducked my head and slurped at my warmish milk.

Once again I gave myself permission to take it easy, since I was sick. Once again, I did not. Following the advice of the desk clerk, I caught a tuk-tuk to the zoo. Lisa is fond of going to zoos wherever we go, even though she is sometimes sorry (the zoo at Tarsus in Turkey depressed her terribly as the animals were so ill-treated). I resolved that if I had the energy at the end of today's journeys, I'd go to the zoo just for her.

There were a number of the fire-engine tuk-tuks (as I'd taken to calling them) lined up in front of the zoo. A large sign advertised the very places I wanted to go: the King and Queen's summer palace, and the Golden Mountain Wat.

The price was certainly right, about 150 Bot ($4.50) for both ways, up and down the mountain. After only about a half hour of driving on a steep road through dense forest, we pulled over to let some folks out at the wat. The rest of us continued on for another fifteen minutes, until we reached another parking lot. The driver pointed at our tuk-tuk. "One hour. Back here!" He was very insistent.

I wondered if an hour was going to be long enough, especially after I paid and received a map of the palace grounds and saw that the footpaths around the place were about 2.5 kilometers, total. It turned out to be just about right, because, much to my disappointment, we were not allowed into the palace buildings. We could only gawk at them from the outside. This saved a lot of time, and turned the focus of the visit onto the truly amazing gardens that surrounded all of the buildings.

Walking briskly, I was able to cover the entire course of the grounds in the allotted hour. Despite my cold, I felt strangely invigorated by my walk in the gardens and forests of the royal retreat. (Don't tell my wife, who might encourage further exercise-laden activities.)

Not everyone was as time-assiduous as I was, however, and I spent the next half hour in the parking lot as the driver paced and cursed the tardy members of our party. I greeted the elderly Chinese grandmother of one of the families in our group. "*Ni how,*" I said.

"*Ni How,*" she responded, smiling.

I walked to the little convenience store nearby and picked up a packet of cola-flavored gummi bears and three small chocolate bars. Walking back to the shaded spot where our party was waiting, I handed one of the chocolate bars to the grandmother. Her face brightened. "*Shay Shay,*" she said. *Thank you.*

"*Bu,*" I replied. *It's nothing.*

Eventually our stragglers—two clueless teenaged girls from Germany—caught up with us, and without apology, tumbled into our fire-engine tuk-tuk. We zoomed down the hill (a little too fast for my comfort), and in between glances at the sun-dappled leaves, I read Crosby's tome on Theravada on my iPhone.

When we got to the temple, we were confronted with a staircase of nearly 400 steps—steep steps, too. Two enormous green dragons ran the full length of the staircase, from top to bottom, providing a handrail of sorts, set at the impractical height of mid-thigh. Taking a deep breath, I began the plod to the top.

I had to stop a couple of times to rest, but I made it, and fairly quickly, too. Stepping into the courtyard, I was met by a jackfruit tree, sporting several of the soccer ball-sized spiky fruits, multicolored scarves wrapped around its trunk. To the left was a large statue of a white elephant. Behind it was a plaque, partially obscured by the statue itself, relating the legend of the Temple's founding. It seems the Thai king had procured a relic of the Buddha, and had declared that the sacred white elephant would know where the relic wanted its temple to be built. So the elephant climbed to the top of this mountain, turned around four times, and promptly died—apparently, right on this here spot.

Taking off my shoes, I ducked through the low doorway into the Temple itself. I emerged not in a building, but in a courtyard surrounding a three-story-high gleaming gold stupa, radiating light, crowned by three crowns, and almost blinding in the bright sun. It wasn't the largest stupa I'd seen, but it was probably the most arresting. It was certainly a fitting symbol for the Dharma—a shining light, an invaluable treasure, sovereign over all other philosophies.

I started to circumambulate deosil (clockwise), taking in the rest of the courtyard. The stupa was surrounded by a fence, painted red and gold, in front of which were various statues of the Buddha in several of his signature poses. Incense burners were set up before them, and people were kneeling, praying, and making offerings. Some of them were shaking noisemakers—really a collection of what looked like chopsticks in a cardboard tube. I had seen this at other shrines, and imagined it to be some nascent form of Vajrayana practice—as long as you're making noise, your prayer is being said. I'd need to check that out, though—it's certainly a question for the Monk Chat booth.

Under a canopy was a bright green Buddha made of glass which I guessed was supposed to remind worshippers of the Emerald Buddha enthroned at the Palace. This one, though, was translucent, and reminded me of a whole set of Buddhas I'd seen the day before, each a different bright color. "Skittles Buddhas," I'd said to myself then.

At the back of the courtyard was a small, dim building housing a "museum." Unable to resist, I stepped in to be greeted by Kenny Chesney and other New Country luminaries playing rather loudly on the stereo. I reveled in the incongruity of contemporary American twang in my ears and medieval Thai Buddhism before my eyes. I paused before a series of tall panels illustrating a beatific world sporting flying Buddhas at the top, and people climbing trees and writhing in agony at the bottom—paintings that rivaled Heironimous Bosch in their surreal and gruesome glory.

Taped to one of the panels was a sign, in both Thai and English, saying, "Heaven is a place where the man who observes the & religious precepts goes after he is dead." Another sign, fixed to the bottom, said, "Hell is a place where bad people who violate the precepts and morality (killing, stealing, sexual mistake, telling a lie and alcoholic drinking) to after they are dead" (grammatical errors are in the original).

I pursed my lips. Going to heaven and hell sure wasn't simply a transfer of karmic energy in *this* artist's Buddhism, was it? Theravada Buddhism seemed to be as confused as I was about the nature of the soul in its own teaching. Or was that just me, leaping to my own religious and cultural conclusions?

What if the artist simply meant that the inheritor of meritorious karma would re-aggregate in a heavenly realm? Or that the inheritor of wicked karma would re-aggregate in a hell realm? That seemed imminently possible, and squared with what I had gleaned elsewhere, but it wasn't the plain meaning of the signs.

I left the musty museum and paused briefly at the wide doorway to a small shrine. Inside, a man was bowing down before a monk. The monk pronounced a blessing over him and sprayed him with holy water, flicked from a bundle of reeds. I smiled, remembering the last time I had sprayed my own congregation with holy water, using a tree branch as an aspergil. Maybe things *are* the same all over.

Stepping out of the temple courtyard, I slipped on one of the flagstones. I didn't fall, thank goodness, but I pulled a muscle in my leg. I beat on it with my fist until it loosened up a bit, and then limped around the outer square.

Every other shop was selling waffles. I frowned. Buddha statue shop, waffle stand, monk chanting CD vendor, waffle shop, quail egg and rice cream thingy stand...and more waffles. What is it with this temple and waffles?

I was sorely tempted by a woman selling corn in plastic takeaway cups. I watched as she filled the cup halfway with large, steaming corn kernels, plopped on a tablespoon of butter, added two teaspoons of brown sugar, and topped it off with a quarter cup of sweetened condensed milk. And then more corn. I walked away, but part of me wishes I'd given her 20 bot and tried it. It seemed like the Thai equivalent of Elvis' peanut butter and bacon sandwiches.

By the time we arrived at the bottom of the hill, I was too tired to visit the zoo, so I caught a cab back to my hotel. Along the way, I saw a restaurant advertising their "Harry Potter menu." From what I could tell from the pictures, this entailed common Thai dishes with lit sparklers stuck in them.

* * *

The next day was my last in Chiang Mai. Sadly, I said good-bye to my hotel room and headed out, rolling my bag behind me. A tuk-tuk dropped me at my destination: the BaanThai cooking school. I got there early, and so I explored the neighborhood a little. When my classmates arrived, I was pleased to see a good mix of folks. I was the only American in our cohort, which included a friendly Swiss couple, a Chinese couple, and a Japanese woman and her five-year-old daughter.

We were each given wicker shopping baskets, and then like a fierce gang of culinary cutthroats, we sauntered down to the local market. There we were given a crash course in Thai fruits, vegetables, and herbs. Each of us walked back with our baskets laden with produce.

As we walked, I introduced myself to the Swiss couple. They were stand-offish at first, but as we started talking, they opened up a bit, and soon were speaking freely and laughing heartily. I told Adrian and Natasha about my project, and they seemed interested but suspicious. Later, I found out why.

As we were eating our first dish, fried cashew nut with chicken, Adrian talked about the disdain that he—and most people in Switzerland—had for Christianity in general. "No one takes it seriously," he said. "It is..." he struggled to find the English word, "it is a relic, a history piece, you know, like in a museum?"

I nodded. "A lot of people in the U.S. feel that way, too. But a lot of us are still pretty religious. That's changing, I think. You're a little ahead of us in Europe on that."

"Yes," he said, laughing, "your TV preachers...."

"They're still going strong, unfortunately." I rolled my eyes.

Adrian set down his fork. "It's nice to meet a Christian who isn't...." he made a face, but I wasn't certain whether he was fishing for the English words or a diplomatic way to phrase something.

I took a guess at what he was trying to say. "Who isn't an 'I'm right and you're wrong' triumphalistic asshole?"

He laughed loudly and slapped his leg. "That's a very good way of putting it. Yes."

"Thanks," I said. "There's actually rather a lot of us, but we rarely make the news. There's a saying in the United States, 'The squeaky wheel gets the grease.' The assholes make a lot of noise, so you only really hear about them."

"Well, it's good to meet one of the good guys," he said. "I'm glad we met you." It was mutual. All along the way, I'd met wonderful folks whom I'd be glad to call friends if we lived in closer proximity. It gives me hope for the human race. It also comforts me that I could, indeed, live anywhere if I needed to. The world has no shortage of good people and potential friends.

It also has no shortage of amazing food. I surprised myself by not completely sucking at the cooking thing. Together with my classmates, I made coconut milk chicken soup, papaya salad, green curry paste (from scratch!) and green chicken curry.

I should have paced myself, and only eaten half of what I prepared. By the end of the day, when we made our desserts (mango sticky rice, in my case) I was a sleepy, bloated toad that could barely move. Did I still eat the mango and sticky rice? You bet I did.

I said goodbye to my classmates and proceeded directly to the train station for an all-night journey back to Bangkok. As the tuk-tuk hit pothole after pothole I held my aching tummy and moaned.

------

1   Questions of Malunkyaputta.

2   Thanks to my friend and Theravada teacher Christopher Titmus for suggesting the cigarette example.

3   Rupert Gethin, *The Foundations of Buddhism* (NY: Oxford University Press, 1998), 78.

Painting a dragon in a temple garden.

Chapter Thirteen: Taiwan—The Mahayana Revelation

When my plane landed, it was night and I was in China. Of course, the meaning of the word "China" is a matter of some dispute. I was in China but not China, neither in China, nor not in China. It was a perfect example of a Buddhist logic puzzle (more about that later). Specifically, I was in Taiwan. The People's Republic of China, over on the mainland, refuses to acknowledge the little island's sovereignty and considers Taiwan a "rogue province" of China. Taiwan returns the favor, officially calling itself the Republic of China, and asserting sovereignty over the mainland, proclaiming the People's Republic an "illegitimate government." It is, delightfully, the mouse that roared.

My driver held a sign with my name on it, and I flagged him down. He was a friendly, wiry, nervous sort of fellow, and he spoke not a word of English. As we drove, I relaxed and surrendered to the unknown while the yellow halogen streetlights cut through the rain and the fog. Neon signs dotted the landscape in every direction, reminding me of a Chinese Las Vegas that just went on and on and on.

Eventually, my driver exited the freeway and steered us into a residential neighborhood. There were no high-end shops here, only hole-in-the-wall restaurants, lottery parlors, coffee shops, and street food vendors. The driver pulled over and honked. A tall thin young woman whirled and waved at us. When I got out of the car, she introduced herself. "Hi, I'm Gina. You're staying at my Dad's place. I'll show you."

Her English was excellent, and her manner was chipper and businesslike. She was dressed completely in black, with black nail polish, straight reddish hair, and tight black leotards under a charcoal miniskirt. Her high heels clacked away into a rain-

222 • *John R. Mabry*

soaked alley, and I pulled at my suitcase and tried to catch up.

We didn't have to go far. The alley had a side-alley, and she climbed three metal stairs to a landing. I followed her into a closet-sized antechamber with a door on either side. She opened the door to the left, and we went inside.

I'd had a devil of a time finding a place to stay in Taipei. I spent literally hours on Trip Advisor and Agoda, but what I discovered was that I really only had two choices: a hostel, sharing a room with 20 other people for peanuts ($10-$30 per night) or a room to myself at well over $100 a night. There was literally nothing in between—at least there was nothing that Trip Advisor didn't have a long beard of reviews attached to saying, "Stay away if you value your life!!" and such things.

I was beginning to despair, when I hit the button for alternative housing. And there, to my great surprise, was a studio apartment for $40 per night. It was clean, with a private bath, and located a block and a half from the metro station. Perfect.

I looked around critically. It was small, all right. The room was about as wide as the bed was long, with an open space next to it a little larger than the bed itself. The bathroom was odd: a washing machine stood in the middle of the room (it was a very small bathroom, so you had to squeeze around the washing machine to get to the sink or toilet), and there was no dryer. There was also no shower—there was, however, a handheld spigot next to the sink, and rubber matting on the floor. Very, very weird. But hey, it was half of the price of a hotel, so I couldn't really complain.

She gave me the key and invited me to try it out as we stepped into the rain again. She wanted to show me the metro station, which I thought an excellent idea. Her heels clacked confidently on the concrete as we walked briskly, breezing by sidewalk diners bundled in their coats, huddled over bowls of soup that billowed clouds of steam into their puckered faces as they sucked up wriggling noodles.

The combination of neon Chinese characters, the pouring rain, and the surreal disconnection I felt gave the whole scene a *Blade Runner* quality that was at once alienating and immensely appealing—the first of many contradictions I would experience in this unusual place.

Gina led me to the end of the block, then turned right. A half block in, there was the metro station with people streaming in and out like the rain's overflow. Gina turned on her heel and led me back to the apartment. I thanked her, and once she left, I turned on the heater and started to get settled.

Only...the heater only emitted cold air. I emailed the owner, and got a quick reply from his son, Tim. Tim came by in ten minutes with a brand new space heater in hand. "That's only an AC," he said, pointing to the cooling unit that looked identical to combo heating/cooling units I'd seen in many other places, right down to the white remote control unit. "But this should do it."

I thanked him and turned on the space heater. It lit up well, but didn't actually throw off much heat. Still, it helped, and I climbed into bed with my long johns on and slept very well indeed.

I'd hoped to find a place to go to church the next morning, but I slept later than I'd hoped, and by the time I got moving, the thought of navigating an unfamiliar metro station with barely enough time to get there—just to attend a service that I wouldn't understand a word of—left me unmotivated. Instead, I spent an hour listening to a Christian band one of my parishioners had recommended, Tenth Avenue North, while I read the lectionary readings for the day and contemplated their meaning for me in this new place. "You are the salt of the earth...you are the light of the world." The words were comforting and familiar, but I wasn't making any new connections. Still, I resolved to carry them with me as I headed out into this cold, wet, alien city.

The first order of the day was breakfast. As I stepped past street food vendors and mom-and-pop eateries, I realized how daunting this was going to be. There were no signs in English, and the food I could see appeared to be remarkably inedible. At least, what with the tentacles, the wheat noodles, the alien vegetables, and the tofu equivalents of Limburger, I was beginning to despair. Then I remembered a little place Tim had recommended the night before when he'd dropped off the space heater. I headed there, and having arrived, was just as dubious as I'd been at the other places.

The Taiwanese seem to have been completely indoctrinated by the Egg McMuffin media blitz. Several of the places I'd passed seemed to specialize in egg-and-something-sandwiches, and they were going fast as commuters snatched them up and ran for the metro. I am allergic to both bread and eggs, so I felt at a bit of a loss.

Things were not quite as tough in India or Thailand, because most people spoke at least a little English. I knew no Hindi or Thai, but could usually rely on the good graces of others. In Taiwan, almost no one spoke English, and if they did, it was very little indeed. Fortunately, I could close the gap a little. I had studied classical Chinese as part of my doctoral work, and we'd used Mandarin as our spoken language in class, largely because our professor was a native Mandarin speaker. I've forgotten most of my skills in written Chinese and spoken Mandarin after twenty years of disuse, but I still retain enough Mandarin to be polite, and I can recognize several characters, which is helpful.[1]

I stepped into the place that Tim recommended and approached the girl at the counter. Between my very little Mandarin and her very little English, I tried to communicate that I wanted the chicken, but not the bread and not the egg. And could I have one of those hash brown patties, too, please?

The only thing they had to drink was coffee and tea. Being

allergic to both of those, I cast around for something else, even if it was less familiar. I pointed. "What is that?" This resulted in quite a bit of conversation, but finally, the man who seemed to be the manager said, "rice milk." I said I'd take one, at which point he said, "Cold? Hot?" I answered, "Hot."

The drink came first, and it was a thick, slimy substance that tasted like coffee. Great. I took a couple of sips, just to see if I could adjust, but then began to feel the same headachy reaction that I get to coffee and realized I should quit while I was ahead. When my meal arrived, it was a chicken sandwich on toast with an egg on top. When I peeled the egg off and set it aside, then did the same with the toast, the waitress finally got it, and replaced my plate with one containing only grilled chicken and potatoes. Perfect. As I happily ate, I noticed a dish that looked like a white translucent bar of soap, only grilled. I asked what it was. "Rice cake," the young woman answered. I resolved to give that a try the next day.

I finally snagged a hot chocolate at one of the ubiquitous 7-11s, and headed for the metro. I'm always nervous about encountering a new metro system, or a new train system, or a... you name it. Probably it's just a variation on the old "fear of the unknown." I fret about it—often rather a lot—and then I actually get there and I figure it out, and it's usually no problem. I should have gotten the message by now, but it's always the same. There's s lesson about Buddhist living-in-the-moment in there somewhere.

As I could have predicted, I got there, found an English language metro map, and to my delight discovered that there was an "English" button on the ticket machine. Getting my ticket and figuring out my route turned out to be as easy as riding the BART at home.

As we neared the station, I found myself growing excited. I was going to the largest and most popular Buddhist temple in Taipei, but that wasn't what I was happy about. Today, for the first time since Lisa left, I'd get to talk to a friend—in unfettered English. Joe was a student of mine, and a fellow Christian clergy person, currently doing missionary work in Taipei. I couldn't wait to see him.

We were supposed to meet at 1pm, but I'd given myself plenty of time to get lost and I arrived much sooner than I'd expected. With about an hour to kill, I wandered around the underground mall surrounding the metro station, then explored the shops that ringed the courtyard surrounding the temple. Everything had a surreal rain-sheened gloss to it.

Eventually I wandered around to my appointed place and read a new scholarly evaluation of Mahayana Buddhism.[2] My head snapped up when I heard, "John!" and saw Joe bounding toward me. He was a shorter man than I, and a little thinner, with wire glasses an open, cheerful face. I gave him a hearty hug and we exchanged "how-the-hell-are-ya's."

He apologized that he didn't have more time to spend with me while I was here, but I told him how grateful I was that he had even a small window, since I knew he was between two trips. I really was taking up his only time between one trip and another, and although I felt bad about that, I was too eager for a friendly face to suggest that he beg off. He didn't seem resentful at all, and I was grateful.

We stepped out into the square and headed toward Longshan Temple. A large pagoda-style archway provided the threshold, flanked by two banks of moon lanterns, twenty in a row on either side, ten rows deep—like a wall of pumpkins ascending toward the sky. We stepped through the archway and into a smaller inner courtyard. Here we saw a platform that almost looked like it could have been a parade float, its primary feature being a horse, standing erect on two legs, wearing a crown and decked out in traditional Chinese dress of regal blue. He was lit from the inside by Christmas lights, and was surrounded by flames and dragons. "Who is he?" I asked Joe.

"He's the spirit of the new year—the year of the horse," he said. I'd just experienced Chinese New Year last week in Thailand, so it made sense that the decorations would still be up. At the other end of the courtyard was a waterfall, surrounded by greenery. It was beautiful.

Distracted by movement, I shifted my gaze to the stream of people entering the gates. Joe must have noticed. "How have you found the Taiwanese people?" he asked.

"Uh...pleasant enough," I said, not wanting to be prematurely judgmental. Gina and Tim were very nice, but most of the folks I'd passed on the way here were in a hurry to get wherever they were going and didn't have much time for lost or clueless Westerners. "The language thing is such a problem that I don't feel like I've got a sense of them yet."

Joe nodded. "I can see that. But they really do warm up to you pretty fast. In my experience, they bend over backwards to be helpful. Even total strangers will go out of their way for you." He paused, fishing for the right analogy. "They're very *grandmotherly*."

I smiled. I hoped I'd have a chance to see that side of them.

Joe cocked his head, making an *on the other hand* gesture. "Of course, they can be smothering at times, too." He leaned in conspiratorially. "Let's just say they do not have a Western sense of personal space."

I nodded. *And why should they,* I thought, *not being Westerners?*

"Shall we go in?" Joe asked.

I agreed and followed him across another threshold where we found ourselves in a very bustly place. Several tables were set up, piled with foodstuffs—offerings, no doubt. Statues of the Buddha and various Bodhisattvas were in glass cases on the tables, and kneelers stretched out behind them. In front was yet another courtyard with the temple proper at the far end.

All Buddhists believe in Bodhisattvas, but the Theravada and Mahayana have very different ideas about them. For Theravadins, Bodhisattvas are very rare. They are Buddhas-in-waiting, or more precisely, in formation—they are beings who are well on their way to becoming Buddhas. In their teaching, there can only be one full-fledged Buddha at a time—in fact, there is only one Buddha for every world age. So there might be a couple of Bodhisattvas working their way up the karma ladder, but the next one isn't due to ripen into full-fledged Buddhahood for another 2,500 years.

Mahayana Buddhists, however, are much more generous with their Bodhisattvas. In their teaching, all beings have the seeds of Buddhahood—what they call "Buddha Nature"—within them, and all can *become* a Buddha, and eventually will. So for Mahayana Buddhists the goal is not to follow the Buddha, but to become a Buddha.

I flashed on the Pseudo-Clementine literature, part of what remains of the ancient Jewish Christian scriptures, where it says that the goal is not to follow Christ, but to *become* Christ. It was an intriguing passage, one that has stuck with me. I thought it strange that it came from the equivalent of *our* Theravadins, the Jewish Christians. Even though we don't use that "becoming Christ" language in the Pauline tradition, the teaching is still there. When we are baptized into Christ, we become his body, and (on good days) we are teaching as he taught, healing as he healed, and loving as he loved.

But there was more to this whole Bodhisattva thing than just *becoming* a Buddha. Unlike Theravadins, Mahayana Buddhists believe that the Buddha, upon his death, refused to enter Nirvana, and chose to stay in the world of suffering (as a disembodied spiritual presence) to assist other beings in their liberation. This is source of the Mahayana teachings on compassion for all beings (there is no emphasis on compassion in Theravada teaching). For Mahayana Buddhists, a Bodhisattva is someone who does the same. For them, a Bodhisattva isn't someone who is on the way to becoming a Buddha, but someone who has already achieved enlightenment and instead of entering Nirvana, has elected to stay in the world to help others become enlightened as well.

This is what "Mahayana" means: it is the "greater way" to renounce one's own happiness and rest until everyone is liberated. This is the ultimate goal of genuine mystics everywhere—not just to get cozy with the Divine, but to be so closely united that you do what the Divine does, you spend yourself in the service of others. This is precisely what Jesus was getting at when he said, "If you want to be my disciples, you must take up your cross and follow me." In other words, you too must be willing to go to the cross, to sacrifice yourself. It is the same teaching, just dressed in different cultural and symbolic clothes.

Bodhisattvas are afforded a pretty high place in the Mahayana pantheon. Many of them specialize in special graces—such as Manjushri, the Bodhisattva of Wisdom or Avalokitesvara, the Bodhisattva of Compassion—and the faithful pray to them when they need help with something that falls within their purview. So are the Bodhisattvas gods? Uh... not officially, not by the Western academic definition of the word. But in my opinion, if it walks like a duck and quacks like a duck...it's *probably* a duck.

All around us, people were holding lit incense before their faces, and bowing three times to the Bodhisattvas, their lips moving quickly, saying private prayers. No one seemed to notice us or mind that we were gawking, they just went about their business as if we weren't there. I snapped a few photos. No one seemed to mind.

We walked up to the main temple building, and watched as

people made offerings before several of the Bodhisattvas, but one statue was getting the lion's share of attention. "He's the Bodhisattva of wealth and success in business," Joe explained. A serious look crossed his face. "It's really a very covenantal relationship."

"What do you mean?" I asked.

"Well, the people have responsibilities toward the gods, and if they fulfill them, the gods are bound by their responsibilities to their people."

I nodded, but I wondered if it was a loving relationship, or more of a business arrangement. I suddenly realized I had been projecting my own devotional feelings onto everyone I was seeing, as per my "method" for inter-religious empathy. As useful a method as it was, it wasn't infallible and I needed to remember that not everyone feels like I do, especially not about religion.

A female Bodhisattva figure was drawing a good crowd, and it was her image that provided the focal point for the temple, not the Buddha's. "Quan Yin," I said, recognizing her.

"The old girl herself," Joe agreed, grinning.

"She's the Chinese manifestation of the Bodhisattva Avalokitesvara," I remembered aloud. "She's depicted as male in India—the Dalai Lama is his reincarnation. Do you know how she got to be female?" I asked.

"No," Joe looked delighted and eager for the story.

"Christian missionaries—Nestorians no less—evangelized China in the seventh and eighth centuries. They brought with them statues of the virgin and child...."

Joe nodded, making the connection. "Very cool," he said. "The same way that Christians picked up that same iconography from the Egyptians' statues of Isis and Horus."

"Exactly!" I said, triumphantly. It's a wonderful feeling to be with someone who is literate enough in your own area of expertise that he or she can finish your sentences.

"You know what's interesting about this place," Joe said, "it's Buddhist, but I've never seen a monk in here."

I looked around, and was a little surprised to see that he was right. But something clicked for me, too. Whereas at a Theravada temple, you couldn't spit without hitting a monk, this temple was packed with people, and every one a layperson. My reading in Williams said that one of the theories regarding how Mahayana split from the older Buddhist schools was that it was an anti-clerical movement.

In the Theravada system, you could live a perfectly good life as a layperson, but you could never reach enlightenment unless you became a monk and worked on your spiritual development full-time—and even then it would probably take you several lifetimes (understand please that I use the word "you" very loosely here, since Buddhism rejects a permanent self). The job of Theravadin laypeople is to support the monks and nuns, and to thereby acquire merit so they will be reborn in a higher station of life the next time around.

In contrast, the goal for Mahayana Buddhist monks and nuns is to achieve liberation, and like the Buddha, refuse to enter Nirvana until all other beings can also enter in. The goal of Mahayana laypeople is to be granted liberation by the Buddha's grace, acquired by their faith and devotion. In fact, the Mahayana tradition promises laypeople that they can be liberated even though they're part-timers—they can even be liberated in one lifetime!

Williams relates a great story from the *Asokadattavyakarana Sutra*, in which a twelve-year-old girl by the name of Asokadatta refuses to stand or bow in the presence of the monks. When confronted about it, she said, "I follow the path of supreme enlightenment, the great vehicle (*maha-yana*) which is like the lion, the king of the beasts; why should I salute these monks who follow an inferior vehicle (*hina-yana*, of which Theravada is one school) which is like a jackal?" Just to mock

them, she turned herself into a man, and then resumed her girl-
ish form, because according to Mahayana teaching, everything
is an illusion, a trick of the mind anyway.[3]

Other scholars dispute the "Mahayana as clerical backlash"
notion, at least as an origin theory, but there is no denying that
there is an element of that to it. The layfolks we were watching
now were not taking a back seat to anyone—they were stepping up and taking charge of their spiritual lives, their temple,
their sangha. And Joe was right, there wasn't a monk in sight.
The Protestant in me rejoiced.

Along one side were several altars, each to gods that were
distinctly *not* Buddhist. "They are pretty syncretistic around
here," Joe commented.

"Yeah, well you know, I've found the same thing wherever
I've gone," I said. "You'd go into a Buddhist temple in Nepal,
and there off to the side would be a shrine to Shiva or Ganesha
or Krishna. There just don't seem to be any hard boundaries
between religions. It was the same in Thailand—there were
statues of Hindu gods in most Buddhist temples."

"And here they're the native Chinese gods," Joe pointed out,
"Taoist gods, of course. Like that angry-looking fellow. I'll bet
he's the one you pray to if you're going into battle." He was
pretty fierce-looking, all right. In an alley fight, I'd definitely
want him in *my* corner.

I wondered what it would be like if the blurry boundaries
between faiths were more prominent in the West. We're certainly doing our part at Grace North Church. Every Sunday
we read a passage from a non-Christian scripture—from the
Upanishads or the Buddhist sutras, or the Tao Te Ching—specially selected as a companion to the Gospel reading. Sometimes the readings echo the Gospel, but just as often they
challenge it, providing a very rich mix from which to preach
and ponder. We also hang a string of flags bearing the symbols
of many of the world's religions behind our altar during serv-

ices. Our music is likewise diverse, often choosing our hymn texts from Sufi poets, the Buddha, and many other sources. It's one way that our community feels connected—not just to other Christians, but to a much larger family of faith. But how would our congregation feel about a giant statue of Quan Yin or Ganesha in our sanctuary? Jeez, who am I kidding? This is Grace North we're talking about. They'd friggin' *love it.*

It occurred to me that for the Taiwanese it just wouldn't feel right if deities from a variety of traditions *weren't* standing elbow to elbow. I envied them a bit for their tolerance, for their embrace of the religious Other—more than that, the complete dissolving of boundaries between self and Other. We took one more turn around the courtyard, and then headed back to the metro station to head to another temple.

"Are you travelling with your computer, John?" Joe asked me.

"Yeah, and my iPad, and my iPhone," I laughed. "I was a little worried about bringing them all, but I'm really glad I did." You just really need a computer to write well and handle internet connections, but the iPad has been essential for reading. "Instead of lugging around a trunkload of books, I've just got every book I need loaded to my iPad. I use it all the time. And that's not counting comic books."

Joe's eyebrows shot up.

I noticed and lowered my head sheepishly. "Okay, I'll let you in on a little secret about me you probably don't know. I'm a huge comic book fan. I'm a voracious reader."

Joe's whole face brightened. "So am I!" he laughed.

"Really? Marvel or DC?" I asked, the comic fan's equivalent of Democrats or Republicans. (In this incredibly specious analogy, DC has more in common with the Republicans.)

"Marvel, all the way!" he said. "I'm a real Spider-Man nut."

"Aww, I'm a DC guy," I admitted. I like Marvel, but I can't

get enough of Batman, Green Arrow, Starman, Sandman Mystery Theater, the whole Vertigo imprint....the list goes on.

For the rest of the ride to the next temple, we were consumed with all things comics—collections, characters, films, the obsessiveness of fandom, and the far superiority of the iPad over paper for comic consumption.

At the same time I was lost in fanboy bliss talking with Joe about our common enthusiasms, I suddenly felt a little sad that he lived all the way across the globe. If he lived in the Bay Area, I could see we'd be great friends, as we discovered more and more that we had in common.

Before we knew it we were stepping into a garden where life-sized figures from ancient Chinese mythology were frozen in time. Standing over a pool, an artist in a flowing blue robe held a brush up to a dragon in flight, painting him or perhaps giving him life. A family of figurines gathered in a cave around an elderly woman in bed. In another tableau, a kneeling man in salmon-colored trousers seemed to be applying some kind of ointment to the open mouth of a tiger.

"Where are we?" I asked.

"This is probably part of the temple," Joe said. The garden was a lot of fun, but small. We exited the other side, and noted that we were right across the street from the temple we sought. So we crossed, and entered the Bao-an Temple, a Taoist place of worship devoted primarily to health. That made sense of some of the tableaus, although I would have liked to have known how painting the dragon fit in.

Stepping into the courtyard, we came quickly to an altar with a golden candle stand in front of it where people had set several lit candles. "That is so amazing. Where have you seen that before?" I pointed. "It's just like what you see in a Greek Orthodox church."

"It sure is," Joe agreed.

It reminded me that technically, Russia is in Asia. In front of the main altar were several large tables, each filled to overflowing with offerings. "This god likes Doritos," I pointed out to Joe. But the lighthearted jest faded quickly, as I realized that most of the people around us were either praying to be relieved of some ailment, or were hoping for the recovery of a loved one. All around us people were bowing with lit incense held before their faces. They were all suffering—precisely the condition that Siddhartha endeavored to fix.

Crossing to the far side of the courtyard, we discovered a statue of a wide Chinese woman, wrapped in silks and surrounded by several female attendants, six on either side. "This is the goddess of childbirth," Joe whispered. "See that woman?" An elderly woman was bowing before the image, her lips moving in a silent prayer. "Her daughter is pregnant— or she *wants* her daughter to get pregnant." He was speculating, of course, but it was probably a pretty good guess.

After we finished with that temple, we set out to find the Confucian temple, which was supposed to be just around the corner. It wasn't that simple but we did find it. In contrast to the Buddhist and Taoist temples, which were buzzing with activity, this one was like a ghost town. We were almost the only people there, and instead of altars, the place was filled with museum-like displays about Confucianism—and they were very good displays.

"It's pretty dead here," Joe commented.

"Well, what do you expect from a religion that doesn't actually worship any gods?" I countered. We both chuckled a bit, and I mused on the puzzle that was Confucianism.

It was really an educational movement that posited a nobility not of birth, but of virtue. Confucius was a bastard child, with a highborn father and a lowborn mother, and so he kind of found himself between social castes. He read everything he could get his hands on and made a name for himself as a teacher, accepting all students (all male students, that is) regardless of their social ranking.

He taught that the "way of heaven" was for everyone to know his or her role, and to perform that role with precision. Kings should act like kings, ministers like ministers, and servants like servants. If everyone performed his or her role well, then society (and the universe) would move along like a well-oiled machine, and everyone would be happy and prosperous.

To Confucius' great annoyance, his ideas never really caught on during his lifetime. After he died, however, he was recognized as the greatest philosopher in Chinese history, and almost everything in Chinese life was laid out according to his teachings. That was, until the Taoists—those nonconformist free-thinking troublemakers—started chafing against the overregulation of society at every level.

The whole of Chinese history can be seen as a push-and-pull between the easy-going attitude of the Taoists and the anality of the Confucianists. I seems to me that this anality is still very much with them. "Taipei" sounds a lot like "Type A" and the Taiwanese are very disciplined people indeed: I found almost no trash on the ground in the whole city, in fact there was no evidence of pollution of any kind—everything sparkled to a high sheen. I saw not a single stray dog or homeless person, and in startling contrast to India, everything here *works*. I realized that what I was seeing was what the whole of China might look like if it were free and democratic—prosperous, clean, and safe.

By the time Joe and I reached the displays on the Confucian canon and Chinese calligraphy, it was time for him to go. We agreed to stay in touch over the next few days in case there was a chance of getting together before my flight back to India, and then he rushed off to the metro. I felt suddenly very alone. And very cold.

* * *

I was awakened by the blaring melody of an ice cream truck. At six in the morning. I thought this very strange until I actually dressed and hit the street, whereupon I discovered that it wasn't ice cream vendors blaring tinny, amplified music-box versions of "Turkey in the Straw" but trash collection trucks. Huh.

I took this bit of weirdness in stride and headed to the 7-11, where I ordered a hot chocolate and picked up an English-language newspaper. Then I walked back to the breakfast place and took a seat. There are no walls on the place, and it was frightfully cold. I ordered grilled chicken, a hash brown patty, and an order of fried rice cake. I sipped my chocolate and flipped through the newspaper. I didn't have to read very long before it became very clear how tenuous the Taiwanese position was, and how much anxiety over Chinese aggression colors daily life. The newspaper was full of polls over what to do regarding China's latest actions, and lots of political hand-wringing over China's threats. China, it seemed, was working both the carrot and the stick pretty hard. You've got to hand it to the Taiwanese—they've got guts.

After breakfast I walked briskly to the metro station and, following the directions in the Lonely Planet, caught the 706 bus to the Museum of World Religions. I was a little early, so I went half a block to a Starbucks, ordered another hot chocolate, and read a bit more in my Mahayana book. A little after 10am, I went back up to the museum, paid for my ticket and rode the escalator up to the 7th floor.

I stepped out into a long hallway, the first twenty feet or so of which was a waterfall built into the window facing the street. The effect was of light coming through a bank of fogged out windows which were rippling with cascading water. Very, very cool.

I walked along it slowly, savoring the mystical ambiance. It reminded me of the many biblical references to "living water," which in the Jewish scriptures just means "running water"—in other words, not stagnant. This is useful information when you come across the similar phrase "living God." It's tempting to think that the phrase means "not an idol," but perhaps it means more than that. Perhaps it is referring to a God who is flowing, changing, and pouring out into new and surprising places.

Perhaps it refers to a God who is not stagnant, but instead is like a river, a torrent that refuses to be dammed up into one conception, one theology, or even one face—a Spirit that "lists where it will."[4] It's that God I'm hoping to discover on this pilgrimage—the God beyond my fixed ideas and images and comfort zones.

The rest of the hallway was a long mural of people from various faiths at prayer spread out along the left hand wall. The pillars along the right had sentences fading in and then out on them, in both Chinese and English. Things like: "What happens when we die?" and "What is memory?"

That hallway ended in a foyer the shape of a giant gold sphere. The inside of the sphere hosted an eleven-circuit petite Chartres labyrinth, ornamented with symbols corresponding to the Chinese zodiac. It would have been cooler if the labyrinth had actually been big enough to walk, but it was just small enough to make it impractical for actual use. It seemed a shame, especially since if you got rid of the gold sphere (the use of which eluded me, beyond the weirdness factor) there would have been plenty of room for a larger labyrinth.

My thoughts were interrupted by a docent in a blue vest, a middle aged woman with pretty good English skills. She pointed behind me, "Movie start at 11:20. It about twelve minutes."

I thanked her and told her I'd set my watch. She asked me if I wanted to rent an English audio guide. I told her no, but thanks. She walked back to her desk, where I noted there were about six docents, all in their blue vests, and staring at me, the only visitor, as if looking for an opportunity to pounce.

I warily turned my back on them and entered the main hall. The first thing I encountered was an installation on Christianity that ran about twenty feet along the wall. There was a large painting of Jesus, a monstrance, a rosary, priest's vestments, as well as several photographs. Along the handrail were signs in both Chinese and English describing the items. There were quotations from the Bible, but there was no sense of what Christianity was *about*. There was no mention of the soteriological dilemma it was trying to solve, nor mention of how it accomplished that. There was no mention of the Protestant Reformation—just some disjointed facts and figures.

I hate to be Professor Grumpypants, but why kick a museum like this off with a display on Christianity, anyway? It made no sense to me, and in fact, it touched a pretty raw nerve. As a teacher of World Religions, I firmly believe that a chronological approach is the only way to present the subject, because every tradition that arises is an adaption of the tradition that came before it.

For instance, Judaism is impossible to understand without knowing something about Middle Eastern native religions, Christianity is impossible to understand without knowing something about Judaism, and Islam is a whole lot easier to grasp if you are familiar with Judaism and Christianity. The same is true of religions in the east—Hinduism grows out of the native Vedic faith, Buddhism and Jainism are reforms of Hinduism, and so on.

But no, this museum started with Christianity. I shook my head at the sheer randomness of it. Buddhism inexplicably followed Christianity, then Islam. Most of the major faith traditions were represented, and I was quite pleased indeed to see a section on Zoroastrianism that looked like it had been added later, as an afterthought—no doubt at the Zoroastrian's insistence, since the museum credited the New York Zoroastrian Society for all of the signage. Go Parsis!

After a few minutes, another of the docents approached me. She didn't have much English, but she did know two words: "Audio guide?" I realized that I would find no peace until I procured an audio guide, so I laid down my NT$200 and then stood around for ten minutes until the docents could find one that worked.

By that time, the movie was set to begin, so I took my seat—the only person in the theater. The film was so unremarkable that now, only two days later as I write this, I can remember almost nothing about it. It was one of those, "there are timeless questions" kinds of things with Hallmark-worthy photography and soothing Japanese flute music. It was light and fluffy and of almost no interest at all. When it ended I returned to the main hall and continued to make my way around.

The audio guide narration was just as insipid as the film and I learned nothing, so I eventually simply stopped pushing the button. (I did keep the headphone fixed to my ear as a prophylactic against docent attacks, however.)

I finished the displays on all the major faith traditions, and gravitated toward the center of the room, where there were several large-scale models of signature houses of worship. I recognized the Synagogue from Prague, and the Dome of the Rock mosque. There was a tabletop-sized replica of one of the Shiva temples at Kahjuharo. Chartres cathedral was there, plus a Shinto shrine and a Buddhist Temple that I've not seen in person (yet).

Overall, it was a very impressive collection, although there were several signage errors that irritated me. A quotation by Krishna from the Baghavad Gita was attributed to Shiva (???) and the caption under the Dome of the Rock said that "the building was sacred to Muslims, Jews, and Christians." Of course, the *land it was built on* is sacred to all three faiths, not the mosque itself. Okay it was a trivial error, but you would think, in a museum as impressive and expensive as this, someone would be fact-checking these things. (In fact, where do I apply for the job?)

Going downstairs, I entered the Hall of Life Passages, with displays marking the various mysteries that religions ritually mark in human life: birth, coming of age, marriage, and death. I decided to give the audio guide a chance to redeem itself, so I placed it near the "Introduction" panel and pressed "play." I was expecting to hear a nice preface to the display on the mystery of human life and the importance of ritually marking the birth event, but what I heard was, "The Hebrew circumcision knife is used to remove the foreskin of the penis...." Ouch. I cringed and yanked the earpiece off my head, finally just stuffing it in my pocket.

The written signage had almost no references to genital mutilation, thankfully, and I actually made the rounds of the displays fairly quickly. Across the hall, I discovered a "temporary" display on Ch'an Buddhism. The idea I got was that every now and then there would be a special installation going into more depth on one of the traditions, or a sub-tradition (such as Ch'an, known more widely by its Japanese name, Zen Buddhism).

But here's the irritating thing: this "special installation" had been here for three years. And guess who designed and funded this museum? Yeah, Ch'an Buddhists. Call me an Xer, but look, dude, I don't care if you want to sell something, just be up front about the fact that you're selling it, okay? I ground my teeth in annoyance as I toured the "special temporary exhibit." It was beautifully done, even magnificent, with a very modern art, impressionistic approach. But all of the signage was in Chinese, so I didn't stay long.

There was only one other thing I wanted to see, and that was the Children's Fantasyland. As an educator, I am especially interested in how an interfaith organization might approach religious education. How would an excellent museum like this one go about introducing children to the world's religions in a fun and exciting way?

Uh…they wouldn't, it turns out. I stepped through the door straight into the Snow White ride in Disneyland, a dark forest where I was startled by a screaming animatronic bird leaping up from a tree top. I followed a path deeper into the plastic forest, passing by rock formations and giant mushrooms. As we turned a corner, there was a place to climb inside a styrofoam cave. On my right we passed a half-human sized family of stuffed bears, getting all huggy with each other and looking sociopathically happy, their manga eyes a little too wide, giving their glee a manic, crazed appearance.

Through an archway I almost tripped over the largest stuffed animal I have ever seen in my life, a big yellow dog that filled nearly the whole room. Disturbingly, a tunnel burrowed through his torso, providing passage from one part of the room to another. Strangely, he also possessed tiny wings.

I tried to take a selfie of myself with the dog, but all I got was myself smiling next to a black eye as big as my head. Cool as the playroom was, I shook my head at the huge missed opportunity. I was hoping to steal candies from Ganesha's sweets pot, see who could hold the Buddha's meditation pose longest without moving, or play pin-the-savior-on-the-cross—but no.

* * *

That evening I huddled in the entrance to the Taipower metro station, trying to stay warm and glancing at my watch. "There's John Mabry!" a familiar voice called out. Looking around quickly, I saw Jen Gallmeyer's face poking out of a winter coat, stocking cap and a muffler. I gave her a hearty hug as I hadn't seen her in a couple of years.

I first met her in a chance encounter at the horserace track in Emeryville. I was there for a birthday party, and bumped into a very good friend, Richard Stevens. Richard had been a Lutheran seminarian whose committee had denied him ordination. I introduced him to the Old Catholics, and he was soon after ordained, maintaining a very active wedding ministry.

Richard was a major horror film addict. He was also a Bob Dylan nut. For years, he came over to my apartment every Tuesday night to watch either a horror film he'd picked out or to view a couple episodes of *The Sopranos*. When he started dating Jen, he kind of dropped out of sight, as friends often do when they are in the first flushes of love. I didn't resent it at all—I was happy for him. Over the past couple of years he'd gone through a very painful divorce and he was overdue for a healthy slice of happiness, in my opinion.

He was just beginning to come back into my orbit when a massive stroke killed him. He wasn't even fifty. I had met Jen a couple of times, but I didn't really know her. But as we planned Richard's memorial service, it became clear to me why she'd captured his heart. She was smart, funny, and had a gung-ho approach to life that was a good compliment to Richard's go-with-the-flow personality.

After the memorial, Jen and I met a couple of times for lunch, and then she was off to see the world. I'd been keeping tabs on her through Facebook and knew that she'd been teaching English in Taipei for a while now. So when I figured out I'd be coming here, I dropped her a note.

"This is pretty weird," she said. "You being here."

"It's surreal, isn't it?" I agreed enthusiastically. "I mean, in the whole of the world, what are the odds?"

As we walked toward one of her favorite restaurants, she filled me in on her adventures. "First I went trekking in Kathmandu, and I met this guy...." She told me a little about him, and we exchanged impressions and memories of Nepal. "You didn't make it to Pokhara?" she asked.

"No, next time," I said. "Lisa is trying to talk her friend into going on a trek there. If she succeeds, I'll tag along. They can go on their trek and I'll sit in a coffee shop in Pokhara and drink hot cocoa."

"That sounds like an excellent plan!"

"So what happened to your beau?" I asked.

"Well, I'm a Westerner, and he's a…he's a Nepalese guy." She scrunched her face up. "It was good for what it was, but it wasn't going to work out, long term."

I nodded. "I get it."

"So I took the ESL training in Thailand, and there was a good job here, so here I am."

We arrived at the restaurant, and took a seat by the window. It was a Western food joint run by Taiwanese, so they were a little unclear on some of the concepts, but it was mostly familiar. We ordered, and Jen asked me how my pilgrimage was going.

"I'm sooo glad I decided to leave India," I said. "If I had to stay there another month and a half I…don't think I would have made it." I might have thrown myself on the burning ghats, truth be told. "I probably would have just come back when Lisa did."

"But instead you went to Thailand!" Jen said. "How cool is that?" Of course, that led to a discussion of Thailand, which, we both agreed, was awesome. After we enthused about the Thais for a while, Jen asked. "So why Taiwan?"

"Well, I went to Thailand to spend some time soaking up Theravada Buddhism, to try to get a feel for the spirituality." I knew that Jen was reading my blog—if not every post, at least a good smattering of them—but there's a lag between when I'm in a place and when I post about it. "And now I'm here to soak up Mahayana Buddhism."

"How would you characterize the main difference?" Jen asked.

"You want the long answer or the short answer?"

"Short for now."

"Theravadins are the conservatives and Mahayanans are the progressives. Theravadins want to keep everything exactly the way it was when the Buddha was alive, and Mahayanans are open to new ideas, and letting their theology grow and evolve."

"That's perfect," she said.

"You know, my own denomination, the United Church of Christ, is the most progressive of the Christian denominations. Our motto is, 'God is still speaking.' I guess you could say the motto of the Mahayana is 'Buddha is still speaking.'"

"I like that!"

"Of course, that's an oversimplification. It doesn't mean that there aren't fundamentalist Mahayana...."

"Of course," she said, mock seriously.

Our food arrived and it was marvelous. I have absolutely no memory of what we had, but it was Denny's diner fare, and as good as you could possibly hope for, even at a Denny's.

Afterwards, we braved the wind and cold again, first in search of ice cream (my fault) but then to one of Jen's favorite coffee shops where she got what is probably the best hot chocolate in Taipei. But I got, marvelously, ice cream. (Yes, I as I write this I am feeling fat and insecure. And I will now have a gummi bear to quell my discomfort. Or three....) Once our orders arrived, I sighed. Jen smiled and licked chocolate off her spoon.

"Are you learning Mandarin?" I asked.

"I started to..." she frowned, looking down into her cup. "But then I stopped."

"Why?"

"I've really been missing home. I'm thinking of going back."

"Oh." I pursed my lips. "Yeah, if you were going to stay, set down roots, it makes sense to learn the language. But on the other hand...."

"Right," she said. A reflective look came into her eyes, and she changed the subject. "It seems somehow fitting that we're here," she said.

"What do you mean?"

"I mean, it was Richard's death that, you know, started me on this journey. It seems appropriate that it's you—that it's his friend—now that I'm thinking about ending it."

"Kind of like bookends," I nodded.

"Yeah. Just like that," she grinned, a little sadly.

We finished up, and walked back to the metro station. I'd hoped we'd get another chance to get together, but our schedules simply did not sync up again. I gave her a hug, and we headed off toward our different trains. I felt sad as I walked toward the platform that would take me to my apartment. Our goodbye seemed too abrupt, as if we'd been cut off midsentence on a phone call. I comforted myself with the thought that maybe soon I'd meet Jen again for lunch—this time at home in California.

---

1   The written Chinese language as nothing to do with the spoken, as the pictograms represent ideas, not sounds. The two main languages spoken in China, Mandarin and Cantonese, bear no resemblance to the other, and speakers of each cannot understand each other. But they can both pick up the same newspaper written in Chinese script and read it perfectly. Chinese could be used as a universal written language for the whole world, if people would just get behind the idea. Any takers?

2   Paul Williams (not the early 70s singer who looks like one of the Banana Splits) *Mahayana Buddhism: The Doctrinal Foundations* (NY: Routledge, 1989).

3   Williams, 23.

4   John 3:8.

Quan Yin, with the baby Buddha on her lap.

Chapter Fourteen: Lukang—City of Dark Goddesses

As the train pulled in to Changhua, it became clear that not all of Taiwan was as bright and shiny as Taipei. It was a busy, industrial town, with little beauty and no glitter to it—unless you count the ubiquitous neon. I showed my hotel voucher to a taxi driver, who scowled at me.

"Yuanlin!" he shouted. I had no idea what he was saying. I shook my head. "Yuanlin, bu Changhua," he said, shaking his finger "no" at the ground. He turned on his heel and consulted with another taxi driver. They spoke loudly and quickly in what sounded like complete gibberish to me. Finally, the driver turned back to me and wrote on a pad of paper, "400."

"What? Four hundred dollars to take me to my hotel room?" I was incensed. Okay, four hundred Taiwanese dollars is only about twelve American dollars, but I expected my hotel to be in the general vicinity. It was not.

"Next town," the other taxi driver called to me. "Far."

I rolled my eyes and silently cursed the online travel gods, who in their capricious mercy, ought to *inform* their worshippers of such things. You know, helpful little tidbits like, "This hotel is listed for Changhua, but it is not actually *in* Changhua." That kind of thing.

I was a little concerned because Changhua was not really where I wanted to be anyway. I wanted to visit Lukang, a town filled with amazing historic temples. But Lukang has limited sleeping options, and several sources recommended staying in Changhua and making a daytrip to Lukang. So how to get from this new place—Yuanlin—to Lukang tomorrow? I reckoned I'd figure it out.

My hopes were dashed as the taxi ride stretched out longer and longer. *Just how far is this place, anyway?* I wondered.

Eventually he pulled up in front of a hotel on a busy city street. I jostled street food vendors getting my bag out of the car, and with a grunt lifted it up the stairs to the lobby.

As I stepped through the door, the woman at the desk bowed. "Agoda?" she asked.

"Yes," I said. I had booked through the Agoda website. "Mabry." She pulled out a roster and I pointed to my name. Strangely, Mandarin speakers can't say the name, "Mabry" as the "bree" sound does not occur in Mandarin. In my Chinese class, my professor called me *Ma Shen-sun,* "*Mr. Ma.*"

"Please," the woman said, indicating the sideboard behind me. "All free."

There was tea and coffee and...a huge freezer with an assortment of ice creams. "The ice cream is free?" I asked.

"All free," she smiled.

I *was* going to like this place; not so much my waistline. I got my key and went up to my room. It was sparkling clean, large, and very attractive. Not bad for US$25. There was one thing that would have to be fixed, however—it was *freezing.* I felt cold air coming from the vents and picked up the remote from the table. Just as in Taipei, it turned on the AC, but did not control heat.

I left my things unpacked and went downstairs to ask about heat. A different young woman was behind the counter, wearing a blue surgical mask. "No heat," she said, her words slightly muffled.

"How can you run a hotel without any heat?" I snapped, edging toward ugly American status.

Her enormous brown eyes just blinked at me.

"Can I at least get another blanket?"

She blinked again, without comprehension. I took out my phone and spoke into the iTranslate app. She read the resulting text in Chinese and nodded. She picked up the phone and in a moment, a middle aged woman appeared in a tan service vest.

She motioned me to follow her into the elevator. When we reached the seventh floor, she took me to a linen closet and handed me a comforter. Then she locked it up, and turned on her heel.

I wasn't at all certain about this, but I'd give it a try. I went back to my room, and lay down for about a half hour. Too cold to actually fall asleep, I decided to explore the neighborhood. I needed to figure out how to get to Lukang the next day anyway.

At the front desk I asked about buses to Lukang. There seemed to be a different woman at the desk every time I visited. I was lucky this time, because this woman knew a little English. Shortish black hair framed her face in a chipper Jackie O look. She pulled out a tourist map and made a circle. "We here," she said, then drew another circle. "Bus there. Leave every hour— nine, ten, eleven. Okay?"

I looked at the map and it seemed simple enough. "Okay!" I said, smiling. One major goal accomplished! The afternoon was turning late, and besides exploring, I needed to find a decent place for dinner. I hit the street, and wove my way through the traffic and the street vendors.

As I was waiting for a break in traffic, I saw a lean Western face coming toward me. "Howdy," I said, sticking out my hand. The man hadn't seen me, and seemed a little lost in his own world. He blinked as he registered me. "Uh...hi," he said.

"I am not from here," I said with a big smile.

"I...live here," he said.

"I'm John. I'm just in town a couple of days. I'm going to go see Lukang. And you?" I asked.

"I'm Vincent. I teach English. I'm from Scotland, but my wife is Taiwanese. I was on my way home from work."

I nodded. "I'm going to Lukang tomorrow, but what should I see today while I'm here in Yuanlin?"

His eyebrows bunched up as he thought. Apparently, Yuanlin did not have much to recommend it. Then he brightened. "There is a pretty big temple nearby," he said. "You could go there."

"Sounds like just the thing!" I said cheerfully. "Where do I go?"

He directed me to keep going the direction I was headed until I came to a main street. Then I'd go left and follow the noise.

"The noise?" I asked.

"Let's just say it's a big religious festival," he said.

"My lucky day!" I said. I realized I was being a little over-effusive, but it was so good to meet an English speaker.

"Well, I better get home," he said, shaking my hand. "Enjoy."

"Will do," I said. It wasn't until I reached the main street that I realized I'd missed a huge opportunity. I should have asked him to recommend a place for dinner. In fact, I'd liked the guy very much, and wished I'd invited his wife and him out for dinner—their choice of restaurant, my treat. But I'd missed that boat, sadly.

It was not a pretty town. It wasn't third-world dirty, it just wasn't built with aesthetics in mind. There were wires everywhere, and neon screamed at me from all directions. It was also raining, which didn't help the damp mood of the place. Would I have felt differently about it if the sun had been shining? Maybe, but not much.

I heard the music from blocks away. As I walked past stores boasting "best buns" and "meo meo hats" (a cute collection knit headgear with sheep-like ears sprouting floppily from the top) the music got progressively louder until it was almost overwhelming. Soon I saw it—blood red pillars reaching out onto the sidewalk.

Next to the pillars were several folding chairs containing elderly parishioners wearing bright yellow robes, chatting away excitedly. Literally hundreds of red paper pumpkin lanterns were suspended from the ceiling of the vestibule. To one side, an oven set into a wall blazed away, ready to carry prayers to the gods whenever someone tossed the paper they were written on into its fiery maw.

Stepping up to the sanctuary, I could see that a ritual was going on. Of course, I could hear it from blocks away, but now I was able to see what was actually happening. Three Taoist priests stood elbow to elbow facing the main altar. Between them and the main altar, however, were about a dozen tables, every one of them covered with candles set about eye-height on tall wooden stands.

It was a Fire Marshall's nightmare, but it certainly made for an impressive religious display. The main god seemed to be female. I'd find out later she was a local favorite, the patron goddess of mariners, Matsu. (Only now as I write this am I remembering that there is a marine shipping company called Matsu—another penny drops.)

The priests' robes were gorgeous, multi-colored affairs. The chief celebrant's vestment was bright yellow covered with a rainbow of embroidery, his assistants on either side were in either passion fruit or hot pink—take your pick. They all wore black birettas with gold topknots set into the crown. The principal celebrant was holding a microphone and chanting more or less on-key.

He was accompanied by a band that consisted of drums, cymbals, and an atonal reed instrument that seemed to be similar to an oboe—but sounding more like a crumhorn. It was played with enthusiastic vigor by someone who seemed to know how to blow but had absolutely no idea what notes to play. Holding the whole ensemble together was a Hammond organ player who looked like a sumo wrestler. He was completely rocking out, and his personal style, keyboard slides, and jazzy rhythms would have been more at home had he been accompanying a Vegas lounge lizard.

The sheer weirdness of the whole scene made it hard to tear myself away, and I did stand there in awed amazement for quite some time. But since there seemed to be no end in sight to the ritual, I eventually wandered on.

After a couple of blocks, the shopping district seemed to be drying up, but looking to the left I saw that the action had just shifted to another part of town. I passed a restaurant that looked promising—it had a wood-shingled façade, and the menu set up on a stand out front had many items listed in English. I had never heard of most of the dishes, but what the heck, I was brave. The restaurant wouldn't open for another hour, though, so I continued to follow the line of stores.

I came across another Taoist temple, but it was empty. It housed an entire pantheon of unfamiliar deities, but most interesting were a collection of ritual implements set on poles and displayed in racks on both sides of the sanctuary. The racks were identical to those that hold pool cues, and the poles were about the same size. Except, instead of cork cue tips at the ends of them there were hands making various gestures and an assortment of ancient-looking weapons. One hand looked like it was making the "hang ten" sign, another was holding a large ring, while one stick bore a dragon's head and another looked like a punching bag—all carved from wood and painted gold.

Walking back out to the shops, I noted that the stores had morphed into street stalls, and soon I'd walked into the midst of a full-scale street market. One stall sold fried squid—its sign ornamented by the cutest cartoon squid I'd ever seen—and another stall advertised "carrot fit jeans." I had no idea what those were, but I'd be willing to guess that I wouldn't fit into them.

It was starting to get dark, and the town felt more rough-

and-tumble than I was used to or comfortable with. I realized that it was a do-or-die moment as far as dinner was concerned. The restaurant I'd seen that looked like it might be good still wasn't open, so I started walking back toward my hotel, keeping a keen eye out for a decent place to eat.

About halfway back, I saw a sit-down restaurant that looked pretty upscale. Not "empty-your-wallet" expensive, but nice. I approached it and noted it served Korean cuisine. I know next to nothing about Korean cuisine, but it looked clean and inviting, so I went in.

To my delight, the menu was subtitled in a "kind-of-English" that was close enough to the real thing for me to figure out what was what. I felt a little gun-shy about meat, which I knew was irrational there, but I couldn't shake the fear. There was a dish called "spicy shredded rice cake" that sounded intriguing, so I ordered that and a Sprite.

As I waited, I watched the large flat-screen television showing Taiwanese kids doing pop songs in front of an audience. It didn't look like a contest, but more of a showcase. A lot of the lyrics were in English, but they were usually pretty badly mangled. It was entertaining on a wide variety of levels, and kept me engaged until my food arrived.

There was a bowl of white rice, and a bowl of the shredded rice cake. The rice cake was more like finger-thick noodles that were *extremely* chewy, stewing in a sauce that tasted like a very sweet, very spicy Chef Boyardee spaghetti sauce, with shreds of…was it chicken? I shrugged. So I didn't avoid the meat after all. I threw caution to the wind and ate it anyway.

The band at the Taoist temple was still going at it when I walked by on my way back to my hotel, but this time they were accompanying a choir of laywomen that was painfully dissonant. I'm sure it was my imagination, but there seemed to be a Doppler effect as I got farther away from them, the key of their song sagging further and further with every step.

When I got back to my hotel room, it was colder than ever. I went down to the desk and spoke to the gentleman who seemed to be in charge. I pulled up the iTranslator app, and said. "I'm freezing. Are there any rooms with heat?" No, there weren't. "Could I rent a space heater?" No, they didn't have space heaters. "What would it cost to upgrade to a room with a bathtub?" At least I could have a good soak and then warm the place by the heat radiating off of my scalded body. "I upgrade you now, no charge," the man said. I was speechless. I hadn't expected that at all. I moved my stuff right away and immediately drew a bath.

The short version: I got warm.

The next day I bounded down to breakfast, eager to get to Lukang. There was a huge spread of Chinese food, none of which seemed identifiable as breakfast fare, but of course I'm sure that's just my ignorance of Chinese culture. In the West we're used to sweet things for breakfast, but this seemed not to be the case in Asia generally.

I followed the map to the bus station, and a bus was just pulling out as I got there. I was twenty minutes early, but I waved him down anyway. "Lukang?" I asked. He nodded yes. I hopped on and hoped for the best.

As the bus snaked around its succession of stops, I remembered what Joe and I had seen at the Longshan Temple, with its proliferation of Bodhisattvas—thousands and thousands of them set into the walls, each illuminated by a Christmas light—and the central figure of Quan Yin, the Bodhisattva of compassion, nudging out the Buddha for the place of honor. It was such a mishmash of images, so chaotic, so disorganized, it seemed to me a fitting introduction to the Mahayana.

The Mahayana is not, after all, a coherent theological system. It is an academic umbrella term for all those Buddhist schools who have leaped beyond the staid, safe boundaries of Theravada conservatism into creatively unbounded metaphysical speculation and reliably wild mythologizing. The Mahayana schools don't agree with one another about much of anything beyond the Four Noble Truths and the Eightfold path, so it's impossible to generalize about them. Nevertheless, it was their creative approach that converted Asia, and is now making incredible gains in the West as well.

I wondered about what it is in the American psyche that might attract us to Mahayana teaching. I flashed back to the hullabaloo a few years ago when *The DaVinci Code* hit. Suddenly, people who thought Christianity was a bucket of yawns were jumping-up-and-down excited about "secret teachings" and Gnosticism.

It was a rich time for people in my field, and I enjoyed a bit of a boom in speaking engagements as I was asked to lecture numerous times on Gnostic Christianity. I really enjoyed that period, not because I think that Gnostic Christianity is superior to orthodox teaching, but because your average person on the street was actually excited by religious ideas and was asking questions. It was a rich time for dialogue, and a great teaching moment.

Alas, it passed, and I was a bit sad to see it go. I understand why people got excited. The idea that the mainstream somehow got it all wrong—or worse, that they suppressed Jesus' original message and replaced it with a controlling, politically driven dogma—is certainly enticing.

The Gnostics claimed that in addition to the "accepted" scriptures, Jesus had passed on an oral tradition too, secret teachings that he told only to those who were ready for them. These teachings eventually got written down in the Gnostic gospels.

According to one prominent school of Gnostic Christians (the Valentinians), the savior taught that we suffer because we're trapped in an illusion of dualism—that in fact, divinity is at the heart of all things, and it is possible for us to receive *gnosis*, experiential knowledge of the oneness of all things, an awakening to our true spiritual nature that would set us free from endless cycles of transmigration. Jesus only seemed to be human, but in fact was a spirit being sent to earth to bring us this saving knowledge. The goddess Sophia was also important in its mythology.

There are a lot of parallels between Gnostic Christianity and Mahayana Buddhism. The Mahayana say that in addition to the "accepted" scriptures cherished by the older schools of Buddhism, the Buddha had handed down secret teachings to those in his inner circle, which had been passed by word of mouth from master to student ever since the Buddha died. These teachings eventually got written down in the Mahayana sutras.

According to these sutras, the suffering that we experience is due not just to our propensity to craving, but because of a deeper, underlying condition—the illusion of duality. In fact not only can all people become Buddhas, but all things possess Buddha Nature—the divine Oneness at the heart of all things. Awakening to this oneness is what liberates one from the cycle of samsara. The Buddha, far from being an extraordinary but normal human being, was the manifestation of a divine principle who only seemed to be human, and he is joined by other Bodhisattvas, some of which are feminine in aspect, such as Quan Yin.

Just as the Gnostics were anti-authoritarian, rebelling against the dogma of the Pauline bishops, the Mahayana, too, were rebelling against the rigidity of the older Buddhist schools (of which the Theravada are the only surviving representatives). Both arose as philosophical movements within the earlier structures, and only later set up parallel communities and lines of authority when driven out of the more "orthodox" communities. But while Gnostic Christianity had been actively and successfully suppressed, Mahayana Buddhism flourished by going East.

At heart, Theravada Buddhism is a method for minimizing anguish in human life. It downplays metaphysical speculation, is agnostic toward divinity, and stays focused on the basics. By contrast, Mahayana is a Gnostic Buddhism, spinning out a gloriously complex mythology that divinizes everything, and is stuffed to the gills with oodles of glorious theological speculation.

Given the American penchant for the underdog, for anyone who challenges authority, and the mystical proclivities of the Baby Boomer generation, it's not hard to see why Mahayana Buddhism—with its secret teachings, anti-clericalism, and an emphasis on unitive consciousness—has captured the imagination of the West.

I rode for about thirty minutes before the driver called to me. "Lukang," he said. I thanked him and asked. "Where do I go for the bus back?" I'm not sure how much he understood, but he pointed to a bus stop across the street. He wrote down "16:00." I nodded and thanked him profusely.

My first stop was at the primary temple in the town, once again devoted to the sailor's favorite goddess, Matsu. The sky was threatening rain, but the courtyard of the temple was still buzzing with activity. There was a carnival atmosphere in the air as street vendors spread out as far as the eye could see in all directions. I wondered if it was like this every day.

I headed into the temple, and breathed deeply of the incense—there were literally hundreds of sticks burning in two great cauldrons near the entrance to the main sanctuary. I waved some of the smoke over me and smiled, enjoying the sensation. I stepped up into the main shrine and stood respectfully as people bowed before Matsu and made their supplications.

The statue they bowed to was made of wood and blackened

with age, depicting a heavy-set Chinese woman with a serene smile. She wore a headdress from which black beads hung down in front of her face, adorning but not obscuring her beauty. I recognized her as Matsu, and wondered at the proliferation of black goddesses in the world: the black Madonnas of Montserrat and Czestochowa, the Hindu goddess Kali, the Yoruba goddess Oshun, as well as the dark Taras of Tibetan Buddhism. What is it about these dark, mysterious deities that have enthralled people around the world, even in places where dark skin is not the norm? The devotion to her seemed particularly fierce here, as scores of worshippers prayed before her earnestly. It reminded me of the fervent devotion I've seen in many Christians toward the Virgin Mary.

I walked past the main shrine through a door in the back, and discovered yet another courtyard. Set into the middle was a large fountain where entwined dragons shot streams of water into the air from their mouths. The base of the fountain was actually a water garden, where about a dozen turtles larger than my hand were perched lazily on rocks. I wasn't sure they were real at first—I thought perhaps they were the testudinal equivalent of the stuffed monks I'd seen in Thailand, but no, one of them puffed his red throat and blinked his eyes.

The rear shrine was two stories high, housing what must have been the lion's share of Taoist deities, each in his or her own glass case, with explanatory text—in Chinese, of course. A side altar housed the shrine of Wen Chang, the patron god of scholars where (my tourist map informs me) students come to pray before their college entrance exams—and, I'm sure, after them as well.

Walking back toward the main sanctuary, I passed a room that seemed stuffed with bright red bags. Stepping in, I saw that they were actually baskets with identical red bags in them—each one an offering from a different family. There were thousands of them, filling two rooms, stacked neatly on shelves that reached from floor to ceiling. The rooms were lit with red bulbs and were presided over by fierce warrior gods, all of which gave the place an eerie, alien, slightly threatening vibe.

Just before leaving, I passed the statue of a long-bearded, avuncular-looking fellow. My tourist brochure identified him as Yue Lao, the god of marriage. On his altar were baskets and baskets full of candy. My heart ached when I saw it, because I instantly knew what it represented: that marriage is sweet. I have tasted that sweetness, and can attest to its goodness. I gave a respectful bow, but didn't take any candy—I'll leave that for someone who needs convincing.

Heading for the main Buddhist temple in town, I walked through the Old Town. And a very old town it was, going back over a thousand years. Some of the streets had been there that long, and like medieval streets you see everywhere, they were often so narrow that I could touch the ancient houses on either side with my arms outstretched.

Some of these shops had likewise been here for hundreds and hundreds of years, and some of the doors and archways were original. Plaques written in both Chinese and English gave short histories of some of the more notable landmarks. The passageways had become a tourist hotspot, and although they weren't crowded, the ancient shops boasted trendy boutique items like artisanal rice cookies, local handicrafts, artists' galleries, and of course kitschy candy stores. Stuffed manga beings were ubiquitous.

It was a delightful blending of old and new—displaying an obvious pride in the city's heritage, and a heartfelt attempt at civic rejuvenation. I was disappointed when I exhausted the ancient streets, and consoled myself that I'd pass through them again on the way back. There was so much variety that I was sure I would see new things when I did.

The road ended not far from the Longshan Temple, the entrance to which was ornamented with a string of red pumpkin lanterns and a line of six bonsai trees. The temple was ancient, but unlike most temples I'd seen, it looked it. Most temples had been restored, but not this one. Its weathered wood and fading paints positively radiated age and venerability.

I stepped through the main door, and found myself on stage—a Chinese opera stage, to be exact, looking down over a vast courtyard guarded by two enormous Bodhi trees (*ficus religiosa*, no kidding). Looking up, the domed ceiling of the stage was weathered and cracked into millions of multicolored chips, each of which seemed to be clinging to the dome tenuously.

I crossed the courtyard and stepped up onto the porch of the main sanctuary, which was supported by two stone pillars carved into dragons chasing one another in circles all the way to the ceiling. Inside, on the main altar, was the Bodhisattva Avalokitesvara, seated in the lotus position, with a smaller statue of Buddha sitting in her lap.

It reminded me of so many statues of the Madonna and child I'd seen throughout Europe, and again I was stunned by the proliferation of common themes, regardless of the actual deities or theologies involved. People were people, and they needed what they needed, no matter where you found them.

But I also wondered at the mutability of traditions. Theravada Buddhism had no capacity to stretch far enough to embrace mother goddesses, but Mahayana Buddhism certainly had. The plasticity of Mahayana theology intrigued me, because it seemed to embrace new teachings, new worlds, new buddhas with a gleeful willy-nilly abandon. I'm sure that's simply a trick of perspective, but it certainly does seem that way from here.

The Theravada insisted that all things are aggregates of the five basic *skandas* (the physical elements, emotion, consciousness, perception, and mental processes). In their teaching, these are kind of like the building blocks of reality. But the Mahayana insist that even the skandas break down until, when you finally dismantle everything, you discover that there is nothing there. (Eerily, contemporary physics agrees with this.) But the Mahayana go even further—not even the Dharma, the truth taught by the Buddha, is permanent. It, too, is a temporary, conditioned construction with no enduring reality.

The Mahayana tell a story about the Buddha that illustrates this very well. He said, "When you use a raft to get from one side of the river to the other, what do you do with the raft once you have arrived? Do you put it on your head and carry it around? No, you discard it. It is the same with my teaching."[1] The Dharma is communicated in order to do a job. It points to the Truth, but it is not itself the Truth.

So while the Mahayana love to debate theology, they hold it lightly, because they know it is not the Truth. They can joke about it, they can consider other possibilities without fear, they can stretch it and not break their faith.

I admire such theological plasticity. I've long felt that *relationship* was far more important than *doctrine*. After all, faithful Christians throughout the ages have believed wildly different things. Who am I to pronounce judgment on them? Better to learn from their sincere and pious examples. Plus, they are often right about many things, where the so-called "orthodox" were wrong.

Also, I myself am no bastion of orthodoxy. If salvation comes as a result of "believing the right things" then I have no hope. If salvation comes as a result of loving and trusting Jesus, then I'm fine, and so are the vast majority of heretics throughout the history of the church.

I'm fascinated by the approach of one remarkable Mahayana theologian, Nagarjuna. He taught at Nilanda back in the day, and he pioneered the subject of Buddhist logic. I once took a semester-long course in the Catuskoti, a series of four propositions that governed Nagarjuna's approach. He taught that four things were simultaneously true:

- all things exist
- no things exist
- all things both exist and do not exist
- all things neither exist nor don't exist

Of course, these are contradictory statements, but they cover a lot of ground. Armed with these four statements, Nagarjuna shot down every doctrinal proposition launched at him. Essentially he was saying that there might be Truth out there, but we'll never know it, and we'll never figure it out, we'll never be able to describe it, and any attempts to do so are not the Truth.

The other day I got an email from Fr. Richard, who said something that really touched me. He said, "Seeking explanations is an excellent way of avoiding experience." I think Nagarjuna would have agreed. So would the Gnostics. And I agree that experience is far superior to theories. You can argue with explanations, but no one can argue with your own experience.

The upshot of all this for Mahayana Buddhists is that they can spin fantastical theologies until the beer runs out, but none of it should be confused with the Truth. The Buddha said that one of the reasons we suffer is because we grasp onto things and we don't want to let them go. Nagarjuna was convinced that one of the things we grasp onto is doctrine. That, too, he said, must be let go of if we are to make any progress at all— *because none of your dogmas are the Truth.* They might point toward the Truth, but they are not the Truth, and people obstinately confuse the two. Better to just let any notions of doctrine go completely.

This reminds me of Meister Eckhart, who said, "God is a being beyond being and a nothingness beyond being. The most beautiful thing that a person can say about God would be for that person to remain silent from the wisdom of an inner wealth. So, be silent and quit flapping your gums about God!"[2]

This is precisely why the goal of inter-religious dialogue can't be about figuring out who's right. Because we can never know. And besides, we're all, to some degree or another, wrong. Truth is not knowable. It is not describable. If you try to boil your experience of the Divine down into a doctrine, at worst your doctrinal statement can only be a fiction (and therefore an idol), and at best it can only point in a good direction.

Nagarjuna also reminds me of Luther (because everything reminds me of Luther—just like everything reminds me of my dog, cue Jane Siberry), and his insistence that we let go of any claim to our own righteousness. In his system, we are saved by the grace of Christ alone, and not at all by our own efforts. Nagarjuna was saying, "You cannot rely on your own under-standing" while Luther was saying, "You cannot rely on your own virtue." Both were advocating a complete letting go, an abandonment of self-effort, a relinquishing of control. Only then can real trust begin.

Just then I got a glimmer of what God's absence has meant for me. Going on this trip, I have left everything familiar, every-thing safe, everything certain in order to throw myself utterly into the unknown. I have tried to cling to my old standards of cleanliness, of privilege, of comfort, and all of these have had to go. I have tried to cling to God as I have known him, but he said, "I'm outta here" as soon as I hit Varanasi, and except for brief glimmers of intimacy, I have had to let him go, too. It has been a painful but transformative process of abandoning the familiar and the known to an alien, unknown Mystery.

Instead, the Divine is this bowl of rice. The Divine is not this bowl of rice. The Divine is and is not this bowl of rice. The Divine is neither this bowl of rice nor isn't this bowl of rice. This is a Schrödinger's Cat approach to theology. The divine is in a state of superimposition (here and not here, this and not this, real and not real, mine and not mine) and always will be until I break through the veil of duality.

Walking behind the main sanctuary, I saw another court-yard, small and green. In its center was a pond full of koi. As I watched, a woman knelt and "called" them by clapping her hands. Sure enough, a whole mob of them bobbed to the surface, like dogs begging for attention. After she walked away, I tried the trick myself, and giggled as they leaped up at me. What did they want? For that matter, what did I want from them? I suppose just the joy of watching a being move.

I rose up on my increasingly creaky knees and said goodbye to the temple. I passed by numerous bakeries, some of them Western in style, and all of them smelling delicious. Being allergic to wheat, I didn't dare try them. But I sure got a noseful.

Out of the corner of my eye I caught a flash of red, and saw that it was another temple, a small one—too small to be on my map. Of course, I had to check it out. As I approached the threshold, I saw that it was a Matsu temple. The goddess image was large for such a small temple, and adorned with what looked like brass. Just that morning I had read an article in the newspaper about priests in one of the Taoist temples being brought up on animal cruelty charges for stuffing a live bird into a cavity carved into one of the gods. It was a sacrifice intended to "energize" or "charge" the god for the coming year. It had been done at the same festival for the past 500 years, the priest had explained. No one had ever raised a ruckus before. He admitted that times were changing and the temple leadership was willing to accede to public opinion.

In India, the most famous and, according to tradition, efficacious sacrifice was the horse sacrifice, in which 2500 of the noble beasts lost their lives each time it was performed. The last time it was performed, for the benefit of the BBC, 2500 gourds were sacrificed instead. I wondered if next year they'll stuff a mango into the god. I wondered if there were a suffocated bird in the body of the Matsu I was looking at now.

I paused when I saw a woman on her knees. She was praying earnestly, and then she flung something on the ground—two red half moons clattered away from her, and she studied them intently.

When I looked this up later, I discovered that it was a form of Taoist divination called *Jiaobei,* in which a worshipper asks the deity a question in prayer, then throws the blocks. The resulting combinations of the blocks after they are thrown indicate the deity's answer: one flat, one round is a "yes"; both blocks round is a "no"; both blocks flat means the god is laughing at your question; and if either of the blocks lands in a leaning position it means that the question is obscure and should be rephrased. They are usually thrown three times to make sure the answer is right.

It struck me that the Jiaobei blocks were embodied expressions of Nagarjuna's propositions. That made me smile. The woman bowed low, and withdrew. I took a few pictures and was about to go when a docent approached me. "Where are you from?" she asked. She was about thirty, wearing an informal slim black dress. Her hair was gathered in the back.

"America," I said, smiling. "San Francisco."

"Oh, I love San Francisco!" she said, a little too excited.

"Have you been there?" I asked.

She scrunched her nose up. "No," she said.

I laughed. So did she. "What can you tell me about this temple?" I asked.

"It is the oldest temple in Lukang," she said proudly. My eyebrows jumped, and I took it in anew. The ancient beams were so old they were almost black. I could well believe her.

"This is a Matsu temple, yes?"

"Oh, yes," she said, with an earnest giggle. "We love Matsu."

"She protects sailors, right?"

She moved her head back and forth, as if equivocating. "Yeees..." she finally said, not sounding too sure. I was about to ask her if they stuffed birds into her, but the young woman spoke first. "...But she is much more than that to us."

Instantly I forgot all about the birds. *This* is the kind of stuff I love. When I go to church, I want to hear a testimony. I want the same thing in other houses of worship, too. "Please tell me about her—and tell me why you love her," I entreated.

Her friendly demeanor softened into something like wonder as she turned to face the statue. "She is our mother. She is the mother of all the people. She comforts us when we are sad or worried. She cares for everyone, so we come here when we need..." she patted at her heart and nodded.

I got it. Once again the parallels to Marian devotion struck me. I have known so many Christians who feel alienated from God the Father because of the harsh way he's been depicted in Christian teaching, but who love Mary with all their heart and pray to her regularly. I even know a few Protestants who fall into this category.

"What is your name?" she asked.

I told her and shook her hand. "And yours?"

"I am Yian Hua. I live in Taipei, but I come here on weekends to serve Matsu."

"Are you building merit?" I asked her.

She looked confused. Then she seemed to understand the word. "Oh, no. I just here because I love her. I know what 'merit' mean. Not Matsu. Buddha."

It was true that merit is a huge part of Buddhism, one that I haven't really written about yet, but it has certainly cropped up regularly in my reading. Basically, the idea is that if you perform good deeds and religious rituals you will win a more favorable place in the next life. I had been wondering if merit was a part of Taoism or the indigenous faith. Apparently not.

"Taoism not about merit. Taoism is about this life. Buddhism is about...er...." she hesitated.

"Taoism is about this life, but Buddhism is about the next life?" I finished the sentence for her.

"Uh...yes," she looked a little embarrassed. It was a bold statement, an oversimplification, and she knew it.

I raised my hand to comfort her. "It's okay, I understand what you are trying to say. I teach religion in America, including Buddhism. It's complex."

"Yes," she ducked her head a bit.

It might have been an oversimplification, but she had told me something useful. Just then a couple of other women came up to her—apparently they'd been shopping nearby. They talked excitedly in Mandarin, and Yian Hua introduced me. I didn't catch the other two women's names, but they instantly shoved pastries at me. I declined, explaining that I was allergic to wheat. "I don't know what I can eat and what I can't," I complained with a shrug.

Yian Hua asked me for my notebook, and wrote a couple of lines in neat Chinese characters. I asked her what it said. She said, "Just show this when you want to buy food. It says, 'Wheat makes me sick. Do you have anything that is made with rice?'"

"That's perfect!" I said. "Thank you so much!"

"You can eat this," she said, snatching a bag from one of the other women's purses. The other women seemed pleased, so I rolled with it. The bag contained bright pink and white lumpy things. Like large, rough Good & Plenties that have been treated with that plaster popcorn they spray on ceilings to make them bumpy.

I tasted one. "Candy coated peanuts!" I said. She couldn't know that my favorite candy is Boston Baked Beans—essentially candy-coated peanuts. "Thank you so much, Yian Hua!" I exclaimed. I was beginning to understand what Joe had meant when he said that the Taiwanese have a "grandmoth-erly" nature.

I felt ready to move on, so I thanked all three women pro-fusely, truly grateful for their kindness and help. Soon, the nar-row ancient street dumped me out onto a much wider modern one, and I went into the first bakery I saw. I showed the man behind the counter the sentences Yian Hua had written for me, and he pointed to a plastic box with about a dozen diamond-shaped cookies in them. They were all white, except for a cus-tard middle. "Rice?" I asked. He nodded. I bought them. They were delicious.

I stopped at the next bakery, too, and showed the sentences to the giggly teenage girls behind the counter. They acted like it was a great game, and ran around the store looking at all the ingredient lists. Finally, they presented me with a bag filled with what looked like doughnut holes, with a light brown dusting. "What the heck," I said and bought them. The dusting was a mixture of sugar and ground peanuts. Inside, they were light and fluffy. They were delicious.

I stopped at a couple more bakeries before I realized that I was collecting *way* more food than I could travel with.

As I got on the bus, I sank into the seat with a great, tired, happy, satisfied sigh. My feet hurt, but it was a *good* hurt. My tummy was full, and a little *too* full of sweet things. My mind was full, too, as I continued to ruminate on the revelations I'd been graced with that day—especially the invitation to let go of explanations and simply enter into the experience. There is something distinctly patriarchal about the drive to nail every-thing down, to figure everything out, to explain it all away—so the invitation struck me as a bit of motherly advice, if not grandmotherly.

That thought reminded me of all the goddesses I had en-countered that day: Quan Yin, Sophia, Kali, Mary, Oshun, Tara, Matsu, and the three angels at the temple, especially Yian

Hua. I had never felt particularly drawn to goddesses before, but they certainly seemed to be finding me lately.

Just then I realized that the bus driver had plastered the same photo of Quan Yin across the top of the bus' windshield, fifteen images across and two deep—an iteration that would have made Warhol proud. She seemed to be smiling right at me.

----

1   Paraphrased from *Majjhima Nikaya* i. 134-135.

2   Matthew Fox, *Meditations with Meister Eckhart* (Santa Fe, NM: Bear & Co., 1983), 44.

Lapis lazuli Avalokitesvara at Fo Guan Shan.

Chapter Fifteen: Fo Guan Shan—Buddhaland

My next stop was the southernmost tip of Taiwan, a monastery called Fo Guan Shan, which means "Light of Buddha Mountain," near the city of Kaohsiung. The Lonely Planet gave it a full page, and described it as a "must-see." Who was I to argue?

As I was planning this stage of the journey, I received an email from one of my supporters, who suggested that if I stayed in a monastery instead of a hotel, I might have a more meaningful experience.

He must have been reading my mind, as I'd already written the guest master at Fo Guan Shan and asked if they had room. They did. Then I asked if it would be possible to have an English speaking spiritual director while I was there. It was.

Of course, had I been in India, I would have said, "No way" as even the best hotels there are barely livable—I can only imagine the conditions of the monasteries. But in Taiwan? I was willing to give it a try. I could put up with spartan conditions and watered-down gruel for two days, right?

The bus out to the monastery site was a little late, and the monk assigned to me called several times to ask, "Where are you now?" I was a little annoyed at this, because first of all I have no control over how fast the bus goes, and second the street signs are mostly gibberish to me, so I had no idea where I was. Finally, I just ignored the phone.

Eventually, though, we rolled by the gates of the monastery, and looking out the window I saw a bald nun in dark tan robes waving at me. My monk was a nun! When I alighted from the bus, she walked up to me with a slightly smug smile on her face. "I think you did not know I was a nun."

"True," I said. I saw that her name was Liu Yang on her

email, but that gave me no indication of her gender. She looked like she enjoyed her little surprise, though, and led me back to a golf cart where a middle-aged man in a polo shirt was waiting for us.

The golf cart stopped outside an ornately decorated pagoda, painted red, black, and gold. "This is Pilgrim's Lodge," she said. "I will show you room." She led me to an elevator and we ascended two floors. The hallway looked like any nice-ish hotel hallway. She handed me my key and I opened the door. The room was small, but seemed clean. There was a twin-sized bed, a nightstand, a desk and a wardrobe, though little room to navigate. I was surprised to see it also had a private bath and shower.

"Okay?" Liu Yang asked.

"More than okay," I said, nodding my approval. "It's much nicer than I expected."

"You don't know about Fo Guan Shan," she said. It was a statement, not a question, but I answered as if it were.

"Only what I've read in the Lonely Planet."

She smiled a mysterious smile that I would get to know well over the next couple of days. "Do you need time to rest?" she asked.

"Heck, no," I said. "I've only got two days here. I want to see all I can."

Her smile broadened. "Then let us go and see."

We stepped out of the Pilgrim's Lodge, and she led me up a long flight of stairs. The clouds were threatening rain, but none was falling. It was sweater weather, but not cold. At the top of the stairs, I gasped.

"This is the main sanctuary," she said. "The Hall of Buddhas."

It was a double-tiered pagoda that stretched an entire city block, lit by red pumpkin lanterns and Christmas lights. A walkway over twenty feet wide stretched the length of a football field from where we stood to the steps of the sanctuary. We traversed it solemnly, and as we started up the steps she whispered, "No camera."

Too bad. As we stepped into the main hall I was overwhelmed by its splendor. The walls on every side were covered with hundreds of thousands of inch-high gold Buddha statues, each one individually lit with a yellow Christmas light. Likewise, four wide, tall pillars supported the ornate ceiling, and every one of them was covered with tiny Buddha statues as well. The hall radiated a serene golden light. A main altar ran most of the length of the building, and on it sat three identical Buddha statues, each one about twenty-five feet tall. They were made of gold as well, and were shimmering in the reflected light from every conceivable direction.

But as I looked closer, I discovered that the Buddha statues were not, in fact, identical. The faces were the same, and the same serene half-smile beamed down at us from each one. Each was seated in a meditative pose. But the Buddhas' hands were different.

I looked at Liu Yang, and she leaned in and whispered, "Not same Buddha." I wasn't sure if she meant they represented different people or just different poses. I must have looked confused, because she explained patiently, "Middle Buddha Shakyamuni Buddha. You know Shakyamuni Buddha?"

"Of course," I said. He was the historical Buddha, the prince Gautama, whose footsteps I had been following. The right hand of the middle statue was turned downward in the "subduing Mara" mudra.

"That Buddha," she said, pointing to the statue on the right, "Medicine Buddha. He hold pearl of great wisdom." She was right, this Buddha was holding what looked like a racquetball. I guess it *could* be a pearl.

"And this Buddha," she pointed at the Buddha on the left,

"Amitabha Buddha. He hold lotus." This Buddha was indeed holding a lotus flower.

"Tell me about the Medicine Buddha and Amitabha Buddha," I said.

"They Buddhas of other places. Not here. Rule Buddha fields, Buddha lands...." she fished for a word.

"They are the Buddhas in other universes?" I suggested.

She nodded, smiling. "You know about Amitabha?"

"I know a little bit. I want to know more."

"Amitabha Buddha in Pure Land, ruler of Pure Land. If you chant name of Amitabha Buddha, you go to Pure Land when you die."

"And the Medicine Buddha?"

"He rule other land. Shall we go on?" She didn't have much to say about the Medicine Buddha, and I got the impression that he was sort of a third wheel in their theology. We walked out of the magnificent sanctuary and back down the long walkway.

"I think I've seen one of your sanctuaries before," I said. "Do you have a temple in southern California?"

She looked surprised and pleased. "Yes, Hacienda Heights."

I nodded, "That's the one." It was the first Chinese Buddhist sanctuary that I'd ever seen, and it was a bit like eating dessert before dinner. I'd gotten it into my head that all Chinese Buddhists temples would be similarly grand, and had been surprised thus far in my Taiwanese travels that they haven't been. I mean, they've been very cool indeed, but they haven't been impressive on the scale that the Hacienda Heights temple had been—not until this one.

"We have temple in Oakland, too," she said, nodding. "I send you link."

"Okay!" I said. We kept going down stairs, past the Pilgrim's Lodge, past a garden filled with 500 white statues of early Buddhist saints. We passed through a large archway, and

Liu Yang pointed up at it. Two Chinese characters were carved prominently into the stone. "What does it say?" I asked.

"It say, 'non-duality,'" she said.

"What does non-duality mean in Pure Land teaching?" I asked.

"It mean that hot and cold one thing. Good and evil one thing. In conventional reality, we see them different things. But in supramundane reality, they not different. Everything one thing." She smiled a little smile. "I tell you story. Sariputta— you know Sariputta?"

"One of the Buddha's first disciples," I said.

"Yes. Sariputta said to Buddha, 'I cannot live, there so much war. It too hard.' Buddha said, 'I do not see war." Sariputta say, 'How can you not see war, it everywhere!' Buddha opened his eyes and Sariputta saw world as Buddha sees world, peaceful, no division, no distinction. No 'our people,' no enemy. Vision last only a little while. Sariputta bow before Buddha, say, 'I understand now.'"

"Samsara is Nirvana and Nirvana is Samsara," I said.

She closed her eyes for a moment, as if cherishing my comment. "This how it really is."

She pointed at a building near the road. "That bookstore have many English books. You browse later."

"Okay," I said, and made a mental note to do just that.

"Come," she said, and led me to a cave built into the concrete. It was, of course, a fake cave, its rough edges applied with plaster and shellacked many years ago. Inside the cave was way bigger than I'd expected. A giant gold statue of the Buddha loomed a story high on my left, his arms outstretched. In front of him were painted statues of people from all over the world, in modern dress. "Buddha embrace everyone. *Everyone*," she said.

To my right there was an identical Buddha statue, but instead of people gathered between his outstretched hands there were animals of every kind. "Buddha have compassion on all beings," Liu Yang said.

We stepped up to an ornately painted door. Above it gold Chinese script stood out in lovely contrast to a cobalt blue field. "That *Amitabha Sutra*. It very short," she said. "I know by heart."

"I'd like to read that," I said.

"I get you copy," she said.

Through the door was an enormous room with hundreds of painted statues of the Buddha's early followers. Signs gave the history of many of the main ones. Liu Yang paused before one who seemed to be stretching back an opening in his chest cavity with his bare hands, revealing a small seated Buddha within. It looked painful.

Liu Yang gave a little bow. "Buddha in your heart," she explained.

We walked past all of the disciples to an altar at the far side of the room where a twice-human sized painted statue of the Buddha was seated. He was flanked by two female disciples. "Which Buddha is that?" I asked.

"That Amitabha Buddha," she said. "He has hand up in teaching gesture. Only Amitabha shown like that."

"Okay," that iconographic information would certainly help me keep score over the next couple of days.

She handed me a red slip of paper and a pen. "You write wish now," she smiled. "Write wish for Lisa."

"Wait, how do you know about Lisa?" I asked.

"I read blog," she said.

"You certainly do your homework," I said, cocking an eyebrow.

"Wish her long life and health," she said.

"Okay," I said and wrote that down. Liu Yang pulled a camera out of a pocket in her habit and snapped a picture of me as I wrote.

"Write in English," she said.

Like I have a choice, I thought. I folded the paper and she snatched it up and put it in a stack with thousands of other requests.

"Come," she said, and I followed her into a narrower part of the cave, this one with great plaster stalactites hanging from the ceiling. As we wound through it, I ignored the musty smell from the industrial berber carpeting and the roar of the dehumidifiers plugged in at regular intervals, and focused on the murals on the walls outlining stories from Gautama Buddha's life, along with the stages of spiritual awakening in Pure Land thought.

The winding cavern ended, eventually, emptying out into another mammoth cave, where a two-story tall red pagoda shown in the floodlights. Amitabha Buddha stood at its top, his hand raised in the teaching gesture, and once again he was flanked by two female Bodhisattvas. On both sides of the pagodas animatronic figures of little girls played musical instruments, danced, and waved flags. I expected "It's a Small World After All" to start playing, but the music was entirely Chinese.

Across a river were several open lotuses that were designed to be used as flagstones, so we could cross over. Each lotus was of a different color. The effect was something like a cross between Tim Burton's depiction of Wonderland and a miniature golf course that had seen better days.

"This represent Pure Land," Liu Yang said, with a grand sweeping gesture of her hand. "Pure Land is Amitabha Buddha's country. You chant Amitabha Buddha's name, you come here when you die." She gestured toward the lotuses. "In Pure Land, everyone has lotus. If you practice, lotus blossoms; if you lazy, lotus withers." I followed her as we began to climb up a rainbow bridge spanned across the river. "There are three hundred Buddha worlds," she explained, as we stood midspan, surveying the surreal landscape. "In Pure Land, you can travel to three hundred worlds and return; you are free to come and go. You understand?"

I nodded. She looked pleased. She pointed to another animatronic tableau, where a giant lotus flower was unpeeling its petals (actually, they kind of snapped open with a crunching sound) to reveal a naked man in the fetal position. "No one born from mother in Pure Land," she said. "Born from Lotus."

"Uh-huh," I said. It was all I could say. Below the lotus, animatronic parrots swooped in circles. "What are those?"

"They Dharma-speaking birds," she said. "They not reincarnated people, they live in Pure Land. They speak Dharma at all time."

We crossed over the rainbow bridge, past several shining gold Bodhisattvas, and saw a blinding light—not a Buddha, sadly, but just the end of the cave and the sunlight from outside. The cave emptied out into a gift shop where one could buy a wide variety of CDs, Buddha statues, malas, cute figurines of baby monks, and t-shirts.

I followed Liu Yang outside, and noted that these gift shops were on nearly every corner, along with numerous food stands—but not homemade street food, these were name brand stands, like you'd see at any amusement park. Liu Yang waved for me to follow and we climbed a long, winding path up a large hill. The hill was covered with ivy and bougainvilleas. Red paper pumpkin lanterns were hung at regular intervals, and everything was meticulously gardened. It was thrillingly beautiful.

I was panting when we reached the top, but it looked like Liu Yang was in better shape. She gestured up. "Standing Buddha," she said. Sure enough, a gigantic Buddha surveyed the countryside, a good six stories tall. It was magnificent.

"I take picture of you with Buddha," Liu Yang said, and gestured for me to move a little to my left. I did, and the camera disappeared back into her habit. Before descending the hill, she took me to a shrine dedicated to the Buddhas of the ten directions, each of them wearing a robe of a different color. She seemed to take special delight in the hall of mirrors, where you could see Buddhas stretching off into infinity—which was not only cool-looking, but theologically relevant. Finally, she paused before a fierce statue of a Bodhisattva. "His name Ksi-igarbha," she said. "He vow to keep everyone out of hell."

"How does he do that?" I asked.

Her brows bunched together, and she seemed momentarily flummoxed by the question. "He teach Dharma. You teach Dharma, you keep people out of hell."

I told her a Christian legend about how Jesus, after his crucifixion, descended into hell. I recounted how he broke down all the walls, smashed the chains, wrenched open the prison doors and set everyone free. Then he led anyone who wanted to go to heaven.

"Jesus is bodhisattva," she said smiling. I smiled back.

As we walked back down the hill, I asked, "Liu Yang, what do you have to do to be born in the Pure Land? Just chant?"

She thought for a moment and then said, "Need three things: faith, vow, and practice."

"Can you say more about those?"

"You must have faith in Amitabha Buddha and Shakyamuni Buddha," she said, as if speaking to a child. "You must vow—"

"What kind of vow?" I interrupted.

"You must desire to go to Pure Land. Never give up. Then you must practice, you must chant at cri-, cri-...." she seemed to be having trouble pronouncing a word, making several false starts.

"Critical?" I suggested.

"Yes," she closed her eyes, as if momentarily embarrassed. "Chant at critical moments. Don't wait until last minute. You practice to live in Pure Land now!"

"Why is the Pure Land important?" I asked. "In other forms of Buddhism, you just become enlightened."

"Enlightenment is hard," she explained. "Here on earth, we have many distractions, much bad karma. It hard struggle. But in Pure Land, practice is easy, make very fast progress. Get enlightened very quick, not difficult. It okay if you not good at practice. Just chant Amitabha's name, get to Pure Land, everything be fine then."

"So the Pure Land isn't like heaven?"

"No. It very very nice, though. You like it there, I know."

"But it's temporary?" I asked.

"All things temporary. All things dependent. All things empty."

"Even the Pure Land?"

"Yes," she said. "But it very very nice. You see."

We reached the bottom of the hill, and she looked at her cell phone. "Come with me," she said, as if I hadn't been shadowing her all afternoon.

"Liu Yang, is Amitabha Buddha a metaphor? Or is he real?"

She stopped in her tracks. She smiled. "Hard to answer." Then she started walking again.

I understand what she means. I'm not sure how I'd answer that question about Jesus, either. Is he just a face of God or is he a real person? Is he the same person who walked around in Nazareth, or is he just one of many ways that the Divine Mystery connects to people? Is he just a comfortable guise that makes it easier for us to cozy up to a superessential darkness? It struck me that if the Divine Mystery were a computer, Jesus and the Buddha would be user interfaces. I kind of liked that idea.

Liu Yang stopped at a door. "My office," she explained. "Package for you."

I smiled. It was Valentine's Day, and I had suspected that Lisa might try to send something when she asked me the address of the monastery several days ago. Sure enough, there was an FTD box inside with my name on it. Opening it, I pulled out a small bouquet of roses. A card was included as well, saying, "Happy Valentine's Day, Cutie-Pie." My heart swelled. I missed Lisa terribly in that moment. I really wished she were with me to explore this weird and fascinating place.

"You want eat?" Liu Yang asked.

I looked at my watch. It was about 4:30—a good time to eat, in my book. "Sure." I was dreading mealtime here, but I needn't have. In addition to the Pilgrim's Hall, there were numerous restaurants. Liu Yang took a shortcut through another garden, and descended some stairs to a restaurant with a breathtaking view of the river. "My treat," she said, handing me a menu.

I couldn't believe how attentive she was being, and wasn't sure I entirely liked it. She was sticking to me like glue, and seemed to be riding the line between great hospitality and intrusive baby-sitter. But the lunch was delightful, partly because I was introduced to foods I wouldn't normally order, and instructed in how to eat them!

After lunch, Liu Yang led me through another archway, this one emptying out onto a street from which you could see a vast river. In a couple of moments we were walking through a park that was rapidly filling with people. "You come on lucky day," Liu Yang said, walking serenely with her hands behind her back. "This first full moon after New Year's. Big festivals. You like fireworks?"

"Who doesn't like fireworks!" I said. "I really did come on a good day!"

She smiled. A curve in the road brought us to a broad boulevard. Half of it was covered by a long canopy, about five city blocks long, consisting of a series of arches made of ochre fabric lit from within by Christmas lights. Strings of Christmas lights connected each arch. Ornamenting the arches were fabric mushrooms, palm trees, flowers, and birds—each of them lit from within as well. Between the arches were large animals made of the same material—tigers, zebras, dragons, dogs, you name it—each of them lit by an interior glow. Did this represent the Buddha nature within all things, or was I over-thinking things?

"How you like my English?" she asked.

I felt a little on the spot, but I stammered, "For...for someone in China, your English is *excellent*." That was certainly true. Her vocabulary was outstanding, but like pretty much every Chinese speaker of English I have ever encountered (and that includes graduate school professors), she tended to skip articles, both definite and indefinite. There are no articles in Mandarin, or in written Chinese (nor, I assume, in Cantonese), so they must seem like alien intrusions and are simply ignored. Not that it mattered much. We were communicating swimmingly.

"But?" she asked.

Oh, dear, I thought. *I'd hoped she'd leave it at that.* "But, if you were in America...we'd grade a little harder." It was a lame thing to say, but I didn't know how to answer her truthfully. I avoided the awkwardness by deflecting. "How did you learn English so well?"

"Middle school English classes," she said.

"That's amazing!" I said. Those classes must have been superb. I can't remember anything from my High School Spanish class, after all. She also must have been a stellar student.

It was nearly dark by now, so the lighting was amazing. About halfway down the lane, a series of lit tableaus appeared on the right. We stepped through the arches and wandered over. Here was Snow White and the seven dwarfs cavorting with a pack of pandas in what was surely an apocryphal addition to the story. I wasn't sure what Snow White had to do with Buddhism, but I was keeping an open mind.

A woman's sweatshirt read, "Sweetie Duck Scorn." I frowned, trying to figure it out. Surely something had gotten lost in the translation. After several more tableaus, many of them depicting traditional Buddhist fairy tales, the final one ended in an enormous dragon that curled up onto the roof, looking back the way we'd come, bobbing up and down at regular intervals, fabric flames shooting out of its snout.

I was just shaking my head at the enormity of this complex when the street ended in a parking lot the size of about four football fields. The parking lot was nearly full, and I saw that one entire lot was devoted to tour buses.

I followed the path of the lights and my jaw dropped. Yet another complex stretched out before me, much larger than the one I'd just spent all day exploring. This one consisted of a massive front building, followed by a long stretch of open space reminiscent of the Washington mall, flanked by a row of five four-story pagodas on each side. The mall ended at another building, equally as large as the first, but sporting a six-story gold Buddha, sitting on the roof in a meditative posture, surveying all his lands. Floodlights lit the entire scene, and the outlines of every building twinkled with Christmas lights.

"Okay. Wow," I said. *This is not a monastery,* I thought. *This is friggin' Buddhaland.* It was certainly not what my friend had in mind when he said, "Why don't you go stay in a monastery?" We climbed the long stretch of steps leading up to the first building along with an entire mob of other folks, passing by story-high statues of an elephant and lion.

"Okay, I'll bite," I said. "Why the elephant and lion?"

"Elephant is spirit of Buddha," Liu Yang answered matter-of-factly. I remembered that soon after Siddhartha's mother conceived, she dreamed that an elephant entered her side. So that must have been the spirit of the Buddha connecting with the fetus. Fascinating. "And lion is Dharma."

Going through the massive doors, we stepped into a large complex that was part shopping mall, part art gallery, part museum, part theater complex, and part educational institution. Looking to my left, I saw a Starbucks going full tilt. Behind it was a 7-11, and off to the side a whole slew of local confectionary shops. On the right were several trinket shops, many of them large and pricey. I almost hopped up and down in anticipation. Who knew that enlightenment could be such a shopper's paradise? I shook my head, remembering that the greatest evil in Buddhist thought is *desire*. The irony was exquisite.

I looked up and saw that there were several more floors above me—but they looked like offices, not shops. We passed a vegetarian restaurant on our left, and several more shops on our right. At the end of the building, the large double doors were sealed shut, forcing you to go through the shops on one side or the other to get out.

Once we emerged into the cooling night, the mall was mobbed with people pressed way too close together for my comfort. A parade had started, with a large float bearing a horse (it was the year of the horse, after all)—once again, lit from within by thousands of tiny lights. A contingent of marchers passed by in unidentifiable uniforms, all of them riding hobby-horses. Another group was wearing large illuminated flowers on their heads like floppy hats—they made me think of one of Peter Gabriel's early stage costumes.

As I beheld the jubilant congregants here, it occurred to me that this complex must serve, in some ways, as their cathedral. There were major, major bucks in play here. I had seen several references to their beloved founder, Venerable Master Hsing Yun, and it made me wonder how the FGS organization was governed. "Okay, Liu Yang, this is obviously a huge denomination—"

She pursed her lips and shook her head, not understanding the word. "Uh, sect, religious group, the FGS I mean. How is it governed?"

She cocked her head. I pressed further.

"I mean, the individual temples, are they governed by the laypeople, or are they administered by the clergy? Is the polity from the bottom up or from the top down?"

I must have hit a nerve, because for the first time, she sounded impatient with me. "We talk about that later." *Okay,* I thought. *That shut me up.*

A woman's voice came over the loudspeaker, sounding sickeningly peppy in a way that I usually associate with Japanese media. After a lot of preamble, she eventually started a countdown in which everyone joined: "*...san, er, yi!*" And the fireworks began.

They were launched from the tops of the pagodas, and I've never seen fireworks that were so low to the ground. They were spectacular, but kind of scary, too. I kept expecting still-burning detritus to fall into my hair. The air was thick with smoke and the smell of spent gunpowder. The odor brought me back to my childhood, popping long red strings of caps on the sidewalk with a rock.

Fireworks lit up in the sky from what seemed like every direction, the majority of them seeming to come from behind the gold Buddha statue that towered over the entire complex, framing his serene countenance in a sparkly halo of fire. It reminded me of the scene where Mara tempted the Buddha under the Bodhi tree. In some versions of the story, Mara attacked him with armies, but he simply ignored it all, remaining calm and composed under the Bodhi tree. The large Buddha statue seemed to be acting out that myth now. Fire raged all around him, but the Holy One did not budge from his meditation.

* * *

At Liu Yang's invitation, I arose at 5:15am to join the monks and nuns for morning prayer. The south Taiwanese air was slightly chilly as I walked up the dark stairs toward the main sanctuary. The only brightly lit building visible, it was an inviting oasis of warmth and light. A gigantic bell hanging just outside the main doors boomed the call to prayer as I stepped inside. The three Buddhas were there, meeting the early morning with their trademark serenity.

I was directed to stand in formation off to the right. As I took my place next to a monk on one side and a laywoman on the other, I realized that there was going to be no chance to be a backseat Baptist for this ritual. Everything was strictly regimented, and there was no way to say, "I think I'll just hang out over here and watch, thanks." We faced the center aisle, and on the other side was a neat formation of nuns, their faces betraying nothing.

The liturgy began abruptly with the booming of drums and the clang of symbols. Someone handed me an interlinear liturgy in Chinese, English, and transliterated Chinese. It was a mixture of doctrine and entreaties to the Amitabha Buddha. I had a devil of a time finding my place, and in fact it wasn't until the third chant that I was able to match up what I was hearing with what I saw on the page. But then I got lost again. Oh, well. I read the translation, soaked up the meaning, and sighed deeply as the chant washed over me.

It was truly beautiful, but I suspected it wasn't a very ancient chant. It had the lilt of a more contemporary composition, but like our labyrinth chants at Grace North Church, it felt both soothing and sacred.

Every now and then someone would come up behind me, snatch the booklet out of my hand, and replace it with another, pointing at a line too quickly for me to register what was being indicated as another chant began. This went on for about forty minutes, but was so novel that the time passed quickly. I didn't really chant along, but spent most of my time marveling at the architecture and the sheer golden splendor of the place.

Without any warning the nuns filed out, and then we followed. Outside, Liu Yang was waiting for me, a patient smile on her face. "Go to breakfast now," she said.

"Lead the way," I said.

We headed back toward the Pilgrim's Lodge, but had to stand aside as a group of laypeople—literally a hundred or more of them—were moving in formation. They took three steps—no doubt one each for the Buddha, the Dharma, and the Sangha—and then prostrated themselves. "It's going to take them a long time to get to the sanctuary that way," I noted to Liu Yang. I didn't think to ask how far they'd already been walking in that fashion.

At the Pilgrim's Lodge a yard-thick cauldron of rice stood next to another cauldron of gruel. On a sideboard were steamed mushrooms, steamed greens, and pickled vegetables. I gave the gruel and mushrooms a pass, but stocked up on the others.

The food was bland, so I opened my shoulder bag and took out a small baggie of capsicum powder, my private stash. Liu Yang seemed fascinated by this, and asked if she could put some on her own food. "Of course!" I said, handing her the bag. "There's plenty."

I took a bite and then said, "Those people going to the temple—"

"Big festival today," Liu Yang said. "Auspicious day for pilgrimage."

"Are they acquiring merit by walking and prostrating themselves that way?"

Liu Yang nodded as she flicked some gruel into her mouth with her chopsticks. "Yes," she said. "They gaining merit for better living in next life—or for loved ones."

Merit is a hugely important concept in Buddhism, and not one that you hear very much about. I can imagine, given the emphasis on the clergy in the Theravada tradition, why a person might say, "So why do the laypeople support the monks? What's in it for them?" and the answer, of course, is merit. If they support the monks, it eats up bad karma and ensures them a better incarnation the next time around.

Merit is not an alien concept to Christianity, of course. In the atonement theory that held sway during the middle ages, God the Father was pictured as a feudal lord who was so affronted by human sin that he could not stand to look upon us. In order to reconcile God and humans, Jesus came to earth and lived a perfect human life, saving face for God and making him very pleased indeed—so pleased that he offered Jesus a "boon" of grace (remember, it's the middle ages, so nobody gives gifts, they give *boons*). But Jesus, being God, didn't need the grace, so he gave it to the church to distribute to the people. The saints likewise pleased God and added to this "storehouse of merit" that Jesus had built up.

Christians believed they were tapping into this storehouse whenever they received a sacrament or purchased an indulgence from the church. An indulgence usually took the form of a certificate that promised a certain amount of time off of Purgatory. People purchased them for themselves, or for family members who had died. Martin Luther thought that this was not only unbiblical, but ridiculous, and in most cases simply represented the church hierarchy preying on the gullibility of the poorest of the laity.

There's a bit of this fleecing of the sheep present in Buddhism as well. Around the third century or so, the Buddhist monks were becoming quite wealthy, because they believed (or at least they taught) that it was the duty of the clergy to receive gifts and property from the laity in order to give laypeople an opportunity to gain merit. You can just hear them, "Oh, yes, I'll accept your land. But this is for your own good, of course, not for ours," wink-wink. Some scholars think that the Mahayana school arose in part as a reaction against the corruption of the monasteries, among monks going off to live in the forest where they could practice their faith free from hierarchical corruption (much like the Desert Fathers and Mothers did in the Christian tradition).

So did Mahayana arise from disaffected clergy, or from fed up laypeople? The answer is probably *yes*—both factors contributed to the success of a system that afforded the laity a lot more power and a more significant place in the faith, and also provided a self-imposed check on clerical excess.

There are other ways to gain merit, too, of course—giving money or labor to the monks or to the monastery, praying or meditating, doing prostrations, chanting, and any act of kindness or charity. Another way is to go on pilgrimage, which was precisely why Martin Luther denounced pilgrimages in his own day. He saw people going on them in order to mechanically rack up points for themselves, instead of offering their whole hearts to God. What he missed was the transformative element to pilgrimage. I agree that we shouldn't undertake it in order to gain God's favor, but it is a marvelously immersive way to pray.

My pilgrimage feels not like a duty to be performed but as a gift I am not worthy to receive—which is certainly a more Lutheran approach. I don't feel like God loves me any more because I've gone and done this thing, instead I am so much more mindful of how dependent I am on God, now that most of my support structures are gone.

Liu Yang broke my reverie. "Now you must excuse me, but I have a group of two hundred pilgrims coming from Korea. Will you be okay by yourself today?"

"I'll be just fine," I promised, actually relieved to have some time to myself.

"Okay. Here, I pack you lunch." Opening her shoulder bag she took out a box containing mushroom sticky rice and two apples.

"Uh, wow, that's above and beyond the call of duty," I said, a little flummoxed by all the attention. "You didn't need to do that—you can't turn around without bumping into a restaurant in this place."

She ignored my protest, bowed, and headed out. I finished up and deposited the food in my room. Maybe I'd eat it later, maybe I wouldn't—I detest mushrooms and the water outside of Taipei is not safe to drink. I'm sure the apples have been washed in it. But I didn't have to decide now. I had stuff to see.

I first checked out the main bookstore and picked up a CD of classical Chinese music, along with a couple of tracts on Pure Land Buddhism and a graphic novel on the life of the Ch'an saint Bodhidharma.

Across the courtyard from the bookstore was the Museum of Buddhism. It was wonderfully curated, if a little flashy. There were rooms that could compete with some of the best museums in the world, showing ancient Buddhist art from around the world, but then the very next room would be a fun-house-like hall of mirrors filled with Buddhas. Very strange. Overall, though, it was impressive, and I was fascinated by the ecumenical scope of their collection. From what I'd been able to gather, FGS was primarily Pure Land in orientation, but they honored and incorporated elements of eight different Buddhist sects, including Theravada and Ch'an.

I spent quite a bit of time in the room devoted to Buddhist missionary efforts and the spread of Buddhism across the globe. Colorful maps represented the campaigns of various schools, and indicated which had taken root where. I was utterly engrossed when I turned the corner and discovered myself in...a lollipop museum?

Inexplicably, the Buddhism displays gave way to a historical and geographical study of lollipops. A wall-sized map was devoted to the unlikely subject of lollipop migration across the globe, and several rooms were devoted to displays of lollipops from various countries. I scratched my head, and went back into the hall looking for some kind of transitional signage. There was none.

It crossed my mind that perhaps lollipop consumption accumulates merit in this sect. If so, that is a form of Buddhism that I could excel in. I suck at meditation, but I'm a sucker for lollipops...well, any candy really.

Having exhausted the history of lollipop innovation I headed over to the other large complex of buildings, and walked straight to the Starbucks for a hot chocolate. It was so good I was sure it had coffee in it. I asked, but no, it was just really good chocolate. I picked up some trinkets as gifts for folks back home, and splurged on some peanut mochi that was better than any I'd ever had, anywhere.

I went into another museum, this one dedicated to the history of FGS. Unfortunately, the museum turned out to be less devoted to FGS than it was to its founder, Master Hsing Yun. As I passed display after glowing display gushing about the Master's wisdom in the face of all opposition, the Master's incredible vision, and the Master's generous charity, I started to feel a little disturbed.

I wondered if the members of FGS had any idea how the museum appeared to those of us on the outside looking in. I mean, if you want to avoid being labeled a cult—and I'm sure that FGS wants to avoid that very much—the first thing you do is seriously downplay your charismatic leader and put your focus squarely on your deity. It was the first installation I'd seen that seemed completely tone-deaf to how others would perceive it, and from my perspective it did enormous harm to FGS's credibility.

I had wondered about the money that had been sunk into

this place before, but now I was downright suspicious. No wonder Liu Yang didn't want to talk about polity. If there were any lay oversight at all, surely someone would have said, "Is it really *ethical* to spend a billion dollars to build a place like this? I mean, aren't there better things we could do with that much money? What would Amitabha do?" I walked out of that museum a lot warier than I walked in.

Still, these sprawling complexes were here, and their glory was not to be denied. I exited that museum and walked across the mall to another one. This one had the unlikely name of "The Museum of Underground Buddhist Palaces," and I think I can safely say that it is the only one of its type in the world. Sure enough, inside were displays depicting replicas of great cavernous ruins bearing time-faded Buddhist iconography.

My enjoyment was hampered somewhat by the annoying "squeak-squeak-squeak squeak-squeak-squeak" of a little girl running around in tennis shoes that, strangely, had been fitted with squeak toys in the heels so that every time she took a step it sounded like Donald Duck quacking in agony. I'm not sure what genius invented those shoes, but surely they have contributed to more toddler homicides than any other footwear in history. Sometimes when Lisa and I are watching a movie, our boxer Sally will get hold of a squeak toy and squeak the life out of it until we're grinding our teeth and we finally banish the toy to the outer darkness. This was even worse.

I snagged another peanut mochi and headed out the back door toward the pagodas. I explored every one of them on the left side. One was a photography studio where you could get your portrait done with a statue of the Buddha. They specialized in babies and weddings.

At another I talked to representatives of the University of the West, which has a campus in southern California. They have masters' and doctoral programs in inter-religious studies, which interested me. They also have a campus in Australia. I don't remember what the other two pagodas contained, but I eventually made my way to the large building at the end of the mall, the one with the great golden Buddha sitting on top.

Inside, I took in a couple of exhibits from native Taiwanese painters, which I enjoyed immensely. Then there was a lapis lazuli display, the highlight of which was a human-sized Avalokitesvara, looking like she was made entirely of glass. She had several arms and a halo that contained a thousand hands with an eye in the palm of each one, representing her omnipotence and omniscience.

Having finished there, I passed by a life-sized bronze statue of the founder, Master Hsin Yun, looking fit in mid-stride with a walking stick in one hand. It was a statue that said, "This man is going places."

Liu Yang had given me a ticket to a performance by Chinese acrobats, but the theater was full when I got there (isn't the idea of tickets to limit the number of people? Someone obviously did not get the memo), so I took in the museum of the Buddha's life instead.

It was Gautama Buddha's life, strangely enough. I wondered why they placed so much emphasis on Gautama Buddha in their exhibit, when he was almost incidental to their theology—it was entirely Amitabha Buddha's show there.

The displays were terrific, illustrating key moments in the Buddha's life. Here was the baby Buddha, newly born, stepping forth to proclaim his final birth, lotuses opening and closing along his path. Here he is, a life-sized figure, cutting his own hair as he renounces his kingdom and becomes a monk. Here he is wasting away to nothing practicing asceticism. The next display was a positively psychedelic time-tunnel-like experience as he became enlightened. It was the closest thing Fo Guan Shan had to a ride, and it was pretty good.

The display continued in that vein, but I kept thinking about Amitabha Buddha. According to Williams, he first made his appearance in about the third century CE, but really came to prominence under several medieval thinkers. One of these, Honen Shonin, who lived in the 12th century, wrote, "In the ghastly era in which we live, only Other Power, the power of Amitabha's infinite compassion, can save us. What is more, simple recitation of the name of Amitabha is alone sufficient for that salvation."[1]

One time Honen met some fishermen who were lamenting the state of their souls, since, making their living by killing other beings, they knew they were bound for hell. Honen preached to them the good news of salvation through chanting Amitabha's name alone, and they went away rejoicing, killing fish by day and chanting by night—so it all evened out. Honen wrote, "When I consider deeply the Vow of Amitabha...I realize that it was entirely for the sake of myself alone! ...Any sinner who chants Amitabha's name is saved as a sinner.... Salvation...is certain, even if he expires on a battlefield...."[2]

This reminded me of the Evangelical Christian world in which I grew up, where the only thing needed to be saved was to pray the Sinner's Prayer, and *boom!* you're going to heaven. As I got older, I grew to have grave reservations about this theology, favoring a more gradual (and thorough) change of heart that comes about simply by following Jesus into deeper and deeper levels of intimacy and commitment.

Honen was succeeded by his disciple, Shinran, who was attracted to Amitabha because he just really sucked at being a decent person. He knew the only chance he had was if he made it under someone else's steam, because his own was wholly unreliable. He projected his own sinful state onto the whole human race as well, and taught that because everything we do is driven by ego, no truly good act is possible.[3]

This sounds a lot like St. Augustine to me, who also embraced his faith because he was incapable of being a good person, and then granted us the favor of insisting that we were all

just like him. Of course, it also sounds a lot like those
came after Augustine and were heavily influenced by him, ᵢᵢ.ᵣᵉ
Luther and Calvin.

When Shinran asserts that we only do good deeds due to
egoistic motivations until our minds are transformed by the
Buddha's power, he sounds a lot like Luther, who said that the
work of God in us is to convert our self-serving love into self-
giving love. He also sounds a lot like Luther when he insists
that our own efforts are completely meaningless and our merit
is totally worthless. Only the merit of Amitabha Buddha will
succeed in saving us, and we can only claim that salvation
through trust.[4]

As I walked out of the Buddha museum, I saw a man wearing a bright red t-shirt that said, "I'll believe anything!" I
laughed out loud when I saw it. I have to admit that when I
first heard about Amitabha Buddha and his other universe, I
thought it was absurd, and that everyone who believed it was
crazy. But really, is it any more far-fetched or absurd than what
Christians believe?

I mean, if you haven't been steeped in it, Christianity does
sound a little ridiculous: God was so pained at the distance between himself and creation, that he became a part of creation,
made it part of his life, and set about healing everything broken. Putting it like that, it might sound far-fetched, but it's really, really beautiful, too.

They're both good stories, with different endings, but great
ones. In Christianity, the goal is the healing of all things that
are broken, while in Buddhism it's the liberation of all beings
in bondage. What is most amazing to me, though, is that the
spiritual process that the Christian faith works in believers
seems to be nearly identical to the process at work in those
who follow Amitabha Buddha. The names and faces of the
deities are different, but the actual spiritual process—an aware-
ness of one's sinfulness, self-abandonment, trust, and personal

transformation by the power of the Other alone—is very similar indeed.

This night, too, there would be fireworks, so I took my place near the front this time to get a better look at the floats. I arrived at Fo Guan Shan expecting an austere existence that I would have to endure. What I found was a wholly entertaining, if mildly disturbing, experience that utterly delighted me. Not what I had intended, and not what I was expecting, but amazingly rewarding on many levels. And how often is the spiritual journey just like that?

———

1   Williams, 255.

2   Williams, 261, 256.

3   Williams, 178.

4   Williams, 261-262.

Dried fruit salesmen in Leh, sitting on the steps of a large prayer wheel.

Chapter Sixteen: Leh—The Vajrayana Revelation

I stepped off the plane in Leh, a tiny little town and the largest city in Ladakh. Ladakh is in India, but just barely. Officially, it is an "autonomous region" which pretty much governs its own affairs without interference from Delhi. Most of the people here are Tibetan refugees, and it is one of the last surviving places on earth where Tibetan culture remains intact.

Too bad I didn't get to see it—but let's not get ahead of ourselves. For most of the year, Ladakh is cut off from the outside world. The only way in or out is by airplane, at least until May when the roads melt enough for a few months of use. Leh is ringed by the Himalayas, and is so high—nearly 12,000 feet—that visitors must factor in 24 to 36 hours of lying flat on their backs doing nothing until the altitude sickness subsides.

Which is precisely where things went wrong—but let's not get ahead of ourselves. As I leaped down the steps of the plane to the tarmac, I felt the icy bite of frosty air in my lungs. The wind whipped at my hands, and my legs felt naked. Everywhere I looked there was snow, and postcard-worthy mountain scenes smiled down at me 360 degrees around.

A shuttle bus brought us to the terminal. The building was made of crumbling cement and the only doors were large woven blankets, stained by years of grime. Indian soldiers in jungle camouflage were stationed in ridiculous numbers, almost more numerous than the passengers, loaded machine guns hanging from their shoulders with disconcerting nonchalance. I snagged my luggage and saw a sign on the wall, its paint flaking away. "Leh is 3524 meters above sea level. Travelers are strongly advised to rest for a day or more." I frowned and pursed my lips. I didn't remember anything in the Lonely Planet about that. I took a deep breath. I felt fine. As I got into the taxi, I worried a bit about the whole high-altitude thing. The problem was, I was only going to be there for a day and a half. I decided I'd make it a light day today, only walking around the old town for a couple of hours, and see all the major sites tomorrow.

It seemed like a good plan, a reasonable plan, a plan to move forward with. If only I had known—but let's not get ahead of ourselves.

As a town, Leh pretty much shuts down when the roads do. There are oodles of guest houses, hotels, hostels, restaurants, and gift shops, but they are all closed. When I was searching for lodging on Trip Advisor, I found very few places open during the winter, and those that were fell into one of two categories. Most were of the half-star variety, with travelers' evaluations running some variation on, "Run for your lives!" The other category had exactly one entry, the Grand Dragon Hotel, the only five-star lodging in Leh open year-round.

Was it expensive? Well, yes, running about five times what I've been paying in India. It was also my only reasonable option. Gee, could I put up with a luxury room and a hot bath for two nights? Twist my arm.

After a short ride my taxi pulled up at the Grand Dragon, and as I walked through the doors, I saw that it was grand indeed. Not grand by European standards, mind you, but by tiny Himalayan kingdom standards, pretty darn nice. White marble covered every surface, and through large plate-glass windows I could see the dining room, its ceiling supported by multi-colored Tibetan pillars that looked like they were looted from a monastery when the monks weren't looking.

My room was lovely. It was clean as a whistle, with a soft king-sized bed that just begged you to lie down on it, just for a minute. The bathtub was large, and the bathroom was separated from the bedroom by a plate glass window. A privacy screen could be raised or lowered at will. The green marble floors of the bathroom were heated from below, meeting my bare feet with lovely warmth.

But warmth was a bit of a problem in that room—there was *way* too much of it. I turned off the heat, and never turned it back on. The room must have been over a boiler or something because it was running between 80 and 95 degrees the whole time I was there. I opened the window frequently.

The only wrong note in this beautiful room was the artwork. There was exactly one painting in the room, hung over the bed—a wartime scene of two combat helicopters kissing in mid-flight. I squinted at it to make sure I was seeing it right. I was.

I stowed my gear, put on my cold weather clothes, and feeling like a million bucks, headed out for the old town, a short walk away. As I walked I noticed that I was very quickly short of breath. An employee from the hotel drove by and stopped, offering me a ride. I thanked him profusely, and he dropped me off at the main drag.

I oriented myself to the map in the Lonely Planet, but didn't really go anywhere I'd planned, because I kept getting distracted, going, "Ooh! What's that?" and heading in a different direction.

Apparently there wasn't much to do in Leh in the winter, because the entire population seemed to be loitering on the street. Steel garage doors were drawn down over most of the shops, but I found a market where there was lots of activity. Long johns were a big seller there—no surprise. I bought a pair of yak wool socks for a friend, and hoped they would be large enough for his feet.

I passed by the main gate of the city, painted in the same wild assortment of colors you see in Vajrayana temples—deep blues and reds, poignant greens, and musty yellows. Just in front of it, across the street, was a prayer wheel about one and a half times the size of a man, in constant motion from passersby. A couple of blocks past this was a series of stupas, surrounded on all sides by shops, with electric wires strung over them.

There were fewer cows than in other parts of India, but they were still there, popping up in the most unusual places. In Leh, however, the cow patties are 33% less dangerous because they're frozen solid.

I finally returned to the old town and stepped into the mosque. Like a lot of small mosques, it was utilitarian, although there was some impressive woodwork. Next to the mosque was a little café called The Coffee Sutra. Nice. As I descended the stairs, I started to feel dizzy and a little nauseated. Then my head started hurting.

By the time I'd gone two blocks, I started to feel a rumbly pressure in my bowels. I was also weaving. My head started pounding, and I felt confused and a little scared. I finally walked up to a travel agency and steadied myself against the man standing by the door.

"I don't feel good," I said. "I need a taxi."

"Just sit down," he said, in good English. "I'll call one for you."

After he called he snapped his cell phone shut. "How long have you been here?" he asked.

"I just got in," I said.

He tsk-tsked me disapprovingly. "You should not be out. If you just come, you should go to bed for two days before walking anywhere."

"But I'm only here two days," I said.

His eyes said, 'You're an idiot" but his mouth remained politely closed.

It took the taxi driver all of 90 seconds to deliver me to my room, but he still charged me 400 rupees (US$8). I paid it without complaint and stumbled to the front desk. They sussed the situation out quickly.

"You go to bed, lie down, do nothing, and take these," they handed me a packet of prescription medicine.

I read the label. "Diamox."

"It make you feel better faster," the man said. I thanked him and went up to my room. I went straight to bed.

I found it hard to sleep, however, because my headache grew progressively worse. So did the rumblings in my bowels. I've never had altitude sickness before, thankfully, so I don't know what it feels like. But I have had Delhi Belly, five times, and I know what the first stages of that feel like. And it feels an awful lot like this.

I'm not sure how clearly I was actually thinking, but my best diagnosis was this: the meal I'd had at my guest house in Delhi was not Westerner-approved, and I had a case of Delhi Belly coming on fast. *And*, I was suffering from the altitude. The best thing to do was to take an Azythromyacin as fast as possible, but I'd just taken this "Diamox" and didn't know if the two medications were safe to take together.

I went downstairs with my laptop to try to find out. And— you can bet on it—the internet connection was down. In my oncoming delirium I became mildly hysterical—or not so mildly, it's hard to tell, and everything is a little foggy.

One of the hotel managers understood English, and I was able to communicate my dilemma. "You go to hospital," he said, and snapped his fingers at one of the bellboys for a taxi.

By this time, I was cradling my head in my hands from the pain, and practically rolling on his desk. My tongue might have been hanging out of my mouth. I don't remember. I was certainly drooling.

"I...don't...want...to...go...to...a...hospital...in...India." It was an offensive thing to say, but my filters were off playing pinochle. And it was true. I would dread going to a hospital in Delhi, but *here*? You've got to be out of your mind.

But then there we were, speeding toward the hospital. "Uh, this is it?" I asked when the car stopped. It was a small concrete building in what looked like a military compound. Of course, its only door was a filthy blanket.

As we went inside, I saw that all the doors inside were filthy blankets, too. And the walls were crumbling—little piles of concrete dust and pebbles gathered near the corners. Peering in doorways I saw tiny rooms with four or five beds crammed into them with barely room to navigate between them.

My driver spoke to a woman who must have been a nurse. She was seated at a desk on which a heap of needles and surgical equipment was just, well, heaped. I shuddered. I was led to a bench and told to sit. After a few minutes, a Tibetan-looking family emerged from behind a dirty blanket and I was summoned. I parted the dirty blanket and saw a middle-aged Tibetan woman at a desk, positively reeking authority.

I sat down near the desk, as she instructed a nurse to take my temperature, blood pressure, and oxygen level.

"This should be very short," I said, gasping for breath. "All I need to know is if there are any drug reactions between Diamox and Azythromyacin. That's all."

"Please describe your symptoms," she said patiently, adjusting her librarian glasses. So I did. And my diagnosis. The nurse put a small clamp over my finger and clicked a switch on a portable machine. "Your oxygen levels are fine," the doctor said as the nurse prepared to take my blood pressure.

"Wait, how can you tell my oxygen level from feeling my finger?" I asked. What hoodoo was this? But she ignored me. When my blood pressure had been recorded, she let her glasses fall to her breast, hanging from their lanyard. "You are suffering from acute mild altitude sickness. I am prescribing complete rest for 24 hours. You are to continue the Diamox, and if you begin to have watery stools, then you may take the Azythromyacin."

I started to protest, but she glared at me and I shut my mouth. The moment I got back in the car, I popped the Azythromyacin. I know my body, and I knew what was happening to me, and it was more than altitude sickness. I'd gotten the information I'd needed.

The amazing thing was that it only took fifteen minutes, tops. If I'd gone to an American hospital, I'd be sitting there for another four hours before I even spoke to the doctor. I wonder if "the best health care system on the planet" really just means we don't have blankets on the doors.

Back at my hotel room, I dutifully lay down and for the first time in two months, turned on the television. I found an episode of *The Practice*, the excellent David E. Kelley lawyer show from about ten years ago, and settled in with it. Strangely, every now and then an ad would pop up on the screen saying, "If you use tobacco, you will die" and then disappear. And whenever I changed the channel, another ad would pop up saying, "Worship revered shrines on your television, 25 rupees a month from iDarshan." I shook my aching head in disbelief.

The hotel manager had made prescriptions of his own: hot ginger tea and garlic soup—plenty of both. Both turned out to be delicious, and I kept room service busy bringing round after round of them.

That night I dreamed I was back home, and was late for church. I waited until 20 minutes to 5pm to leave the house—just time enough to make it, if there was no traffic. But I realized that I had prepared no sermon. When I awoke I was in a fit of anxiety, my blankets twisted around my body almost painfully. When I realized where I was I breathed a sigh of relief. I might be in India (bad) but I wasn't late for church without a sermon (good).

My headache had diminished substantially, and my guts were quieter. I blessed God for antibiotics, but my thoughts kept returning to the dream. What did it mean? Perhaps it meant that I was hesitant to come home without a sermon prepared—in other words, I had gained no great wisdom, I had no message to impart. God had certainly been working on me, but I would be coming home the same clueless schlub who left, and I suppose I expected to have gained a bit more insight.

This felt right, like at least one good meaning for the dream, but it depressed me. It seemed to take forever to dress and get downstairs for breakfast, even though I didn't shower.

Most of that day was spent in bed watching TV or working on my blog. But to be honest, I didn't have much energy for it. So I gave myself permission to just actually rest. Later in the afternoon I was feeling almost human again, so I contacted the front desk and asked if they could arrange a driver to take me to the main sites in the city itself. Of course, all the really impressive monasteries were twenty kilometers or more out of town, but I didn't have the stamina for that. And I had to leave early the next morning.

So a little after three, I was speeding toward the city limits with a Tibetan driver named Tzilly, whose parents had fled Tibet in 1959. "Why did they come here?" I asked. "Why not Nepal?"

"No working in Nepal," he said. I nodded. I liked Nepal a lot more than I liked India, but what did I know about their comparative economies in the late 1950s?

We passed a convoy of trucks, edging way too close to a steep cliff to let them pass. And the pavement didn't look in great shape, either. I decided it was best simply not to look. Adrenaline can't be good for altitude sickness. So I studied the trucks. These were cargo trucks, the Indian equivalent of our eighteen-wheelers. But unlike the corporate billboards our trucks are, these were painted from one end to the other, so colorfully it would make the Partridge Family bus jealous. And it wasn't just these buses—all the buses in India are painted the same way—all of them festivals of color, and each different from the other. I smiled at the sheer whimsy of it.

Our first stop was a small monastery overlooking the city. There were a number of stairs up to the sanctuary, and I was panting before we got a quarter of the way. I wasn't sure this was wise as we were going higher and higher. "How many (gasp) monks live (wheeze) here?" I asked.

"Two," he said. Okay, then, this *was* small.

It was also locked. I got some great pictures of the city and the mountains surrounding us, but was sad that I couldn't see the inside. I felt angry at the Lonely Planet for not including this very important information about altitude sickness. If I'd only scheduled one more day, I could have seen the monasteries. But it was impossible now. My Leh trip was a bust.

Our next stop was a large stupa—the Shanti Stupa—built as a gift from Japanese Buddhists. I walked around it, but shrugged. It was a big white stupa. I don't really *get* stupas. I mean, they can be impressive, and yeah, they mark important places, but what was important about *this* place? I didn't have a clue.

As I circumambulated the stupa, however, I was charmed by large blue signs that had been erected every twenty feet or so. The last three said, in order: "No Smoking," "God bless," "Come again." Um...*God bless*? Which god was that referring to, exactly?

That night I dreamed again. I was being given a test on the meaning of the Sanskrit word "Muktananda." I knew what *ananda* meant (bliss), but I'd forgotten what *mukta* meant. I tapped a man on the shoulder and asked him what *mukta* meant in English. "Sickness," the man said. I gave my answer, "The bliss of the disease."

I woke a little disturbed, and the images were very vivid. I was feeling much better by then, and I showered and packed in no time. As I did, I wondered about the dream. There had been a great Indian guru named Muktananda, in fact he founded Siddha Yoga—there is a large Siddha center in Emeryville. I've been there once or twice, and it's kind of a Hindu megachurch.

But I knew the answer given in the dream was not correct. It has been twenty years since I learned my Sanskrit terminology during my Hinduism studies. What I was not recalling was that *mukta* is a derivative of *moksha*, which I very much remembered. *Moksha* means "liberation." Muktananda means "the bliss of liberation," not "the bliss of illness" or "the bliss of the disease."

But the dream was so powerful, I knew there must be something there. As I stood around in the crumbling airport waiting for my flight back to Delhi, I had a couple of good hours to study my books on Vajrayana. As I did so, understanding dawned.

Theravada Buddhists are mostly concerned with this world. For them, it is real, and the suffering it causes is real. The goal is to escape it, once and for all. Mahayana Buddhism denies the reality of this world, or any of the innumerable other worlds it posits. For them, the worlds are an illusion to be rejected, but one should stay ensconced in the illusion until everyone can escape it.

For the Vajrayana, the world is an illusion, but a very *useful* illusion. The world might be empty, but it still matters. For them, emptiness and form are entwined, inescapably joined, and one leads to the other. It is by understanding and using the world in skillful ways that we can become enlightened and so liberate others. The illusion of the world becomes the tool that we use to achieve the highest good. Enlightenment is the gift of the illusion. It is the bliss given to us by the disease of maya.

I was thunderstruck—not a bad descriptor since the meaning of the word *vajra* (as in Vajra-yana) is thunderbolt. "Okay, God, I'm listening," I prayed.

On the plane I was seated next to a young monk. He spoke very little English, and after a while we gave up trying to talk. Instead, we spent most of the flight just looking over at one another and smiling occasionally. It was another good lesson. Interfaith dialogue doesn't really rely on words, only on kindness and mutual admiration. Now I wish I'd taught him to play patty-cake.

On the street in McCleod Ganj.

Chapter Seventeen: Dharamsala—the Vajrayana Vatican

I headed to Dharamsala with both excitement and trepidation. On the one hand, this is where the Dalai Lama lives, which is grand. On the other hand, by all accounts, there's not much there there. And finding safe food is always a challenge when there isn't much there. But I set my hopes on seeing a grand temple—the Vatican City of Vajrayana Buddhism, after all.

Ironically, just as I was going to the Dalai Lama's stomping grounds, he was on his way to mine. Having breakfast in the airport, I read about his meeting with President Obama. Later in the week, he'd be at Berkeley and Santa Clara. Just my luck!

On the plane, my seat-mate was a woman going home. Her name was Clara, and she was from Belgium. She was married to an Indian man and together they ran the Ladies Venture Guest House. I thought it was an odd name, and perhaps I was mishearing it, so I didn't comment. She'd originally come to Dharamsala to discover Buddhism. Instead, she found a husband. She still liked Buddhism, but didn't consider herself a Buddhist.

Our conversation lapsed and resumed in a comfortable, natural flow. I liked her. When we landed (a mere hour and a half later) she said, "Let me see how many people my husband is picking up. If we have room, we'll give you a ride."

"Thanks!" I said effusively, but not getting my hopes up. The airport was nicer than most of the tiny airports I'd seen in India. This one, at least, did not have blankets for doors. I grabbed my suitcase and wheeled it quickly to catch up with Clara. Out by the curb, she was hugging people (their employees, I assumed) and kissing one (her husband, I assumed).

They'd brought two cars, and the back seat of Clara's husband's was empty. I had lucked out.

Clara asked if I minded if she smoked while we drove. I did, of course, but lied and said, "Not at all." It seems there was a price to pay for the ride after all. Fortunately, it wasn't too bad. Her husband, whose name I couldn't quite grasp even after he'd told me twice, seemed to be a very nice man in his sixties, handsome and dignified. 1980s pop played on the stereo all the way up, heavy on the David Bowie—a snapshot of these two in their prime. It made me smile.

For some reason, Dharamsala is the name given for the Dalai Lama's residence, but in fact, it's just the name of the town the airport is near. Nothing is actually *in* Dharamsala, which is a tiny fleck of a place, mostly mud and hillside and scabby dogs and storefronts. You have to ascend up the mountain another forty-five minutes to get to the real action, such as it is. The Dalai Lama actually lives in a little town called McCleod Ganj, and that's where everyone *means* when they say Dharamsala. Delightfully, the drive up the mountain was breathtakingly beautiful. It was a dense pine forest, reminding me of northern California.

The road was narrow, winding, and dangerous—but at some point you just stop looking because the freaking out for your life every few seconds doesn't actually do any good. At one point, traffic stopped completely because a cow had decided to chew her cud in the middle of the road. No cars could pass. No one thought to shoo the cow out of the way. We just waited until, after what seemed like a very long time, she moseyed off.

Eventually we pulled into town, and it was about what I'd been expecting—mud, scabby dogs and storefronts—only more of them. The views, however, were astounding. Snow covered mountains were off to one side, and a lush green valley fell nearly straight down on the other. After the smog of Delhi, the air seemed so clean it sparkled.

Clara didn't actually know where my hotel was, but it was on the same street as hers, so I got off where they stopped and offered my sincere thanks. I gave her a card and invited her to check out the blog. Then I wheeled my bag to a store and asked about the hotel. The guy gave me good directions, but I misjudged the distance and thought he'd misled me.

So I flagged down a taxi, which wound its way around the town and eventually brought me to the hotel, which was a mere 300 yards from where the driver had picked me up. To be fair, I found out later that he had no choice—it was a one-way street. So I'll give him a pass. He gave me his phone number and said, "If there's anywhere you want to go, call me." I told him I would.

My hotel wasn't the Grand Dragon, but it would do. I decided I had evolved beyond objecting to the hair and dirt on the floor. I was in India. Limbless orphans were dragging themselves through the streets on skateboards just outside the door. I could put up with a little grime.

I stowed my stuff and headed out to see the town. What I discovered was that any direction I walked was almost completely uphill. I huffed and panted, but eventually made it to a street lined with trinket booths on one side, and trinket shops on the other.

There's really only one loop to follow around the town, which is about eight blocks long (with a few capillaries that peter out after a block or so), so within an hour, I'd seen all there was to see. I hadn't really gone into any of the shops, but I'd leave that until tomorrow. My most exciting discovery was an Anglican church about a kilometer out of town, called St. John's-in-the-Wilderness. The next day was Sunday, and service as at 10am. I was so there.

But it was still Saturday night, and there was supper to be found. I hadn't seen any place that looked inviting, so I checked Trip Advisor for a more or less safe place. The highest rated places were coffee shops, but that wasn't what I wanted. Scrolling down I found a place that got rave reviews, even if it looked like a bit of a hole in the wall. It took me an hour to find Gyaki, and when I did it was closed.

The light was beginning to fail, and I was beginning to feel the first stages of hypoglycemic disorientation—a pretty dangerous condition that happens to me a lot if I don't eat regularly. I get into this cycle where I can't make up my mind where or what to eat, so I don't eat, and I start to spiral down into a progressively worse delusional state. At home, when this happens, I have a rule that I head for the nearest restaurant—no matter what it is—and order something, anything. Here, that could be fatal. So biting back on my panic, I turned back to the app. My second choice was Snow Lion. I'd passed it a couple of blocks back. I made a beeline for it.

Inside, it was warm and clean-ish. The tables were full, but they sat me with a Croatian fellow who didn't seem to mind—too much. Eventually his girlfriend arrived, and I felt awkward, so I moved to the next table, which had since opened up. Then a gaggle of twenty-somethings came through the door. "I guess you guys are stuck with me," I said, moving back to their table. He seemed friendlier in her company, and they said they didn't mind at all.

The twenty-somethings were very vocal and very grateful. As it turned out they were all doctors, and had just finished doing a series of medical camps in Northern India. They were loud, funny, and very friendly indeed, and I was often brought into the conversation. One of them said he was thinking of going to St. John's in the morning. I said I would see him there.

It turned out that I saw most of them there. I left my hotel room at 9am sharp, climbed the staircase of streets that is McCleod Ganj, then walked the kilometer through the woods, and made it to the church by 9:30—and I wasn't even hurrying.

The church was built in a Gothic style, seeming very out of place in India. The door was locked, but a side door was open. I peered inside and saw no one, although I'd seen what looked like a janitor from a distance, washing out pans under an outside spigot.

I toured the grounds and snapped some pictures. The wind was cold, so I let myself in through the side door. Just then I heard voices outside. Other people started to come in. Then more. Then the doctors arrived. It was about ten 'til, and no altar was set. There was no sign of a priest. It occurred to me that if there was going to be a service that day, it was probably going to be up to me to do it.

I surprised myself by thrilling to the challenge. First, I prayed for help (always the best start). Then I went to work. I had two *iBooks of Common Prayer*, one on my phone and one on my iPad. There were too many people here to all look on one iPad, so it would have to be a simplified service. I pulled up my iLectionary app and looked at the gospel reading for the day. In my head, I quickly outlined a three-point sermon: opening story, unpacking the text, applying it to our lives. Easy.

Normally, I would freak out at the idea of preaching extemporaneously in front of so many people. But a strange calm came over me. I remembered the words of the Gospel where Jesus said, "Don't worry about what you will say; the Spirit will give you the words."[1] Somehow I was able to just relax into trusting that.

At 10am sharp, even more people had arrived, and we all just sat there in silence. There was no priest. I started to get up, when suddenly, from seemingly out of nowhere, a large, red-headed man in a Roman collar took the floor. "Well, since there's no clergy here, we'll have to make our own service," he said, in what sounded to me like an Australian accent. "Let's begin with the Lord's Prayer in Aramaic." Then, with large, loopy dramatic flourishes, he launched into a loud recitation, ꞎy himself, in Aramaic. Then he invited anyone else to get up and talk, and sat down.

Everyone sat there in silence, a little stunned. *So much for starting formally*, I thought. I rose and invited someone to read the collect for the day, and held out my phone to read from. One woman had her Catholic missal with her, and read from that. She read the antiphon instead of the collect, but I didn't correct her—it was just odd. Then I asked if someone would read the Gospel. No one stirred, and so the same woman read the text from her missal.

I silently prayed it would be the same text I'd prepared for— to my great relief it was. When she finished I rose and said, "I've only given one sermon without prepared notes in front of me, and it scared the dickens out of me. Let's see how this one goes!" Smiles all around, but people looked uncertain, too.

I wasn't. The Spirit had given me a good message, and now as I opened my mouth she filled it with her words. It was an amazing experience, a bit like being possessed. It was me, I was in control, but at the same time I was being spoken through. It was ecstatic. I've had that experience before, but it's rare.

The text was Matthew 5:38-48, where Jesus says, "You have heard it said x, but I tell you y" where y is always much harder than x. It ends with him saying, "Be perfect as your father in heaven is perfect."

I started with a story I'd read recently about Bodhidharma. He'd brought Ch'an Buddhism to China, but had been so disgusted with the corruption of the monks there that he went off into the wilderness by himself. Eventually one young monk found him and asked to be his disciple. Bodhidharma rebuffed him. He asked again and again. Each time the master told him to go take a hike. So he cut his own arm off—that got Bodhidharma's attention, and he accepted the young man as his student.

I said, "A lot of us have been given horrible images of God. We were told he is a punishing monster just waiting for us to trip up. And we've been given terrible messages by our churches, that we have to conform to some cookie-cutter image in order to be acceptable to God. We grew up feeling that in order for God to love us, we had to lop off huge chunks of who we are. Like Bodhidharma's student, we feel we have to cut pieces off of ourselves in order to win God's acceptance.

"But the Good News is that this just isn't true. God doesn't just love the shiny bits, God loves all of you. In his day Jesus didn't hang out with the 'acceptable' people who were following all the rules. He went out and found those folks who had been told that they were outcast, and he embraced them and hung out with them and called them his friends."

I finished by saying, "When Jesus said, 'Be perfect, as God is perfect,' that is a terrible translation. It doesn't mean without fault. It means *complete*. Jesus is saying, 'Be whole, as God is whole.'" I invited them, the next time they prayed, not to just put on their best face for God, but to bring before God every part of themselves—the stuff they're proud of, and the stuff they're not proud of, too. I asked them to take a leap of faith, that if they showed up before God with all of their parts, that God would embrace them completely.

As I watched the faces of the congregation, I knew that the words were hitting home. The woman with the missal was crying. The uncertainty left their faces, and they leaned in as I spoke.

Martin Luther said that every sermon should bring good news. Ever since I read that quote it has been my guiding light in preaching. Good news was spoken in Dharamsala that morning.

I sat down, expecting that we would enjoy a few moments of silence. To my surprise, the priest sprang to the front of the room, and began to give another sermon. This one bore no resemblance to the Gospel passage, but instead was on the theme of "wars and rumors of war," and to be frank, it sounded a little unhinged. It also didn't really go anywhere.

I was confused, because I really didn't understand what he was up to. All that was really needed to put a cap on the service were some prayers and a blessing, but it seemed like this guy was turning it into a pissing match. I patiently waited until he ran out of steam. He invited someone else to add something. Of course, they didn't.

After some silence, I suggested we recite the Lord's Prayer together, this time in English. I was too flustered to realize that the Prayers of the People would have been a really good idea at this time, and when we got to the doxology, I flubbed it. God really does know how to keep us humble.

I asked the priest to give a final blessing. I forgot what he did, but it was *not* a blessing. So I gave one, and closed the service. People started milling about, and instantly the priest introduced himself. I was irritated at him, but intrigued as well, so I shook his hand. He said he was a Jesuit from New Zealand engaged in refugee work in Nepal. After a few minutes, I put my hand on his arm and said, "We should go and be pastoral. We can catch up later. Sound okay?"

He agreed, and I headed out to shake hands and talk to folks. Afterwards, Fr. Tim (as I'll call him here) and I walked back to town together. I told him how ironic it was that I was here when the Dalai Lama was in California, and he talked about the several times he'd met the Dalai Lama. Then he talked about the "poor lost souls" under the spell of Buddhism, and started talking about demonic activity associated with Vajrayana practice. Then he told me about his early study of Taoism, and the demonic influences that assaulted him when he used the I Ching.

Strangely, he counted himself a liberal. I simply could not figure out how someone who held opinions like his could be effective in interfaith work, or in inter-religious dialogue. I did-n't argue with him, however, as I long ago discovered that it is pointless to argue theology, and I did not trust him to respect my perspective. So I just said, "Uh-huh," and listened.

I did offer differing opinions on minor matters, such as when he said the *Book of Mormon* was a load of crap—I countered that the *Book of Mormon* is an entirely orthodox fantasy novel (it supports none of the heterodox teachings of the LDS church), and if you put it on the same shelf as the Narnia books it can be both entertaining and very edifying indeed.

He told me about his work and some of the colorful characters he had encountered, and I told him about my journey from my Southern Baptist childhood to Old Catholicism, and finally to my reception into the United Church of Christ.

He introduced me to a restaurant (which was not listed on Trip Advisor) and it turned out to be excellent. We found a table on the roof with an astounding view of the mountains. He drank two very large bottles of beer, and as our meal progressed he called over to an Australian couple dining next to us, saying progressively more offensive things to them. I was so embarrassed I wanted to crawl into my Aloo Gobhi.

I excused myself to go to the restroom and asked him if he would watch my bag. Then, as I'm doing my business, it occurred to me, "Who is this guy? Is he even a real priest?" I remembered that when he'd pulled off his collar he wasn't wearing a clergy shirt at all, but had stuffed a plastic tab into a rugby jersey. "And is he and my bag (and my iPad!) still going to be there when I get back to the table?" I raced to finish up, kicking myself for my lapse in diligence, and figuring that if he did skip out with my stuff, I'd probably be left with the bill, too.

But no, to my great relief there he was. I gave him my card, and he said he wanted to introduce me to his friend who lived in Dharamsala, a guy who had been practicing Tibetan Buddhism, but had quit because of—*say it with me, everybody*—demonic activity.

We shook hands and went different ways once we hit the street. I wasn't sure what to make of Fr. Tim. I'd enjoyed our lunch together, and was willing to give him the benefit of a doubt—he hadn't absconded with my bag, after all. He was gregarious and a hell of a lot of fun, even if he was a bit of a theological bully. I realized, however, that it would be difficult if not impossible to be friends with someone who could not respect your opinions when they differed from his. This deflated me a bit.

But I was headed to the Dalai Lama's temple, so even momentary depression was not an option. I entered the compound and passed the only beggars I had yet seen in McLeod Ganj. No cameras or electronics were permitted in the temple (damn!) so I left my iPad and phone at the coat check.

The bookstore was closed, I noted with a frown, but the museum was open. I'd hit that last. I bounded the steps to get to the temple. I removed my shoes and went in. And it was…disappointing. First, it was very small. Second, it was mostly concrete walls with very little ornamentation.

There seemed to be two main rooms, and neither of them were very special. They were not even a dim shadow of the beauty and magnificence I had seen in most Vajrayana temples. Here was the Dalai Lama's throne, and there were some impressive statues of the Buddha and Bodhisattvas. In the other room were some mats for meditation and prayer, and some more statues, one of which depicted two multi-armed Bodhisattvas going at it doggie-style, and neither of them looked happy about it.

"Well, that's tantra for you," I said, cocking my head sideways, trying to take in the erotic, horrific splendor of it. Tantra began around the 5th century CE as a Hindu sect, and not a very well respected one. It is often referred to as "the left-handed path," because in India, the left hand is defiled—it's the hand you use to wipe yourself with, after all. It is unclean, and tantra makes conscious use of that impurity.

In Hindu tantra, the male assumes the identity of Shiva (spirit), and the female assumes the identity of Shakti (matter). In their sexual intercourse, performed in a highly ritualized way, the dualisms are transcended as the two become one. There is no longer male and female, no longer god and goddess, no longer spirit and matter. All is one, and in that oneness the practitioners can—if they are skillful—achieve full unitive consciousness. This breaks the power of samsara, ends their cycle of reincarnation, and makes them conscious of their true identity in God.

The worshippers may or may not be married in regular life, and the scandal of unmarried partners doing such work together actually adds to the *tapas*, the spiritual power involved. Tapas is invoked through the breaking of other taboos as well. In the same ritual context, tantric worshippers may drink blood, kill animals, eat animal flesh, drink alcohol, or do other forbidden things. The point of all this is that good/bad, acceptable/unacceptable are all false dichotomies from the non-dual perspective, and when forbidden acts are conducted in a ritual setting, the duality can be transcended and the taboo can actually trigger enlightenment.

Whether it actually does or not is the subject of some debate, but tantra has been around for a very long time, and a lot of people swear by it, although never in polite company.

The sexual and taboo aspects of tantra are especially pronounced in Hindu tantra, but few people give these much thought when turning to tantric Buddhism, which I think is strange. True, Buddhism seems to have expanded the definition of tantra to include any use of the physical world to mediate spiritual benefits. Vajrayana Buddhists believe that the body, ritual tools, and many other material things can provide a "shortcut"—or at least expedient access—to enlightenment.

You almost never hear of the more taboo aspects of tantric practice in reference to Vajrayana Buddhism. In part that is because there is so much else going on in the religion that the taboo aspects (unless you consider all matter taboo) are shuffled to the margin. In part that's by design—there is much about Vajrayana practice that is secret. Are the taboo rituals, including sex, still there? Yes, but you'll never see them unless you decide to devote your life to Vajrayana practice.

There is some debate over whether the sexual aspects of it are acted out physically or in active imagination, and undoubtedly both methods are employed. It is logical that the married Vajrayana monks, such as the Dewari of Nepal, do tantric sexual practice with their wives, but otherwise celibate monks practicing with otherwise celibate nuns is not unheard of. Does the Dalai Lama do it in his head or in the flesh? Come now, *that would be telling.*

We can shake our heads and say how bizarre this all sounds, but there has been tantric practice in Christianity, too. The Valentinian Gnostic Christians (and no doubt other early Gnostic sects as well) practiced a sacrament known as the "Bridal Chamber" in which the male would assume the person of Christ and the female would assume the person of his consort, Sophia (in many Gnostic systems, Christ and Sophia were mated syzygies). They would have intercourse in a ritual setting, and the union of opposites would break the power of the evil archons who hold the world in the bondage of dualistic illusion.

Now, since there are 365 archons who must be defeated in order to achieve liberation, the Bridal Chamber ritual needed to be performed on 365 consecutive days, each time with a different partner. Now that's what I call spiritual discipline! But the method and the end result of Christian, Hindu, or Budhist tantra is the same: to break through the illusion of dualism, and end the cycle of reincarnation.

I took a break to use the restroom, and cringed when I entered—as I often do. In India, every restroom is soaking wet. It's one of the reasons I prefer squat toilets—you don't have to sop water off of the seat before you sit down. This one was no different. Of course, there is no toilet paper anywhere in India either, so I fished my tissue packet out of my pocket and used the last tissue. I threw the plastic wrapper toward the waste basket...but missed. To my great horror I watched it disappear down the toilet hole.

Now, in India, you aren't allowed to put toilet paper into the toilets. You must put them in the waste can next to the toilets. The pipes are too finicky and they get clogged very easily. If the pipes can't handle tissue paper, what would happen with a plastic wrapper? "Oh, great," I mumbled to myself, "now I will forever be known as the guy who broke the Dalai Lama's toilet."

Cringing and hoping no one saw me emerge, I went down the stairs to the Tibetan Museum. It was a simple display, but emotionally powerful. It told the whole history of the Tibetan people, from the first immigrants in pre-history, to the Chinese occupation of the region and their brutal and systematic efforts to eradicate the Tibetan religion and culture. It was the face of pure evil, but the display was matter-of-fact and even-handed. It let the facts speak for themselves, and the facts spoke powerfully.

Exiting the temple, I saw an Indian guy with a sweatshirt that read, "Bring God Back." That made me smile, although I really had no idea what it meant, or to which god it referred.

By mid-afternoon I had poked my head into every shop in the town at least once. I kept hoping to find something unexplored, but I had to admit defeat: I had *done* this town. It was okay—it was time for dinner anyway.

Checking my e-mail on my iPad, my fork froze halfway to my mouth. There were several messages from Fr. Tim, but the last one was puzzling and disconcerting. The message read:

am sorry I lost the dutch coo\nnection, in fact I find that most dutch lost God way before you mentioned the Utrecht connection, maybe you can connect with the dutch "Christians" who follow the Toronto Blessings scam and have set up camp near Mcleaod...

By "Dutch" and "Utrecht" he was referring to the Old Catholics, who originated in the Netherlands. The Toronto Blessing is a Pentecostal movement in which the Holy Spirit grants the gift of holy laughter. He went on:

Frankly I found you sermon and our lunch to be full of your own mental projections rather thann the essence of even one of the faiths you have chosen to try to dissect

My stomach sunk. I felt very sad. I had liked Fr. Tim, eccentric as he was. The tone and the numerous typos led me to believe that he had been drunk when he wrote this, and I hoped that when he sobered up he would write to apologize, and perhaps begin a more civil discussion. I decided not to reply to see if, in fact, he would do so. As of this writing, I have heard nothing further from him.

The email put a tense spin on the evening. My nerves were jangly and I obsessed over our conversation. I do like to be liked, and when that doesn't happen, I feel depressed and stressed. I wished it were not three in the morning back home so I could call and talk it over with Lisa. So I talked it over with Jesus instead. I paced my room, and poured out my frustration and feelings. Finally, my feelings spent, I rested in him. I felt embraced and loved. The jangly energy dissipated and I was able to relax and let it go.

The next day, in fact, I hardly gave it another thought. I'd called the taxi driver who had picked me up on my first day in Dharamsala and had asked him for a tour of the outlying monasteries.

As it turned out, there were three rather glorious ones. The taxi driver was named Ram—after the incarnation of Vishnu—and we hit it off splendidly. He spoke excellent English, and he was friendly and funny. We chatted and laughed the whole time, and I felt grateful to have found a friend after all.

First, he took me to the Karmapa monastery and university. It was a great complex of boxy, yellow-colored stone buildings with deep red accents. The place was crawling with monks, dressed in the same deep red robes that all Vajrayana religious wear. I noted that their clothes and the building accents were exactly the same color. Nice.

The monks nodded and smiled when they passed us, and I took off my shoes and ascended the stairs to the main temple. I gasped as I entered it. Unlike the Dalai Lama's lame place, this was what I had been expecting. Well lit by a row of windows at the top, nearly every inch of wall space was covered in thangkas and tapestries. It was a riot of color and beauty.

The main altar had the requisite enormous gold Buddha statue, but in front of it, seated on a throne, was a life-sized cardboard cutout of the Dalai Lama, grinning that disarming grin of his. It was so comical I actually giggled when I saw it. I was tempted to look around to see if there were cardboard cutouts of Captain Kirk and Farrah Fawcett in the house as well. Streching out on either side of the main altar were statues of various Bhodhisattvas, two of them in wild sexual embrace.

On our way back to the car, Ram and I saw a horse on the ground. It seemed healthy, except that it's front right hoof stuck out at an impossible angle. I couldn't quite comprehend what I was seeing. In America, deformed horses are immediately put down, but at least among these Buddhists, they were given a place to live and cared for. I had mixed feelings about the quality of life a horse can have lying on the ground its entire life, but it didn't look depressed. I'm still not sure how I feel about it.

Ram drove me to our next stop, the Norbulinga monastery. We went first to the school, which looked very much like a temple to me. The two long choirs that face each other in all Tibetan temples were filled with students—young teenage boys in deep red robes. Two older monks sat on thrones overlooking the students. They were finishing up lunch, and at first I was hesitant to go inside. Ram had a few quick words with a monk emerging from the hall, and he assured us it was okay to go in.

The boys tried not to steal glances at me as I explored their classroom, but they failed. I did not try to hide my curiosity, but instead just openly gawked at them. As I walked around the temple, snapping pictures, taking in the amazingly garish altar display, they finished their lunch and a group of musicians in the corner began to blare away on trumpets. Then the students opened the long "books" in front of them and began reading.

Tibetan books are interesting. The pages are about three inches tall, and about fifteen inches wide. Sometimes the pages are "bound" together with two strings that run through all of the pages. But these pages were not bound, only stacked. As I circled back around to the front, one of the older monks leaned over to me and whispered. "Where are you from?"—the most popular question in India.

Just down the road was the main temple complex, and it was an amazing site. This temple definitely had some moneyed supporters, because the entire complex was beautifully landscaped, and the buildings were immaculately maintained. We passed the guest house, which was nicer than the place I was staying at (and about three times more expensive, I discovered later). Just in front of this was a most amazing shrine, built of heaped, rounded stones, and painted in bright colors. It had six sides to it, each one sporting the image of a different deity.

Prayer flags were strung between most of the buildings. We walked over an arched bridge under which a fountain flowed, mimicking a forest stream. To our right were various buildings housing the monastery's art workshops—thangka painting, stone cutting, woodcarving, etc. To the right was a gift shop. Ram steered us into the metal-working shop, and we watched as several young men beat designs into bronze plates. Near the door were schematic drawings for large Bhodisattva statues. I found the juxtaposition of ancient iconography and modern geometric measurements and descriptions fascinating.

Emerging from the workshop, I saw a sign for a "Doll Museum." I thought that odd, and how could I resist, really? Ram gave a head waggle and followed. It took a few minutes for the light sensors to realize we were there, but once the lights came on, we were met with a much more interesting museum than I expected. The place was filled with miniature dioramas of Tibetan culture—religious ceremonies, village life, and court pageantry. I snapped several photos, and took my time soaking in the information on each one. The one that fascinated me most was of a shamanistic ritual, where several dolls in frightening deity masks were frozen in the midst of a ritual dance.

Emerging into the sunshine again, Ram and I stepped up to the temple complex, walking through an entryway lined with about twenty prayer wheels. Ram had no interest in going into the temple itself, so I took off my shoes and headed up the stairs. I was the only person there, and for a moment, I just breathed and enjoyed the calm quiet.

The temple was dark, the only light coming through the open door. In front of the main Buddha altar was a row of small butter lamps. Behind them sat two larger lamps with what looked like a reliquary in between them. The real sight to behold there, however, were the thangkas.

I have always loved thangkas. They are colorful Vajrayana icons, often affixed to silk banners of various sizes. Sometimes there is a cloth that hangs in front of the thangka to protect it from the light that you can tie up at the top when you want to look at it. These had no veils, however, and were each about ten feet in length, hanging from the ceiling. One depicted the Buddha, one was a mandala, and others various Bodhisattvas.

Thangkas are a fascinating part of Tibetan Buddhist practice. In Vajrayana teaching, the first turning of the Wheel of Dharma was the Buddha's first sermon to his disciples in Sarnath (the Theravada revelation); the second turning of the Wheel was the revelation of the emptiness of all things (the Mahayana revelation); the third great turning of the wheel was the Vajrayana revelation, that the Buddha nature within you is already and always working on you for your liberation.

The goal of Vajrayana practice is to get in touch with this already-active Buddha nature within, and one way of doing that is through many series of guided meditations in which the ego gets set aside, and the practitioner "imagines" him or herself as the Buddha, or gets in touch with various aspects of his or her spiritual psychology through the visualization of Bodhisattvas. Often this involves using the thangkas as focus points for meditation.

We have a similar tradition in Christianity, called icon gazing, which comes from the Eastern Orthodox tradition. In gazing at the icons one receives "divine rays" from heaven which, in collaboration with the Holy Spirit within, work to divinize and sanctify the believer. The soteriological language differs, of course, but the practice is similar.

As I walked around the sanctuary taking in the beauty of these enormous thangkas, I wondered at the transformations they had wrought on those who meditated on them. The lamps caught my attention again, and I thought about how much the Vajrayana approach resonates with my own experience.

In my spiritual direction practice, being a successful guide is directly proportional to my ability to get myself out of the way and allow God to lead the session. The ego has to be set aside—not just the ego's wanting to take credit for things, but also its fears about not doing well. This creates space for God to show up, and for a true encounter with the Holy to ensue. I am very clear that I am not guiding these sessions. I am just holding space and watching as the inner Christ emerges from both myself and my client. Insight and transformation often follow.

It is this inner sacred essence that the Vajrayana are pointing to, using their own proprietary images and language. I know it well, and I am impressed that they have designed a system by which people can consciously connect with this essence. Too often in Christianity that connection is hit-and-miss, and sometimes we are our own worst enemies. St. Paul clearly said, "It is not I who live, but Christ who lives within me,"[2] but Catholics get lazy by relying on the sacraments for this connection, while Protestants get lazy by making it a completely neck-up affair. Both will nod their assent to the indwelling Christ, but few have a lived experience of their ontological union with him. The Vajrayana have preserved the mysticism of their tradition. We desperately need to recover ours.

I walked out of the temple wondering how to do that. I wondered if the Vajrayana techniques of thangka gazing and guided meditations might be adapted for Christian usage, to help us get in touch with the Christ within. The Vajrayana say that the Buddha nature transforms us from the inside out. Christian theology (especially Luther) affirms this in regard to the indwelling Christ, and the possibility of experimenting with some new forms of prayer and contemplation excited me.

I left Norbulinga relunctantly—it felt like a beautiful, holy oasis, and the short time I was there felt healing to the soul. But I had to think about Ram's time, so I climbed back in the car. On the way back to my hotel, he surprised me with a couple of unplanned stops. The first was to a cricket stadium that he was clearly very proud of. It was, without a doubt, the biggest building in the Dharamsala area. The grounds were green and close-cropped. The bleachers surrounded it on all sides, and held, Ram told me, 20,000 spectators. "We host state matches here," he said, "they're on TV all over India." I'm not much of a sports fan and I know next to nothing about cricket, but I agreed that it was a fine stadium.

After that, he took me to a Hindu temple that his family goes to frequently. It was a Durga temple—Durga is the main goddess in Hinduism, and she takes many forms. Many of those forms were on display—there were altars to Lakshmi, Kali, Sita and others. Ram knelt by the main Durga altar as a priest poured water on his head, and then into his hands, and then gave him a handful of candy—presad.

As we walked away, it struck me how much more grand Buddhist and Christian places of worship are than Hindu ones. Every Hindu temple I had been to in India—with the single exception of the University Temple in Varanasi—had been small, humble affairs, with little thought or concern for beauty.

Back in the car, we had to wait a while as a herd of marauding cows, up to no good, took their time moving out of the road. I asked Ram to let me out in the main square, and I shook his hand with gratitude for his wonderful companionship.

This was the last time I was going to be in a Vajrayana area, so I decided to take the rest of the day to shop for gifts. I did the full circle of the town a couple of times, buying a Ganesha statue here and a bracelet there. I paused outside of a barber shop. Should I? It was about time for a haircut anyway, and I liked the way the monks looked, with their hair shaved short.

I decided, what the heck, and got a monk-cut myself.

That night I dreamed that Lisa was wearing a large, colorful turban with a peacock feather in it. I said, "Hey, you're wearing a maharaja hat!" To which she replied, "Yeah, so?"

In the morning I packed quickly, and had some time on my hands. I opened my book on Vajrayana theology and read a most amazing story: It involved King Indrabhuti, who invited the Lord Buddha to dine with him, along with five hundred of his disciples. After the meal, the king asked the Buddha to instruct him. The Buddha told him to abandon sensual pleasures and to train himself morally, practice meditation, and to seek wisdom.

The King said, "But I want a way of attaining Buddhahood that doesn't require me to abandon my enjoyment of my harem." He must have winked. Then he recited a poem:

In the Rose Apple Grove so joyful to experience,
Even if I were to become a fox in my next life,
A liberation that abandons the sense pleasures
I could never desire, O Gautama.[3]

Reginald Ray comments that although it sounds as if the king was too attached to sensuality to seriously pursue enlightenment, the Vajrayana path affirms his reluctance, because there is value in the material world, in the body, in sensuality.

The Buddha cleared the room and gave the king secret teachings. He showed him a huge mandala, initiated him into the Vajrayana mysteries, and the king was enlightened.

My taxi arrived, and as it sped away, leaving the dusty, steep, winding streets of McCleod Ganj behind, I meditated on this story. We Christians, too, value the Rose Apple Grove of the world. In fact, we believe it is so important that God became a part of it, and wedded himself to it forever. We call this "incarnational" theology—and even though some deviant teachings, both Catholic and Protestant (and most notoriously,

Calvinist) reject and despise the physical world, the Good News is that God does not. He loves it and saved it by entering into it, subsuming it into himself.

In both traditions, the world, the body, and the senses are all important. The Buddha, after all, realized his body was his only vehicle for reaching enlightenment. And Jesus did not abhor the virgin's womb, but entered into the fullness of human life. For him, too, his body was the vehicle of redemption, for it was his body that healed and loved and died and rose again. Ritual is important to both traditions for just this reason. The body isn't a distraction—it is the instrument of salvation.

------

1   Luke 12:12.

2   Galatians 2:20.

3   Reginal A. Ray, *Secret of the Vajra World: The Tantric Buddhism of Tibet* (Boston: Shambahala, 2012), chapter 6.

Buddha statue at Norbulinga.

The Lotus Temple in New Delhi.

Epilogue

I hired a car from Dharamsala to Amritsar, to see the famed Golden Temple—the holiest site in the Sikh faith. Toward evening of my first full day there, however, I started feeling sick. Then I felt sicker. Eventually, I succumbed to the worst case of food poisoning of my trip so far. Azithromycin got me under control enough to fly to Delhi, but then things took a sharp turn for the worst. I ended up flat on my back for five more days, writhing in intestinal agony. You haven't lived until you've careened through the streets of Delhi in the dead of night on the back of a motorcycle (no helmet, of course) when you are already so dizzy you can barely stand. If I'd come to India for adventure, I'd found it.

I had planned to spend my last few days at the Ajanta caves near Aurangabad. This World Heritage Site was a Buddhist community around the 2nd century CE. The walls of the caves boast some of the most splendid paintings of the ancient world. I thought that this would be an appropriate place to close my journey. But alas, human beings plan and India sneers. I was still shivering and moaning when my flight was due to leave, and I missed it. Instead of cave paintings, I stared at four white walls of a budget hotel near the Delhi airport.

When I finally began to feel human again, I was left with just a couple of days in Delhi. Late in the evening I lay in bed and went through the Lonely Planet, making a list of the things I had not yet seen. One of them jumped out at me: the Lotus Temple—the center of activity for the Bahia's in India. I put that at the top of the agenda for the next morning.

That night I had a dream: I was floating in a boat with a Chinese monk. He looked up at me and smiled dreamily. Then he said:

337

With the beauty of a mountain stream
and the quiet of a lake
writing has it all wrong.

The moment I woke I grabbed a pen and wrote the poem down. The dream haunted me all day, in part because it was speaking to an anxiety I've been carrying throughout this entire trip—my desire to write both well and accurately. This has not been easy, because when it comes to memoir, the two goals are sometimes at odds.

Accuracy is especially tricky. One person I encountered on my journey wrote me an ongoing string of about twenty emails correcting every last thing I got "wrong" about our encounter in my blog. I wrote back and explained that this is a record of *my* experience—and no one else's.

Our experiences are always colored by our prejudices, fears, and expectations. And of course, they are limited by what we perceive. Memory further distorts them by replacing solid structures with emotional ones. Memory is plastic, it distorts the past according to the needs of the present. In the long arc of time, this is how myth evolves. In the shorter arcs of our lives, it's why I tell a story differently now than I did ten years ago. None of us can ever know objective reality—the best we can do is to report our subjective experiences with as much integrity as we can.

Things get even more distorted when you set them to paper. A well-written account leaves out *most* of the experience, and includes only those things that the writer deems pertinent to his agenda. Time is distorted, sometimes events are reported out of order, events and sometimes people are conflated in the service of better narrative flow. Dialogue is reconstructed from quickly-fading memory. Memoir is always a suspect form of history. The dream was right: writing has it all wrong.

And yet I have worked very hard to remain accurate in these chapters. There are times when I was tempted to give myself a better line than I actually said in the moment. Sometimes I even wrote it down, but these never survived the first proofreading pass. I like to be clever, but I want to be honest even more. There is no part of this record that is fiction—unless you classify theology under that category, that is. (And feel free—much of it, in any religion, is a bunch of rather glorious nonsense.) But everything that I wrote is, to the best of my ability to recall, accurate. But in the interest of a well-written account, it is also selective, re-ordered and conflated. Believe me, if it weren't, it would be three thousand pages long and utterly unreadable. You're welcome.

My guts were still a little shaky as I entered the metro station. I went to change trains, but quailed when I saw the mad press of people in the cars. There was no way on earth I was going to squeeze in there. Yet, despite my irritation at so much involved in travelling in India—the cutting in line, the constant badgering, and so on—I was not prepared for what happened as those doors slid open.

I saw a solid wall of human flesh. The train was just about as packed solid with people as it was possible to be. It reminded me so much of those telephone-booth packing contests I'd heard about as a kid that it was comical. I stepped back, resigned to waiting for the next car. But seeing my reaction, nearly everyone crushed against the doors laughed at me. One of them reached out and took my arm, and pulled me toward them. Somehow, everyone shifted and I had the experience of being subsumed into a grand mass of humanity. I was absorbed by that wall of ankles, elbows, and odiferous bodies. I became one with them, the doors slid shut, and I laughed out loud, joining in the general merriment of the car.

Soon, I was exiting the train, and walking out into the sunshine. I hailed a rickshaw and negotiated a price. I quickly discovered I'd been taken advantage of, since my destination was a full block and a half from the metro station. I paid a dollar for the privilege of riding for that distance. *Oh well,* I told myself, *it's hard to fault a person for trying to make a living.*

Walking through the gates, I saw a large green garden rolling out the length of several football fields. At the far end was the temple itself in the shape of a white stone lotus blossom, opening its petals to the sky. It was awe-inspiring.

I'd read that the building design had won many awards, and I wished my friend Greg, an architect, were with me to appreciate it. I'd actually had that thought a number of times on this trip, as it was so architecturally mind-blowing and I would have liked to have had Greg's expertise at hand to explain what I was seeing and why it was significant.

But since Greg wasn't there, I turned to the Visitor's Center, hoping there would be a display that could tell me more. I was not disappointed. In fact, I lost a lot of time in the Visitor's Center, as they had numerous displays—most of them on Baha'i history and theology.

I came to India to engage with Buddhism, but ending my trip here, at a Baha'i holy place felt strangely appropriate. After all, my pilgrimage had been an interfaith endeavor, and Baha'i aspires to be an interfaith religion—a religion that hopes to unite all religions, and therefore all of humankind. They honor several of the world's great prophets: Adam, Noah, Krishna, Moses, Zarathustra, Buddha, Jesus, Muhammad—and their own Bab and Baha'u'llah.

It is a noble vision, though not a unique one. There's something in the DNA of Islam that lends its liberal wing to ambitiously ecumenical schemes. The Sufis, the Sikhs, and the Baha'is are all derived from Islam and yet they strive beyond it to a larger religious unity that would include all other religions as well. I think, in part, this is due to the extreme monotheistic impulse at the heart of Islam—if there is only one God, should we not all be serving him in peace?—but it is also part of the Islamic dream of the Ummah, the Just Society, now universalized and projected onto the whole world.

This striving for oneness is conscious, a dream driven by sincere desire. Yet the Sufis, the Sikhs, and the Baha'is remain relatively small in number. Strangely more successful is Hinduism, which, in amoeba-like fashion unconsciously subsumes everything it comes in contact with. "A new god? No problem. Welcome aboard!" *Sluuurrrrp.* Now it is part of Hinduism.

The school I teach at in Berkeley is struggling with articulating a grand vision similar to the Baha'is—a universal theology that will include all religions. I kept being reminded of that as I read the tragic history of the Baha'i prophet, Baha'u'llah, and the generations of followers who came after him who were persecuted by the authorities of the Ottoman Empire.

Some people assume that my journey was similarly inclined, but that is not the case. I didn't come to India to find a theological unity. I enjoyed seeing the convergences and divergences between Christianity and Buddhism. Exploring those is one of the great joys of my professional life. But I wasn't trying to forge a new teaching or to impose a unitive structure on both, as some others have done (such as Aldous Huxley or Ken Wilber or John Hick).

I admire what these thinkers and the Baha'i prophet were aiming for, but I don't think it a reasonable or even a desirable goal. When it comes to religion, you'd have to label me a multi-culturalist.

And yet to my great surprise, I discovered a unitive structure much closer to the ground, in the realm of shared human experience. Or perhaps, like the solid wall of people who pulled me into the train that morning, it discovered me. Theologies are flags flapping in the intellectual ether, but people are solid things rooted in blood and soil. As I saw people connecting to Mystery, I connected to *them*. I understood the hunger that drove them, the desperation behind that connection, the devotion and the supplication. The names and images and clothes that Mystery wears when interacting with me differs from those it wears interacting with them, but I encountered nothing alien to my own religious experience. Eccentric at times, but never alien.

I left the Visitor's Center behind and strolled through the gardens toward the main sanctuary. The giant lotus was even more impressive, the closer I got to it. I stowed my shoes with the clerk and got in line.

They were allowing visitors to enter only in cohorts. When a sufficient number of us had gathered, they gave us the spiel, first in Hindi, then in English: *No photography, no talking. This is a place for prayer. So feel free to go in and sit as long as you like. Please pray, and leave when you are ready.* Elsewhere I'd read that nothing may be read inside a Baha'i temple except scripture—any scripture.

I went in and took a seat on one of the many hundred white marble benches. I thanked God for keeping me safe during this trip. I was especially thankful for surviving my many illnesses. Then I went ahead and offered my daily petitions. Then I just rested in the Presence, held by such a beautiful, moving, and holy place.

When I opened my eyes, I didn't really feel like leaving. So I thought about all the things I'd learned on this trip:

• Australians travel about four times as much as Americans. At no time in my travels could I have spit and *not* hit an Australian.

• The Taiwanese have the world's most amazing queue etiquette. The Indians have the worst.

- If you don't position yourself exactly over a squat toilet, bad things happen.

- Chinese taste buds are just wired different. Have you tasted the licoriced plums? I don't want to hear any argument about this.

- You never get used to the smell of mothballs—this smell is everywhere in India.

Of course, I learned some *important* things too:

- I learned a method of approaching the Religious Other that would help me tremendously in my teaching. I imagine it will also help me in my ministry in ways that have not yet occurred to me.

- I learned that India wasn't resisting me. India was just India. It was I who was resisting her. She was more than willing to take me in, to make me a part of her vast, multi-limbed body. I fought it—or more exactly, I fought the grime, the pollution, the illness, the horror, and the superfluous, egregious, phenomenal waste of human life and potential. I fought everything I valued and loved being ground under the great unheeding heel of Shiva. I fought in vain. I never did learn to completely let go—that would take more time, I'm sure—but I did stop thrashing.

- I learned to have a much more profound level of trust in God. I found that I can't always have the experience of God that I want, because I can't control God, understand God, or even fully know God. I learned that to truly trust is to trust without result, to rest without feedback, to lean into nothingness without feeling any pressure at my back. I'm not saying I'm good at this, but that I had to do it, and did.

It was scary, but valuable. Am I angry about it? Yes. God and I are working on that. I love him too much not to forgive him. I also love him too much to just let him off the hook. We have work to do. It will be fine.

Flashing light caught my attention as the doors swung open and closed. People were leaving. Feeling the creak in my knees, I rose, bowed toward the front of the sanctuary (there is no altar) and headed back outside. Getting back on the metro, I set out for the Lodi Gardens to enjoy a stroll in one of the most beautiful oases in Delhi before heading back to my guest house for the night. I saw three Indian men near a large patch of wild-flowers. One of them was sitting among the flowers, and another was taking his picture.

"What a great idea!" I said, approaching them. "Will you take one for me?"

The photographer seemed pleased that I'd asked and eagerly accepted my camera. I knelt amidst the flowers and smiled up at the sun as he clicked away. (The resulting photo graces the back cover of this book.) I thanked him profusely.

"Where are you from?" the man asked me.

I constrained my eyes from rolling. "California."

"What you do?" he asked next.

"That is a very good question," I said. One of the things that pilgrimage does for you is dissolve the strands of identity that tie you to place and occupation. After three months of not being a pastor, not being a husband, not being a teacher, not being an American, I wasn't sure how to answer. I wasn't con-fused, but it certainly did make me think about how tied up our sense of self is in what we do, our sense of place, and other people. The quick answers I would have given a few months ago to his question no longer seemed to apply. Sure, I would resume those roles when I returned, *but I was not those roles.*

The me I had come to know over the past three months was

more than my jobs, more than my web of relationships. I had a much better sense of self, but found myself completely incapable of describing it.

I was reminded of a story about the Chan patriarch Bodhidharma who had been summoned to the throne of the Chinese emperor to give an account of himself. "Who are you?" the emperor demanded.

Bodhidharma answered back with equal vehemence, "I have absolutely no idea!"

It was tempting to say that. But I didn't. Instead, I said, "I pray. And I write." It wasn't an answer that spoke to identity at all, but very directly to the young man's literal question: What do you do? *I pray. And I write.* More than that doesn't really need to be said.

Had I reached clarity? I know what I'm not. As for what I *am*, Bodhidharma's answer is the best I can think of. I thanked the men, and headed off toward one of the Moghul tombs. As I walked, Nagarjuna's syllogisms rattled off in my brain: "I am a pastor. I am not a pastor. I both am and am not a pastor. I'm neither a pastor nor not a pastor. I am a husband. I am not a husband...." All true. And not true. None of this seems confounding. Is that strange? (If you've come along on this journey with me, surely not. Who are *you*, by the way?)

Some people get to India and decide it's their heart's true home. I am not one of those people. I am ready to go home. I am ready for sane traffic and safe food. I am ready to resume the duties and identities I laid aside three months ago. I imagine that when I walk through the door, our mutt Judy will turn to our Boxer Sally and say, "It's clearly him, but he smells funny."

So it's clearly *me* at the end of this journey, who ever that is. But I do smell funny. I smell like India—ash, decay, and black pepper. I smell like Thailand, China, and Nepal. I smell like wonder, like the smoke of incense and the wafting of prayer. I smell like that great mass of humanity, clutching at me and pulling me in. I smell like ignorance, like delusion, like passion, like illness. I smell like tens of thousands of thoughtful miles, and a few hundred thoughtless ones as well. I smell tired.

I heard the beep of the taxi and I picked up my bag, turned off the light, and closed the door on a room labeled "India."

Martin Copenhaver
To Begin at the Beginning

CPSIA information can be obtained
at www.ICGtesting.com
Printed in the USA
FSOW01n1529100914
3108FS

9 781940 671307